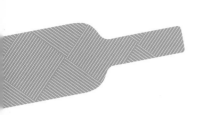

lonely planet FOOD

WINE TRAILS

PLAN 52 PERFECT WEEKENDS IN WINE COUNTRY

INTRODUCTION

We've all experienced it on our travels - whether watching
a sunset in Italy with a glass of chilled Prosecco or at a
barbeque in Australia with a beefy Shiraz - when a local wine
could not be more perfectly suited to the moment.

Tasting wine in the place it was made can be a revelation.
This new, updated edition of Wine Trails plots a course
through 52 of the world's greatest wine regions, with weekend-
long itineraries in each. We encounter California's cutting-
edge wine scene, and the idiosyncratic wines of France's Jura
mountains, and we venture into Spain's extraordinary wineries
and along Portugal's beautiful Douro River. And we even reach
the cultural frontiers of winemaking in Lebanon and Georgia.
In each, our expert writers, including wine buyers, reviewers
and sommeliers, select the most rewarding wineries to visit
and the most memorable experiences to seek out.

This is a book for casual quaffers; there's no impenetrable
language about malolactic fermentation or scoring systems.
Instead, we meet some of the world's most enthusiastic and
knowledgeable winemakers and learn about each region's wines
in their own words. It is this personal introduction to wine,
in its home, that is at the heart of wine-touring's appeal.

CONTENTS

[Argentina]
MENDOZA

Saddle up for some adventurous tasting in the mountainous capital of Argentina's thriving wine scene, where old-world expertise meets new-world innovation.

Maybe you can't distinguish between Italian wine regions on a map, or explain the difference between French and American oak barrels. But unless you've been living under a rock, chances are you've noticed that right now Argentina is hot on the international wine scene. Think about it: you can't glance at a wine list without seeing the word 'Malbec', or turn on the radio without hearing a chef talk about the best-value Argentinian bottles for your summer barbecue.

If the runaway popularity of Argentinian wine strikes you as sudden, you're not alone. Even Argentinian people didn't realise how fantastic their wine could be until relatively recently, though it's safe to say they were always fully aware of the natural beauty of Mendoza. The nation's wine-producing capital occupies a spectacular stretch of sun-drenched landscape at the foot of the snowcapped Andes. Even if there weren't any vineyards around, it would still be a popular travel destination thanks to its gorgeous weather and picture-perfect opportunities for hiking, horseback riding, skiing, fishing, whitewater rafting or cycling. Luckily for travellers there is indeed a glass – or several – waiting for you at the end of a day well spent in the great outdoors.

The wine produced in Mendoza, whether in the longer-established region of Luján de Cuyo or the up-and-coming Uco Valley, isn't just the product of the natural landscape. It's the result of a new generation of winemakers that knows the rules of French or Italian winemaking – and knows how to break them. It's a South American playground for innovation, the meeting point between tradition and new technology. Raise your glass: here in Mendoza, it's a brave new world.

GET THERE
Mendoza El Plumerillo is the nearest major airport, 8km (5 miles) from Mendoza. Car hire is available.

Courtesy of Casa de Uco

01 BODEGA TAPIZ

You'll know you've arrived at Tapiz when you spot the llamas. Dozens graze in the fields around the vineyards, controlling weeds, producing fertiliser and providing wool that local artisans use to make the traditional blankets and ponchos sold in the winery's boutique.

The picturesque llama family is a pleasingly old-fashioned counterpoint to the state-of-the-art (and sustainable) winemaking technology Tapiz employs inside. The two signature wines are Malbec and Torrontés, made with grapes harvested here, in Agrelo, as well as in the Uco Valley and further afield in Argentina's northernmost wine region of Cafayate in Salta. They're presided over, in part, by the

world-renowned French winemaker Jean-Claude Berrouet, who works as a consultant with the brand. For a particularly memorable experience, book a tour of the vineyard by horse-drawn carriage, followed by tasting wines straight from the barrels and a meal at the Club Tapiz restaurant. *bodega-tapiz.com.ar; tel +54 261-3640 7814; Ruta Provincial (RP) 15, km32; by reservation 10am-3pm Mon-Fri, to 12.30pm Sat* 🟦✕

'We have found this place where I think we can make the best wines in the world because of the climate and soil combination'

– Laura Catena, President of Bodega Catena Zapata

02 RUCA MALÉN

According to the co-founder of Bodega Ruca Malén, you don't need to hear descriptions of his wines: you need to taste them yourself. 'As is the case with any work of art,' Jean Pierre Thibaud has said, 'pleasure can only derive from personal discovery.'

Perhaps the best way to discover this particular wine experience – Ruca Malén's offerings include Pinot Noir, Petit Verdot, Cabernet

Courtesy of Casa de Uco

© Nassima Rothacker / Lonely Planet

Courtesy of Catena Zapata

Sauvignon and Chardonnay as well as Malbec – is through a leisurely meal at the on-site restaurant. The eight-course tasting menu with wine pairings, served in a sun-filled dining space overlooking the surrounding vineyards, is considered one of the finest in Mendoza. A word to the wise: after indulging in a feast like this one, you may not have any room left for tasting more wine until the following day. Although the winery takes its name from an old Mapuche legend, the wine tastings and blending classes at Ruca Malén are all about modern winemaking techniques. *bodegarucamalen.com; tel +54 261-15 4540974; RN 7, km1059, Agrelo; tastings by reservation Mon-Sat* 💲✖️

03 CATENA ZAPATA

Like Mendoza itself, Catena Zapata represents an appealing balance between old traditions and contemporary winemaking. The vineyard was founded by Nicola Catena, an Italian immigrant to Argentina who planted his first Malbec vines in 1902. It later became the experimental playground for Nicolás Catena Zapata – arguably the most celebrated winemaker in Argentina – and his daughter, Laura, current president of Bodega Catena Zapata and author of the lauded 2010 book *Vino Argentino: An Insider's Guide to the Wines and Wine Country of Argentina*. Her energetic and unpretentious approach is revolutionising the face of Argentinian wines. There are several tour and tasting options available for visitors. Do seek out Luca, Laura's line of small-quantity, artisanal-quality wine made from Argentina's old vines; and taste the winery's classic Malbecs straight from the barrels or the fermentation tanks. *catenazapata.com; tel +54 261-413 1100; Cobos s/n, Agrelo; tastings by reservation Mon-Fri* 💲

04 BODEGA SALENTEIN

Located in the Uco Valley, the Dutch-owned Bodega Salentein is as much an architectural landmark as a destination for wine enthusiasts. The main building was designed in the shape of a cross: each of the four wings serve as a small winery with two levels – stainless steel tanks and French wooden vats on one floor, and an underground cellar for aging wine in oak casks on the other. The central chamber, or the crux of the cross, functions as a state-of-the-art amphitheatre modelled after the look and feel of a classical temple.

Check the calendar ahead of time: in addition to regular tastings, Salentein hosts a line-up of musical performances and art exhibitions in its barrel room and gallery. Where better to sample the brand's famous Reserve Pinot Noir? Make a weekend of it and check into the 16-room Posada Salentein. Overlooking the vineyards, the restaurant serves succulent meats grilled in a clay oven or sizzled on a barbecue. *bodegasalentein.com; tel +54 026-2242 9500; RP 89, Los Árboles, Tunuyán; tastings by reservation Wed-Mon* 💲🍴

WHERE TO STAY
HUENTALA HOTEL
Complete with a wine cellar, this elegant 81-room hotel is located near one of Mendoza's main squares, and makes a good choice if you'd like to stay in town. *huentala.com; tel +54 261-420 0766; Primitivo de la Reta 1007, Mendoza*

CASA DE UCO WINE RESORT
This sleek, sustainably built lakeside getaway within the Casa de Uco vineyards, featuring a stylish restaurant and offering horseback riding on its large property, is located within easy reach of many other great wineries in the Uco Valley. *casadeuco.com; tel +54 261-476 9831; RP 94, km14.5, Tunuyán*

WHERE TO EAT
OSADÍA DE CREAR
Part of the Susana Balbo winery, this elegant restaurant offers a beautifully presented five-course wine-paired lunch that's one of the

area's best; or go for brunch or afternoon tea. *susanabalbowines. com.ar; tel +54 261-498 9231; Cochabamba 7801, Agrelo; daily*

AZAFRÁN
Gourmet cooking Mendoza-style, Azafrán serves innovative versions of classic Argentine meat and fish dishes. Head to the 500-label wine cellar with the sommelier to choose a bottle for your meal. *azuca.com.ar; tel +54 261-429 4200; Av Sarmiento 765, Mendoza; Mon-Sat*

WHAT TO DO
Arrange a hike, a horse-riding excursion, a rafting adventure, or even a side trip to Aconcagua – the highest point in the southern hemisphere – with one of the many outdoor outfitters in Mendoza. For an active excursion closer to the city centre, rent a bicycle, either independently or as part of an organised winery tour. And for easy-access touring around even more Mendoza wineries, board the hop-on, hop-off BusVitivinicola services. *busvitivinicola.com*

CELEBRATIONS
Mendoza's main event is the Fiesta de la Vendimia, or the annual harvest festival, taking over the city for 10 days in early March. Although the celebration honours all of the region's fruits, the grape, of course, takes centre stage. Highlights include traditional foods, folkloric concerts and a colourful parade and pageant to crown the queen of the festival. Be sure to book ahead: Vendimia draws huge crowds, both from Argentina and abroad. *vendimia.mendoza. gov.ar*

[Australia]

MARGARET RIVER

Margaret River is an oasis of amazing food and wine in vast Western Australia. A weekend here combines wine with Indian Ocean beaches and magical landscapes.

The sunsets off the Western Australian coast, whether you're sitting in a harbourside bar in Fremantle or on a deserted beach, are absolute showstoppers. Time seems to slow down and you find yourself pondering life's biggest questions, such as 'how many bubbles are released in a glass of Champagne?'

The sun is definitely rising on the Margaret River wine region. It's never been a secret to Australians that much of the country's finest wine is made way out west, but with competitively priced flights to Perth, Margaret River is opening up to the rest of the world. And what a treat it is! The region, which is 275km (170 miles) south of Perth, is bounded by the Indian Ocean to the west and extends about 90km (56 miles) north and south between Cape Naturaliste and Cape Leeuwin. Around Margaret River are some of the world's tallest trees and cave systems dating back 40,000 years, plus whales, wildflowers and wild coastlines with world-class surfing. There's an eye-opening clarity to the light, and Western Australia's colours seem to be turned up to 11. Beyond the state's cities – Perth and near neighbour Fremantle, far-out Broome – the natural world rules in primary colours: red deserts, blue oceans and the yellow sun.

Except, that is, for the temperate oasis that is Margaret River. Quality not quantity is the watchword

GET THERE
The Western Australia capital of Perth has the closest airport. Margaret River is about 3hr to the south by car.

here: Margaret River produces 3% of Australia's wine, but a quarter of its premium wines. Which is perhaps another reason why wine critic Jancis Robinson said: 'Margaret River is the closest thing to paradise of any wine region I have visited in my extensive search for knowledge.'

Talking of knowledge: the answer to the Champagne question is around 20 million...

01 CAPEL VALE

Start the trip at the most northerly winery, which is about an hour's drive from Margaret River. Capel Vale was founded by Perth-based Dr Peter Pratten in 1974, with a single vineyard beside the River Capel, making it one of Western Australia's pioneers. Now a much larger producer, it grows a huge range of grapes – including Sangiovese, Tempranillo and Nebbiolo as well as Margaret River's staple crop of Cabernet Sauvignon and Chardonnay – in a variety of locations along the coast. Many of the wines are rated highly by James Halliday, Australia's most prominent critic.
capelvale.com.au; tel +61 08-9727 1986; 118 Mallokup Rd, Capel; 10am-4.30pm daily 🅢🗙

02 DEEP WOODS ESTATE

Up in the Yallingup Hills, with views extending across forests of jarrah and marri trees, Deep Woods occupies a prime position in Margaret River, and in the disparate wine empire of Perth businessman, Peter Fogarty.

Grapes are sourced from far and wide, with most ranges produced in small batches by talented winemaker and James Halliday's Winemaker of the Year 2019, Julian Langworthy. The Reserve Cabernet Sauvignon, in particular, is a tour de force. Stock up on the good-value, red, white and award-winning rosé – Ebony, Ivory and Harmony – in the Margaret River range.
deepwoods.wine; tel +61 08-9756 6066; 889 Commonage Rd, Yallingup; Wed-Mon 10am-5pm 🅢

03 CULLEN WINES

Cullen was founded in 1971, when Margaret River pioneers Kevin and Diana Cullen planted a plot of Cabernet Sauvignon and Riesling here. The winery has a habit of being in the forefront of a movement: it was one of the earliest to become organic and it was the first vineyard in Australia to be carbon neutral.

Led by daughter Vanya, who gained experience in Burgundy and California before becoming chief winemaker in 1989, Cullen Wines became a fully biodynamic winery in 2004. Biodynamic lore says that key processes such as planting and harvesting should be done in tandem with the cosmic rhythms of the planets; for example, planting should take place

01 Sunset at
Leeuwin Naturaliste
National Park

02 Vines at Vasse Felix

03 Alfresco bubbles at
Vasse Felix

04 Wining and dining at
Vasse Felix

05 Cullen Wines'
restaurant

when the Moon and Saturn are in opposition. There's much more to biodynamics than the Moon's movement, but the core of the ethos is about working in harmony with nature so that chemicals are eschewed and nothing extra is added to the wines. A spiral garden has been planted at Cullen to explain biodynamics, and it's fascinating to explore.

Vanya's wines are essentially natural wines, expressing the land on which they're grown, which is an old, granite and gravelly loam. Red or white, the results in the bottle are unerringly sublime wines that wow critics the world over. *cullenwines.com.au; tel +61 08-9755 5277; 4323 Caves Rd, Wilyabrup; 10am-4.30pm daily*

Courtesy of Leeuwin Estate, Vasse Felix

Andrew Watson © Getty Images

04 VASSE FELIX

Luck is at the heart of Vasse Felix. The winery takes its name from French seaman, Thomas Vasse, who was swept overboard when his ship was surveying the Australian coast in 1801. Founder Dr Tom Cullity added Felix – meaning lucky – to the lost sailor's name when he established Margaret River's first winery in 1967. But he didn't find much fortune at the outset: the crop for the winery's first vintage in 1971 was mostly eaten by birds. A peregrine falcon was brought in to scare off the pests, but promptly disappeared into the distant trees; a falcon motif was added to the logo.

Things soon looked up, and under the present winemaker, Virginia Willcock, the wines, especially the Premier Chardonnay, have become classic examples of what Margaret River does best. To understand what that is, take the two-hour tutored tasting at the cellar door. And check out the art gallery and the sculpture walk in the grounds. *vassefelix.com.au; tel +61 08-9756 5000; cnr Tom Cullity Dr/Caves Rd, Cowaramup; 10am-5pm daily, tutored tastings 10.30am Mon-Fri* 🍷🍴

05 VOYAGER ESTATE

Continuing south, homing in on the town of Margaret River, you should choose between Voyager or Leeuwin, both among Margaret's grandest estates. If you want to check out elegantly understated Cape Dutch architecture and manicured gardens, Voyager's the one. The walled gardens, designed by South African landscape designer Deon Bronkhorst, are a beautiful place to wander when the rose bushes are flowering. Voyager was established in 1978, but under winemakers Travis Lemm and James Penton it retains a spirit of adventure, using wild yeasts for white wines, and experimenting with project wines. There'll always be something interesting to sip. *voyagerestate.com.au; tel +61 08-9757 6354; 1 Stevens Rd, Margaret River; 10am-5pm Wed-Sun* 🍷🍴

06 LEEUWIN ESTATE

Superlative wines await at this family-owned winery, another of the estates in Margaret River dating

Courtesy of Leeuwin Estate

from the 1970s. The Art Series Chardonnay is regarded as one of Australia's finest, alongside the Cabernet Sauvignon and Shiraz. The ethos at Leeuwin is to always reflect the land and the weather in the wine, as winemaker Tim Lovett says: 'Every vintage is different. It's about showcasing a sense of place.' All Margaret River's finest ingredients – the maritime climate, the ancient Australian soils, the skilled winemakers, such as Tim Lovett and Phil Hutchinson – come together at Leeuwin. Add to that winning formula the annual outdoor concerts, which have attracted thousands since 1985. *leeuwinestate.com.au; tel +61 08-9759 0000; Stevens Rd, Margaret River; 10am-5pm daily* 💲✕

06 Leeuwin Estate's Art Series

07 Voyager Estate

08 Vasse Felix's Barrel Hall

09 Live music at Leeuwin Estate

ESSENTIAL INFORMATION

WHERE TO STAY
BURNSIDE ORGANIC FARM
These rammed-earth and limestone bungalows have spacious decks and designer kitchens, and the surrounding farm hosts a menagerie of animals and avocado and macadamia orchards as well as a winery. *burnsideorganicfarm. com.au; tel +61 08-9757 2139; 287 Burnside Rd, Margaret River*

EDGE OF THE FOREST
Update your expectations of what a motel should be. This delightful spot is set in bird-filled gardens next to a State Forest, with walking trails from the front door. *edgeoftheforest.com. au; tel +61 08-9757 2351; 25 Bussell Hwy, Margaret River*

WHERE TO EAT
BOOTLEG BREWERY
Take a break from the grape at Bootleg. *bootlegbrewery.com. au; tel +61 08-9755 6300; Puzey Rd, Wilyabrup; Wed-Sun*

WHAT TO DO
Surfers will want to hit the powerful reef breaks of the beaches between capes Naturaliste and Leeuwin; around Dunsborough the better locations are between Eagle and Bunker Bays. The annual surfer competition is held around Margaret River Mouth and Southsides.
From June to September, humpback and southern right whales make a pitstop in Flinders Bay, off Augusta, south of Margaret River. And from September to December, whales – including the rare blue whales – frequent Geographe Bay to the north; take a whale-watching cruise. *westernaustralia.com*

CELEBRATIONS
The annual Margaret River Gourmet Escape showcases the region's world-class food and wine over a weekend in November. It draws guest chefs and has plenty of open-air events. *gourmetescape.com.au*

[Australia]

ADELAIDE HILLS

Discover a different side to Australia in this cool-climate region where jacaranda trees, fruit orchards and weekend cyclists offer a distinctly European vibe.

Welcome to another side of Australia. From the jacaranda-lined streets of Adelaide's CBD, the M1 freeway climbs southeastward and the trees get thicker, the road quieter. You'll probably pass a few cyclists out for a spin, and apple or cherry orchards. Just half an hour later you'll be in the heart of the Adelaide Hills. Unfortunately, the region was hit hard by the December 2019 bush fires, with vineyards suffering significant damage; many wineries were affected but happily most were soon back up and running.

This part of South Australia was settled in the 19th century by Germans and Lutherans fleeing persecution, and there's a certain European feel to the winding roads that link twee towns like Hahndorf. These days it's a popular weekending destination for residents of the South Australian state capital, intent on trying and buying up-and-coming wines from the Hills' small-scale producers. This is a true cool-climate region; as other grape-growing regions in Australia wonder about rising temperatures, the Adelaide Hills enjoys ideal growing conditions for Sauvignon Blanc and a fresher form of Shiraz. There's not much of a Germanic connection in the vineyards (Australia's best Riesling is still found in Clare Valley) but some have had success with Grüner Veltliner. The Hills is a young wine region but it's growing up fast.

Adelaide itself is a city for gourmands, with one of Australia's best food markets and a thriving farm-to-fork local produce scene. The only time the city gets busy is during the Adelaide Festival in March. The rest of the year, this sedate city makes a great base.

GET THERE
Adelaide has the closest airport with car rental and is about 40min from Hahndorf. Tours from the city are also available.

From top left: © Robin Barton (3); kwest / Shutterstock; courtesy of Shaw and Smith

01 GOLDING WINES

Although Golding Wines' first vintage was in 2002, the winery has close connections to Adelaide Hills' fruit-growing heritage: Darren Golding's father was a local apple and pear merchant. Together they designed and built the cellar door with an Aussie aesthetic: a tin roof, bare wood, brick and stone. While the building was spared from the devastating 2019 fires, 90% of their vines were lost. The recovery process has been remarkable and with the help of its elegant new cellar-door restaurant Gingko, it is still one of the Hills' best wineries.

They started with parcels of Pinot Noir and Sauvignon Blanc but quickly became more adventurous, including planting what they thought was Albariño. 'The plants were given to Australia by the Spanish government,' says Darren. 'It was only a few years later that we were alerted that the Albariño was in fact Savignan, a grape from the Jura in France, where it makes Vin Jaune.' Michael Sykes, Golding's winemaker, uses it to make Lil' Late (Harvest), a sweet wine with tropical flavours.

But the staples of the winery are the Handcart Shiraz, which shows the fruity spicy side of Shiraz, and a Burgundy-style Pinot Noir. 'The cool nights in the Adelaide Hills preserve the acidity,' explains Darren, 'leading to vibrant, elegant wines, red or white.' The Hills, reckons Darren, have a huge future. So where else would he recommend in the region? 'Head up to Mt Lofty Ranges,' suggests Darren. 'The wines are good and if you go out the back you can look over Piccadilly Valley.'
goldingwines.com.au; tel +61 08-8189 4500; 52 Western Branch Rd, Lobethal; tastings by reservation 11am-5pm daily ⑤✖

02 MT LOFTY RANGES

'All I want is to produce wines representative of this place,' says owner Garry Sweeney, whose wife, Sharon, picked the location for Mt Lofty Ranges. She chose well because the cellar door's spot is enviable, with views into a verdant valley from its perch at 550m.

Growing grapes gives entry into a close-knit community. 'Everyone

The region was settled in the 19th century by Germans and Lutherans, and there's a certain European feel to the pretty winding roads that link twee towns

lends a hand,' he says. 'If your tractor breaks down, someone will come round. In my first year I didn't know how to prune and other winemakers came over to show me.' Their lessons were learned: Mt Lofty Ranges' Pinot Noir, Riesling and Chardonnay are delicious.

The tasting room features reclaimed materials, an open fireplace and a terraced decking that leads down to the vines; there's also an on-site restaurant. If you arrive any time from mid-March to early April you may catch Garry and the team among the vines, hand-picking the year's harvest.

mtloftyrangesvineyard.com.au; tel +61 08-8389 8339; 166 Harris Rd, Lenswood; 11am–5pm daily 💲✕

(06)

03 SIMON TOLLEY

An airy, bright cellar door that opened in 2021 means that more wine fans can enjoy a taste of Simon Tolley's hard work. The viticulturist, a fifth-generation grape grower, now concentrates on cultivating interesting clones of Chardonnay, Syrah, Sauvignon Blanc and Pinot Noir at the family estate outside the town of Woodside. That might sound slightly nerdy but if you book a bespoke tasting with Simon he can explain the nuances of each grape, which brings an interesting perspective to your glass of wine. Additionally, a luxury lodge is available for overnight stays. *simontolley.com.au; tel +61 08-8389 9407; 278 Bird in Hand Rd, Woodside; 11-5 Thu-Mon*

04 SHAW + SMITH

Shaw + Smith is one of the larger cellar doors in the Hills. The focus is on five wines: a Sauvignon Blanc, a Chardonnay, a Riesling, a Pinot Noir and a Shiraz. For $25 you can taste a flight of all five with a platter of local cheeses; the Sauvignon Blanc is perhaps the most successful, lying someway between a fruity Marlborough, New-Zealand style and a spartan Sancerre from France. *shawandsmith.com; tel +61 08-8398 0500; 136 Jones Rd, Balhannah daily 11am-5pm* 🅢✕

05 HAHNDORF HILL

At Hahndorf Hill, which is pioneering several Austrian grape varieties, you'll not only be testing your tastebuds at the cellar door with interesting wines but also some tongue-twisting names. The warm days and cool nights of the Hills suit Grüner Veltliner, which owners Larry Jacobs and Marc Dobson first planted in 2006; South Australia's first Grüner Veltliner vintage has gone on to win many awards. Blaufrankisch, the red version of the grape, has been grown at Hahndorf for over 20 years – both benefit from the high mineral content of the blue slate, quartz and ironstone soil. The pair also make a pear-scented Pinot Grigio, a Zweigelt red and a great cool-climate Shiraz to try while enjoying cheese platters, chocolate pairings and the views over the vines. *hahndorfhillwinery.com.au; tel +61 08-8388 7512; 38 Pain Rd, Hahndorf; 10.30am-4pm Mon-Sat*

ESSENTIAL INFORMATION

WHERE TO STAY

AMBLE AT HAHNDORF

At Amble's country-luxe base in Hahndorf there's the Fern studio, the Wren cottage and an apartment (Amble Over). Wren features a spa bathroom and private deck; Fern a private courtyard with a barbecue. *hahndorf.co; tel +61 04-8464 8464; 10 Hereford Ave, Hahndorf*

FRANKLIN BOUTIQUE HOTEL

The Franklin offers a hip option in Adelaide, a much-needed meeting of demand for twee-free accommodation. The basic ('deluxe') rooms are small but so stylish that you won't mind; pay more for bigger bathrooms and more inventive lighting in the premium and superior rooms. *thefranklinhotel.com.au; tel +61 08-8410 0036; 92 Franklin St, Adelaide*

WHERE TO EAT

CHIANTI

With local growers as suppliers, the chefs at Chianti, Adelaide's long-standing and much-loved Italian restaurant, are spoiled for choice: the menu champions the local origins of dishes such as spaghetti *vongole* with Coffin Bay clams or rabbit from the Adelaide Hills with porcini and speck. *chianti.net.au; tel +61 08-8232 7955; 160 Hutt St, Adelaide; Mon-Sat*

WHAT TO DO

Kangaroo Island is a popular excursion from Adelaide. It's not only inhabited by kangaroos but lots of amazing marsupials, and, in the ocean, dolphins and seals. *tourkangarooisland. com.au*

CELEBRATIONS

The Adelaide Hills wine region stages events throughout the year: Chardonnay May sees wineries across the region throw open their doors for special events celebrating this well-loved white; October's Sparkling Spring is a three-day jamboree in honour of the local fizz. *adelaidehillswine.com. au/events*

[Australia]

CLARE VALLEY

Take the Riesling Trail through sleepy Clare Valley to meet friendly winemakers and sample some of Australia's most food-friendly wines.

Follow a back-road south out of a town called Clare – a left, a right, and a left under a canopy of blue-green gum trees – and a few minutes later you could be sipping from a glass of chilled Riesling on the porch of Skillogalee. Skillogalee is one of around 40, mainly family-run wineries in South Australia's Clare Valley, an Edenic plateau (not a valley) about two hours' drive north of Adelaide. Most of the wineries have cellar doors offering tastings and often platters of locally sourced produce, and the welcome at each is as warm as the Australian sun. Base yourself around the town of Clare and you'll be within easy reach of most cellar doors.

Clare is a well-kept secret. This is one reason why it makes the Wine Trails cut; unlike Barossa, the cellar doors don't have parking spaces for coaches. Another reason is that it's extremely pretty, with secluded wineries hiding down shady lanes. And the

final reason is what those wineries make – some of the best Riesling in the world.

Riesling is a distinctive white wine most often associated with northern Europe (especially Alsace in France and Germany's Mosel Valley) but in Clare they've taken the grape, lost some of its sweetness and added a strong mineral edge. What ends up in your glass here is arguably the best possible companion for Asian cuisine.

Most wine-tourers will be arriving from Adelaide – beyond Clare, the terrain gets increasingly rugged until you arrive in the Flinders Ranges and the start of the true outback. Before you arrive in Clare you'll pass through the Barossa, now home to many of Australian wine's biggest and most historic names. Clare too is rich in heritage, with some century-old vineyards. But the place also seems to inspire an adventurous spirit in its winemakers – long may that continue.

GET THERE
Adelaide has the closest airport; Clare is a couple of hours' drive away, beyond Barossa Valley.

01 WINES BY KT

Kerri Thompson's a one-woman band, founding Wines by KT in 2006 after a career making wine in not only Clare Valley but also Tuscany, Beaujolais and McLaren Vale. As a Riesling evangelist, she has set up shop in the right place, occupying a small cellar door on the main street of Auburn in the south of Clare Valley. Her solo venture combines her experience with an experimental edge that allows her to produce the Pazza, an unfiltered, wild-fermented natural wine among more classic single-vineyard wines. It's an interesting place to begin a journey into Clare's world-class Rieslings. *winesbykt.com; tel +61 04 1985 5500; 20 Main North Rd, Auburn; by reservation 11am–4pm Thu–Mon*

02 SKILLOGALEE

Taking over one of Clare Valley's most venerated wineries is not for the faint-hearted but tech businessman Simon Clausen and wife Lisa are up to the challenge. Skillogalee is based around a cute stone cottage little-changed since it was built by Cornish miner John Trestrail in 1851. As Barossa was being settled by Germanic people, so British, Irish and Polish settlers ventured further up to Clare; the Cornish came out to work in the mines. Its history as a winery began in the 1970s but it was the previous owners, Dave and Diane Palmer who took over in 1989, that put Skillogalee on the map. Now the Clausen family aims to build on that legacy: 'Nearly everyone you meet, especially from South Australia, has a Skillogalee story and that is something we are immensely respectful of,' says Lisa Clausen.

They'll continue to focus on low-yielding vines and hand-crafted processes, growing all their own fruit using sustainable techniques. 'We've introduced several biodynamic practices in the vineyard and are planting indigenous flora to strengthen local ecosystems and attract native insect predators to help us control vineyard pests naturally,' explains Lisa. Lending a hand is consultant winemaker Kerri Thompson of Wines by KT, who has a deep connection with Clare Valley.

'We love that Skillogalee is a wine destination where you experience

01 Skillogalee
cellar door

02 Skillogalee's
verandah

03 Meals with a view at
Skillogalee

04 Tom and Sam Barry
of Jim Barry Wines

05 The view from
Paulett Wines

06 Tim Adams wines

'Clare has its own distinct feel, history and wine profile with exceptional landscapes, a great community and climate.'

–Simon Clausen, Skillogalee

it all: you can see where the grapes that made the wine you're enjoying were grown, you can visit the historic cellar door and then have lunch, perhaps on the verandah overlooking the vines.' In addition to the cottage's rustic restaurant, serving seasonal dishes, new accommodation means staying for bed and breakfast is an option. *skillogalee.com.au; tel +61 08-8843 4311; Trevarrick Rd, Sevenhill; 9.30am-5pm daily* ✖

🕒 PAULETTS

It was Penfolds' head winemaker who recommended Neil and Alison Paulett start a winery in Clare Valley. 'It's a reliable region,' says Alison Paulett, 'the elevation brings hot days and cool nights,

which slow the ripening and lend the Riesling its austere style.' Winemaker Neil's Polish Hill River Riesling has waves of citrus and a mineral backbone, helping it to age for 10 years or more. Their Polish Hill River Shiraz, named after the Polish settlers who moved here in the mid-1800s, spends 15 months in French and American oak barrels. 'The most important thing,' laughs Alison, 'is getting people to know where Clare is.' Their wines are spreading the word, as is their excellent Bush DeVine Restaurant, with wine-paired dining. *paulettwines.com.au; tel +61 08-8843 4328; 752 Jolly Way (Sevenhill-Mintaro Road), Polish Hill River; by reservation 11am-4pm daily* 💲✖

05 TIM ADAMS WINES

Brett Schutz, a winemaker at Tim Adams, in the heart of Clare Valley, believes European makers of Riesling are adopting the Australian style, with lower sugar levels. In return, the Clare Valley is adopting a European idea: 'The essence of terroir is important here. No two areas of Clare are the same; there are microclimates so you can blend minerality from Watervale with fruitier grapes from the warmer north end of Clare.' The result is a brisk, dry, crisp Riesling, thanks to a fast 14-day fermentation. 'All Tim asks us to do is express the fruit through the wine.'
timadamswines.com.au; tel +61 08-8842 2429; 156 Warenda Rd, Clare; by reservation daily 10am-4.30pm $

06 JIM BARRY WINES

For some of Clare's most exciting wines, from its highest and oldest vineyards, head up to the far side of town. First planted in the 1960s, the Armagh vineyard, named after the green hills of Irish settlers' home county, makes world-class Shiraz wine. The Florita vineyard in Watervale, one of the area's oldest, produces the monstrously good Lodge Hill Riesling. As well as tastings, you can book tours of the Armagh and Florita vineyards.
jimbarry.com; tel +61 08-8842 2261; 33 Craig Hill Rd, Clare; 9am-5pm Mon-Fri, 9am-4pm Sat & Sun $

04 SHUT THE GATE

With a clutch of recent awards in its display cabinet, including the top spot in Adelaide Review's Top 100 Hot Wines and also the award for 2022's Best Large Cellar Door, Clare Valley from *Gourmet Traveller WINE* journal, Shut the Gate is playing a blinder. The focus for the wine range is approachability, with some delicious examples of Clare's signature Rieslings, laden with tropical lime and other food-friendly flavours, and classic cool-climate Shiraz. But there are some adventurous choices to be discovered in the list, including a raspberry-rich Sangiovese and a bright Barbera. The grapes are generally bought in from premium local growers so you won't see any rolling vineyards from your perch at the cellar door on Clare's main road. However, owners Rasa Fabian and Richard Woods have crafted the look and feel of the cellar door as carefully as their wines so it's a very pleasant place to be. There's vintage furniture to settle into, surrounded by shabby-chic décor. The wine labels are just as artful, adopting a slightly Gothic, gold-tinged grandeur or retro hand-drawn illustrations of animals that sit well with the rest of the venue.

Close by there's a providore that can supply local produce for a picnic in the countryside.
shutthegate.withwine.com; tel +61 08-8843 4114; 8453 Main R Rd, Clare; daily 10am-4.30pm

WHERE TO STAY

CLARE VALLEY MOTEL
The Clare Valley Motel is an affordable base for a weekend away among the vines. It has been renovated over recent years by owners Lee and Jan Stokes but retains the quaint vibe of a traditional country motel. *clarevalleymotel.com. au; tel 08-8842 2799; 74a Main North Rd, Clare*

SKILLOGALEE
An overnight stay at one of Skillogalee's four cottages, perhaps after a home-cooked meal in the restaurant, allows you to wake up to breakfast in the peace and quiet of the vineyard. That's a win-win. *skillogalee.com.au; tel +61 08-8843 4311; Trevarrick Rd, Sevenhill*

WHERE TO EAT

SEED
Newly germinated in Clare, Seed is an all-day bistro in an atmospheric old building. Fresh, healthy, regional cuisine is served, including platters for sharing. In

the evening the wine bar is buzzing. *seedclarevalley.com; tel +61 08-8842 2323; 308 Main North Rd, Clare; Wed-Sat*

WHAT TO DO

RIESLING TRAIL
Following the course of a disused railway line between Auburn and Clare, the fabulous Riesling Trail is 24km of traffic-free cycling trail. The gentle gradient means you can walk or push a pram along it easily. Take your time and explore the dozens of detours to cellar doors along the way. Bikes can be hired at either end of the route. *rieslingtrailbike-hire. com.au*

IKARA-FLINDERS RANGES NATIONAL PARK
Some three hours' drive beyond Clare, the Ikara-Flinders Ranges National Park is a highlight of South Australia. Its saw-toothed ranges are home to native wildlife and, after rain, carpets of wild flowers. The vast Wilpena Pound natural basin is the big-ticket drawcard. There's accommodation at the Wilpena Pound Resort. *parks.sa.gov.au/parks/ ikara-flinders-ranges-national-park*

CELEBRATIONS

Slurp previews of the latest wines from the local makers at the annual Clare Valley Gourmet Week in May. Around 20 wineries participate, with food and live music also on the menu. *clarevalley.com.au*

[Australia]

MUDGEE

Mudgee – higher and colder than it's famous neighbours – is arguably New South Wales' most exciting and rewarding wine region to visit.

Is there a more quintessentially Australian country town than Mudgee? It takes its name from the Indigenous Wiradjuri word *moothi* (meaning 'nest in the hills'), and you can see why. With its historic stone buildings, Cudgegong River, big eucalypts, undulating pastures, vineyard country and forested surrounds, Mudgee is pretty indeed.

The Hunter Valley was Mudgee's closest wine region for most of its history, but the two could not be more different. While the Hunter's weather is influenced by the Pacific Ocean, Mudgee is on the western slopes of the Great Dividing Range and its weather is more westerly influenced: hotter summers, colder winters, less rain in the growing season and less humidity. It's also higher-altitude at 400m to 500m (1312ft to 1640ft), with vines as high as 1100m (3609ft) in the Rylstone area, at Nullo Mountain. This combination of continental climate and well-drained sandy loam or slightly acidic soils, over clay, is suited to robust red wines like the region's deep crimson Cabernets.

Mudgee has a rich past and was a notable gold-mining area; poet Henry Lawson is one of its favourite sons. The local wine industry recently went through a period of radical restructuring during which a third of its vines were uprooted; what remains should be the cream of the crop. Certainly, the wine quality, winery tourism and optimism of the *vignerons* are all on a high, with confident investment in cellar doors and some fine restaurants opening.

Mudgee is the first Australian wine region to be known for organic wine, due to pioneer Botobolar – claiming to be Australia's oldest organic vineyard, established in 1971 – and later subscribers Lowel and Broombee. At under four hours' drive from Sydney and with some 35 cellar doors, it's a great winery-hopping weekend destination.

GET THERE
Mudgee is 128km (80 miles) north of Lithgow. From Sydney, it offers a drive through the Blue Mountains and Great Dividing Range.

From top left: courtesy of Gilbert Family Wines (2); Robert Stein / Amanda Davenport / Smudge Publishing

01 LOWE WINES

The Lowe family property Tinja has been in the family for five generations, but David Lowe was the first to plant vines here. A charismatic 'flying winemaker' (someone who has gained and shared expertise across continents), he wears his reputation lightly, encouraging clear, jargon-free appreciation of the splendid wines at Lowe's award-winning cellar door.

The vineyards are in two discrete locations: at the winery on Tinja Lane where Shiraz and Zinfandel are grown; and in a recently acquired vineyard at Nullo Mountain, near Rylstone. This 1100m high-altitude vineyard excels with Riesling, Chardonnay and Pinot Gris. Lowe also produces wine from grapes grown at Orange. All the vineyards are certified organic and Lowe also makes some no-preservative-added wines. Renowned chef Kim Currie runs an outstanding restaurant, the Zin House, in the former Lowe family homestead, overlooking the Zinfandel vineyard. You can also follow a walking and cycling trail through the orchards and vines, past donkeys and an emu paddock to wooded picnic grounds. *lowewine.com.au; tel +61 02-5858 4026; Tinja Lane, Mudgee; 10am– 4.30pm daily* 🄢✕

02 ROBERT OATLEY VINEYARDS

The Oatley family, founders of the well-established Rosemount Estate, still have two wineries in Mudgee: Montrose and Craigmoor. The latter is Mudgee's oldest winery and vineyard, established in 1858, and now hosts the cellar door, art gallery and, in what was once the underground barrel cellar, a small wine museum. Tastings feature six wines from Oatley's Craigmoor and Montrose estates; these might include Artist Series Chardonnay and Shiraz, with labels by local artist Leonie Barton. Grazing boxes are available if ordered in advance *craigmoor.com.au; tel +61 02-6372 2208; Craigmoor Rd, Mudgee; 11am–4pm Fri-Mon, daily in school holidays* 🄢

03 HUNTINGTON ESTATE

One of Mudgee's most famous wineries, Huntington Estate changed

Mudgee's combination of continental climate and well-drained sandy soils is suited to robust red wines: deep crimson Cabernet Sauvignons lead the way

hands in 2005, when Bob Roberts retired and passed the reins to his neighbours, Tim and Nicky Stevens. The estate's renowned full-bodied, long-aging reds, made from Cabernet Sauvignon and Shiraz, are still here but the focus has shifted a little, with Tim adding some lighter-bodied reds to the portfolio – such as a juicy, succulent little Grenache.

Older vintages are available at the cellar door and the Stevens are still dedicated to bottles that stand the test of time. Mudgee's firm tannins are a pet project: while respecting what the region naturally produces, Tim experiments with fermenting whole bunches and whole berries, as well as making an Amarone-style red from partially sun-dried grapes. You can also enjoy a glass or two and

a cheese or charcuterie board in the Garden Bar.

The annual week-long Huntington Estate Music Festival, initiated by the music-loving Roberts family, attracts some of the best chamber musicians in the world. In partnership with Musica Viva, it is more popular than ever. *huntingtonestate.com.au; tel +61 02-6373 3825; 641 Ulan Rd, Buckaroo; daily* 🅂✕

04 ROBERT STEIN

Winegrowing in Mudgee was established by a German viticulturist named Roth, brought to Australia in the 1830s to work for one of the industry founders, John Macarthur. Another of those German 'vine-dressers' was an

and Tempranillo. Of special interest is a pair of super-premium Shirazes named Ridge Of Tears, one each from Mudgee and Orange, a fascinating taste comparison. *loganwines.com.au; tel +61 02-6373 1333; 1320 Castlereagh Hwy, Apple Tree Flat, Mudgee; 10am–5pm* 🅢

06 GILBERT FAMILY WINES

A descendant of Joseph Gilbert, who first planted Pewsey Vale in South Australia's Eden Valley in 1842, Simon Gilbert is almost wine royalty. He has made wine in Mudgee most of his life, and with his son, sixth-generation winemaker Will, on board has opened a smart new cellar door in prime position out of Mudgee town on the Ulan Rd.

Will Gilbert worked several vintages in Canada's Okanagan and Niagara regions before returning to the family business in 2016. Acknowledging recent trends, he's broadened the range to include a sparkling Riesling pét-nat (*pétillant naturel*), a skin-contact rosé and skin-fermented white wines. These are well-made drops that will appeal to followers of the natural-wine movement. An alternative draw might be the Goose Apple cider, also available at the cellar door. Grazing boards are on offer at weekends. *gilbertfamilywines.com.au; tel +61 02-6372 1325; 137 Ulan Rd, Mudgee; 10am–6pm Sun–Thurs, 10am–10pm Fri–Sat* 🅢

ancestor of Robert Stein, but it wasn't until 1976 that Stein moved from Sydney to Mudgee to return to the family's roots. He planted the vines that his grandson Jacob Stein manages today, producing a flagship, award-winning Riesling range as well as full-blooded reds from Shiraz and Cabernet Sauvignon, some made with organically grown grapes.

Robert Stein had another passion beside wine – motorcycles – and you can check out his vintage collection at the free on-site museum. Also in the grounds, the Pipeclay Pumphouse restaurant has high standards to match the wines. Much of the produce is grown on the farm, including pork from Jacob's own pigs. *robertstein.com.au; tel +61 02-6373 3991; Pipeclay Lane, Mudgee; 10am–4.30pm daily* 🅢✕

05 LOGAN WINES

The modern, stylishly designed Logan cellar door puts paid to any notions of Mudgee as a staid old wine region. Winemaker and owner Peter Logan holds court in this sunny space with its panoramic view over the Cudgegong Valley. He swapped pharmaceuticals for the wine industry, setting up Logan in 1997 to specialise in wines made from Mudgee and Orange grapes.

Logan's schtick is all about wines that accompany food, wines that people enjoy drinking, as opposed to wines that win medals. To that end he's added a skin-fermented Pinot Gris: an amber-coloured wine with tannin, texture and the backbone to partner stronger food flavours better than most white wines. The quirky range Weemala, named after the Logan vineyard in Mudgee, includes Shiraz Viognier

WHERE TO STAY

PERRY STREET HOTEL
Stunning apartment suites make a sophisticated choice in town. The attention to detail is outstanding, right down to the kimono bathrobes, Nespresso machine and gratis gourmet snacks. *perrystreethotel. com.au; tel +61 02- 6372 7650; cnr Perry & Gladstone Sts, Mudgee*

WILDWOOD GUESTHOUSE
This rustic homestead has four comfortable bedrooms individually styled with big downy beds, fine linens and an eclectic mix of antiques. Each opens out onto the wraparound verandah overlooking the tranquil countryside. *wildwoodmudgee. com.au; tel +61 02-6373 3701; Henry Lawson Dr, Mudgee*

WHERE TO EAT

ZIN HOUSE
A highlight of vineyard dining: long, leisurely six-course lunches of simply prepared local

produce (either home-grown, from honey and eggs to figs, quinces and persimmons; or impeccably sourced), paired with Lowe wines. Diners share farmhouse tables in a beautifully designed home. *zinhouse.com.au; tel +61 02- 5858 4026; 329 Tinja Ln, Mudgee; Tue-Sun*

PIPECLAY PUMPHOUSE
On the grounds of the Robert Stein Winery, this farm-to-table stunner is the talk of Mudgee, serving to-die-for light lunches made using a wealth of local produce, perhaps spiced lamb with almond-butter cauliflower or gnocchi with mushrooms and

feta; and six-course dégustation dinners, paired of course with excellent Robert Stein wines. *pipeclaypumphouse. com.au; tel +61 02-6373 3998; 1 Pipeclay Ln, Mudgee; lunch Fri-Sun, dinner Thu-Sat*

ALBY & ESTHERS
Down an alleyway is this supremely pretty courtyard café, serving up fine local fare and good coffee. There's a tempting wine list focussed on Mudgee producers, plus cocktails and keffir. *albyandesthers. com.au; tel +61 02- 6372 1555; 61 Market St, Mudgee; Mon-Sat*

WHAT TO DO

CYCLING
One of the best ways to explore the region is by bike – clear your head with a relaxed ride around town, or take on the more challenging 25km (15-mile) Rocky Waterhole loop. *visitmudgeeregion. com.au*

PUTTA BUCCA WETLANDS
Swap wine tasting for birdwatching at this wildlife park, just north of Mudgee, on the site of an old quarry. *puttabuccawetlands. webs.com*

CELEBRATIONS

September's popular Mudgee Wine & Food Month celebrates the region's wineries, farms and paddock-to-plate restaurants and features live music, cellar-door events, tastings and special lunches and dinners. Check the website for full details, and book accommodation ahead. *mudgeewinemonth. com.au*

06

[Australia]

MORNINGTON PENINSULA

Hightail it out of Victoria's state capital for a weekend among the vines and lanes of this peninsula, and enjoy revitalising beach walks, great wines and local dining.

The Mornington Peninsula has long played an important role in Melbourne society. It's a place where wealthy wine enthusiasts – Melbourne's great and good – have sunk more than a few thousand dollars into their dream project, with the reasonable expectation of seeing the most pleasing results in the bottle rather than on the balance sheet.

Since the revival of the Peninsula's vineyards in the mid-1970s (grapes were first planted here in the 19th century) this 40km-long (25-mile) tendril of land has seen more than 50 cellar doors open, luring weekending cityfolk down the Nepean Highway. The Peninsula is relatively developed along the northwest coast but becomes wilder the further south you go, until you reach the Mornington Peninsula National Park. But along the central ridge around Red Hill, where many of the wineries are located, it is almost quaint in places, with twisty lanes, charming village

GET THERE
Melbourne is the closest city; the Mornington Peninsula is an easy 1hr drive south.

corners and green valleys.

Pinot Noir's spiritual home might be Burgundy, but it has settled very happily here on the other side of the world. Australia's only wine-growing region with a truly maritime climate, the Mornington Peninsula's Pinot Noir grapes love the cool sea breezes that prolong the ripening cycle, increasing flavour. Characteristics of the peninsula's Pinot include a transcendent scent – earthy, spicy, yet fruity – that seems to flick a pleasure switch deep within the brain, as well as a lighter body than Pinots from elsewhere in the New World. Few other grapes are as memorable. Chardonnay is just as distinctive a wine on the peninsula, with a delicacy not found elsewhere; only a few wineries have the know-how to get the best from this partnership. When you've tasted enough wines for the day, drive down to the east coast and watch the sun set from one of the forest-backed beaches.

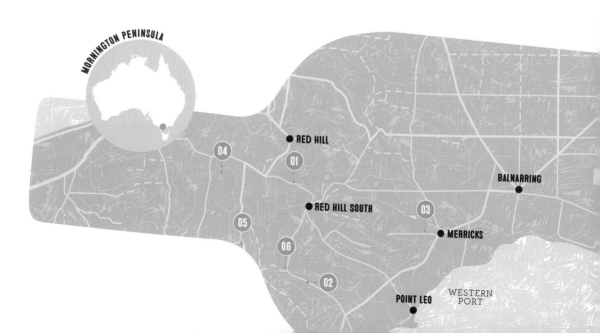

01 ELDRIDGE ESTATE

High on a hill just outside Red Hill, Eldridge Estate winemaker and owner David Lloyd has been chasing the perfect Pinot Noir since taking over the small vineyard in 1995. To that end, he has planted three different Burgundian varieties of the grape and produces examples of each. Note the care he takes over them: bunches are de-stemmed but berries left whole; pressed with an air bag press; fermented naturally without yeast; aged in French oak. The result is a fine example of Mornington Peninsula Pinot – dark cherry fruit but savoury – that demonstrates how food-friendly a grape Pinot Noir can be. It's always interesting visiting Eldridge Estate and one must-try wine is Lloyd's PTG, his take on Burgundy's Passe-Tout-Grain blend of Pinot Noir and

Gamay, a light, quaffable wine that is bright but earthy simultaneously. Compare it with the pure Pinots on the terrace overlooking the vineyard. Mornington Peninsula vineyards are usually a bit higher and a couple of degrees cooler than average, and there's no frost as it's close to the sea. The cooler the climate, the longer the grapes take to ripen and build flavour.

Lloyd's expertise is also applied to Chardonnay – the Wendy Chardonnay, a tribute to David's wife, who died in 2014, is, as he says, 'the best Chardonnay I can make from the estate in any one year.' *eldridge-estate.com.au; tel +61 04-1475 8960; 120 Arthurs Seat Rd, Red Hill; 11am-5pm Fri-Mon* $

02 MONTALTO

Montalto is a winery that succeeds in covering all the bases: world-

class wines, great food and paths that lure visitors deep into the vineyard. But what makes Montalto a must-visit cellar door is its Chardonnay. Once described by James Halliday as 'power and grace personified', it's as enjoyable an example of the grape as you'll find. Picked from Montalto's main north-facing vineyard and from the plot behind the cellar door, the wine, despite its scarcity, has earned accolades from all over the world.

Montalto is owned by the Mitchell family, and the vineyard dates back to 1999, although the modern cellar door only opened in 2001. 'While we see ourselves as a winery, our philosophy is to be a destination to draw people to the Mornington Peninsula,' says John Mitchell. 'No matter where people are in the world, when they drink our wines we want them to remember the

a rock-solid sense of place. Stonier is one of the first wave of vineyards on the peninsula, with its Chardonnay vines dating from 1978 and the Pinot Noir vines from 1982. Today, senior winemaker and manager Justin Pursur, alongside Sam Milne, create Chardonnay and Pinot Noir in several categories, ranging from blends from the younger vineyards to bottles from single vineyards, a dedication to terroir derived from Burgundy. Stonier's distinctive, airy cellar door, designed by Melbourne architect Daryl Jackson, is the perfect venue for these ambitious wines.

Bunches are counted in late December, when some may be pruned (fewer bunches concentrate the vine's energies and flavour). According to one-time cellar door manager Noella 'That's when our viticulturalist starts getting stressed about ordering barrels – at $1200 to $1500 each – and we all take bets on how much will be produced.' Stonier is right on the east coast of the peninsula and the cool conditions suit Chardonnay too: 'Warmer areas produce bigger, buttery chards,' explains Noella. Look for a mineral edge instead in Stonier's Chardonnay, which is as refreshing as a walk on the beach across the road. 'But if you prefer Pinots,' adds Noella, 'go and try them at Main Ridge'.

stonier.com.au; tel +61 03-5989 8300; 2 Thompsons Ln, Merricks; 11am–5pm daily $

whole experience.' To that end, the Mitchells have an olive grove with 1500 trees (you can taste the olive oil in the cellar door), four locations around the valley set aside for picnics, a restaurant supplied by herb and vegetable gardens, and an orchard. Afterwards, there are sculptures sprinkled around the vineyards to discover on a walking trail through vines and wetlands. As John Mitchell says, the Mornington Peninsula offers much more than wine alone.

montalto.com.au; tel +61 03-5989 8412; 33 Shoreham Rd, Red Hill South; 11am–5pm daily %*✕

03 STONIER

Stonier earned a reputation for producing some of the Mornington Peninsula's most expressive Pinot Noirs under former winemaker Geraldine McFaul – wines with

04 MAIN RIDGE ESTATE

The rough gravel track leading to Main Ridge's cellar door might seem designed to deter casual quaffers. Until 2015, it would be the tall, bespectacled figure of Nat White, MP winemaking pioneer, who'd greet visitors. These days he acts as mentor to sommelier-turned-winemaker James Sexton, son of Tim and Libby, who took over from Nat and his wife Rosalie. Tim and Libby Sexton enjoyed a brief retirement before taking the plunge and purchasing Main Ridge from Nat White, having fallen in love with the place, like many visitors do, on a visit to the cellar door.

The Sexton family aims to honour the legacy of the Whites at Main Ridge, which was one of the first wineries on Mornington Peninsula. The 40-plus-year-old vines here were the second to be planted during the Peninsula's revival in the mid-1970s and produce some of the most fascinating wines from Red Hill's volcanic soils.

Handing over the reins seems to have gone smoothly, with the Sextons spending time with the Whites in preparation for the transition, and their first harvest of yielding recognisably classic Pinot Noir. Pinot Noir is where it all started for Main Ridge: after a road trip through France in the 1970s Nat and Rosalie were unable to forget about Burgundy's Pinot Noirs. They aimed to replicate the lighter, fruitier Burgundy style from some of the highest and coolest

05 The wines of Red Hill Estate

06 Barrel testing at Stonier

tenminutesbytractor.com. au; tel +61 03-5989 6080; 1333 Mornington-Flinders Rd, Main Ridge; 11am-5pm daily 💲✕

06 RED HILL ESTATE

Wooden crates are still scattered around the old sorting shed at Red Hill Estate, on the road back to Shoreham, but the space around them has evolved into the tasting room of this 30-year-old vineyard. Out the back, Max's Restaurant has views over green countryside all the way down to the sea and Phillip Island. Chef Max Paganoni selects local produce – strawberries from Sunny Ridge, cheese from Red Hill's own artisan cheesery – for his Italian-influenced menus. On summer weekends you can expect weddings in the gardens.

Back in the cellar door, Red Hill's wines are no less enjoyable. Concentrating on Chardonnay and Pinot Noir, Red Hill winemakers use traditional techniques, including wild yeasts and smaller bunches of berries to up the skin-to-flesh ratio. The result is a complex, earthy Cellar Door Release Pinot Noir and a Chardonnay that is less big and brassy than you may find elsewhere. Both are designed to cellar for a long time; up to 15 years in the case of the Pinot. *redhillestate.com.au; tel +61 03-5989 2838; 53 Shoreham Rd, Red Hill South; 11am-5pm daily* 💲✕

vines on the peninsula. Be sure to taste the difference between the Half-Acre and the Acre Pinots, both produced from the same sloping plot and treated identically. Today, visitors can enjoy a glass or two accompanied by a cheese platter on the sunny deck overlooking the vines. Consider arriving early to avoid having to leave empty-handed – with such small-scale production, the 'sold out' sign is often deployed. *mre.com.au; tel +61 03-5989 2686; 80 William Rd, Red Hill; 11-5pm Sat-Sun and public holidays*

05 TEN MINUTES BY TRACTOR

With its jazz soundtrack and a modern, minimalist interior, Ten Minutes By Tractor is one of the most chic cellar doors on the Mornington Peninsula. Wine is produced from three vineyards, all, you guessed it, ten minutes from each other by tractor. Owner Martin Spedding, who works alongside winemaker Imogen Dillon, believes the region is coming of age now since the first vines were planted in the 1970s: 'Of the 60 or 70 wine producers here, a great majority of them are producing fantastic wine.' This includes TMBT, where top-of-the-range wines go for $80 a bottle. 'These are small-yielding vineyards and the wines are expensive as a result.'

With a deck overlooking a valley and a small plot of vines, the cellar door restaurant offers food tailored to the estate's wines. 'Pinot Noir is better with food than some of Australia's heavier reds,' says Martin. 'The types of foods we're now eating in Australia – a fusion of Asian and Mediterranean flavours – is food with delicate layers of flavours. People are looking for wines that complement not dominate food.'

WHERE TO STAY
CAPE SCHANCK RESORT
Although you can stay in Cape Schanck's actual lighthouse (see below), this RACV resort has a bit more space. It overlooks the wild Bass Strait.
acv.com.au; tel +61 03-5950 8000 Trent Jones Dr, Cape Schanck

WHERE TO EAT
RED HILL BREWERY
Red Hill's brewery grows its own hops, and brews enough European-inspired ales – from strong Belgian-style lagers and German pilsners to English stouts and bitters – to keep beer-curious wine-tourers refreshed. Pair the beers with a decent bar menu, from burgers to maple-glazed ribs.
redhillbrewery.com.au; tel +61 03-5989 2959; 88 Shoreham Rd, Red Hill South; Thu-Sun

PORTSEA HOTEL
At the very tip of the peninsula, Portsea's hotel serves Italian-inspired pub grub, with views on the side.
portseahotel.com.au; tel +61 03-5984 2213; 3746 Point Nepean Rd, Portsea; Wed-Mon

WHAT TO DO
Pack your hiking shoes for the one-hour bush walk to Cape Schanck Lighthouse Reserve's Bushranger's Bay, at the south-east tip of the peninsula. It's an untamed place, rich in wildlife, from the frogs croaking under the tea trees to the kangaroos bounding along the beach at sunset. Look south to see the Cape Schanck lightstation itself, which dates from 1859 and houses a small museum and self-catering accommodation.
parkweb.vic.gov.au

CELEBRATIONS
The biennial Pinot Noir Celebration (February), sees winemakers from all over the world converge on the Mornington Peninsula to sniff each other's Pinots and swap pruning tips. Later in the year the Winter Wine Weekend (June) is an opportunity to meet the producers, attend seminars and taste wine; accommodation gets booked early up for both occasions.
mpva.com.au/events

[Australia]
YARRA VALLEY

Fabulous wineries, attractive towns, innovative art galleries, roaming 'roos: the Yarra Valley easily tempts as a perfect weekend retreat, moments from Melbourne.

Many good things came out of the 1960s. One of the best was the idea by such pioneers as Guill de Pury of Yeringberg winery to plant vines in the Yarra Valley again. Grapes had been planted around the gentle slopes of the Yarra Ranges since the first settlers arrived in the 1830s, but winemaking had petered out until Guill's group of hobbyist winemakers picked up the reins again. Starting with just 2 hectares (5 acres) at Yeringberg, the estate now comprises more than 20 hectares (50 acres). That expansion has been mirrored across the valley, with about 100 wineries and more than 50 cellar doors, large and small, now sprinkled around the country towns of Yarra Glen and Healesville.

Described by wine writer and resident James Halliday as 'a place of extreme beauty', the Yarra Valley is just an hour from Melbourne. But the large numbers of visitors from the big city – especially at weekends – seem to be effortlessly absorbed into this Arcadian retreat. There are more than enough wineries and beauty spots to find some space of your own. The Yarra River, marked by a line of River Red gum trees, runs straight through the middle of the valley, north of the Maroondah Hwy. On a hot day the temptation to find a shady swimming spot and chill a bottle of Chardonnay in the Yarra's waters is irresistible. With all the daytrippers, the valley can sustain a stellar supporting cast of boutique B&Bs, swanky restaurants (often in the wineries), and foodie shops such as the Yarra Valley Dairy and numerous delicatessens in Healesville. This makes the Yarra Valley Victoria's leading wine-touring destination, and perhaps Australia's. But remember that you're more likely to meet actual winemakers like Guill de Pury at the smaller cellar doors – and that's the joy of wine touring here.

GET THERE
The closest airport to Yarra Valley is Melbourne's, around a 1hr hour drive away.

01 MANDALA WINES

Although Mandala's cellar door, with its cantilevered roof, looks contemporary, the vines – primarily Pinot Noir and Chardonnay – have been around for more than 20 years. Picks of the Mandala bunch are the single-site wines: The Rock, The Prophet, The Matriarch and The Butterfly, which are available for tasting on selected weekends. Single-vineyard wines in Australia are an attempt to introduce the idea of Old World terroir, where a wine is imbued with the characteristics of a specific plot of land. Taste the Matriarch and Prophet Pinot Noirs and make up your own mind. Another highlight at Mandala is the DiVino restaurant, which serves Italian-influenced food.

mandalawines.com.au; tel +61 03-5965 2016; 1568 Melba Hwy, Dixons Creek; 11am-4pm Wed-Fri, 11am-5pm Sat & Sun 🏷✖

02 TARRAWARRA ESTATE

No other winery in the Yarra Valley has quite the same visual effect as Marc and Eva Besen's remarkable creation. Shadows cast by concrete columns sweep across a courtyard framed by rammed-earth walls and the arcing glass of the TarraWarra Museum of Art. The complex rests atop a ridge between Healesville and Yarra Glen and is the work of Melbourne architect Allan Powell, who seems to have been inspired by the Yarra's light and its earth.

With a car park often filled with sports cars, an entrance that curls between high-sided walls before opening out to views over vines and landscaped grounds to the north, visiting this winery is certainly an event. Luckily Clare Halloran's wines are equal to the build-up: her Chardonnay, typically aged 10 months in oak, is a well-defined example of the grape. The other big draw here is the TarraWarra Museum of Art (twma.com.au), which hosts exhibitions of modern (post-1930) Australian art from the Besens' own collection. There's also a celebrated restaurant, with Yarra Valley-born chef Joel Alderdice cooking up seasonal, locally sourced food; much of the produce is grown in the kitchen garden.

tarrawarra.com.au; tel +61 03-5957 3510; 311 Healesville-Yarra Glen Rd, Yarra Glen; 11am-5pm Tue-Sun 🏷✖

03 YERINGBERG

It was the gold-diggers who first followed the Yarra Track up to Victoria's goldfields in the 1850s, because the Yarra River couldn't be crossed in flood. The track became a road, and as people settled in the valley, vines started to flower and the first wine boom swept the Yarra in the 1880s.

The second wave of pioneers, such as Guill de Pury, arrived in the 1960s. His Yeringberg winery, now run by fourth-generation siblings Sandra and David de Pury, stands on the site of an original 150-year-old vineyard and many of its features date from that era. Another connection with the past is Yeringberg's Marsanne Roussanne white wine, which uses the grape varieties originally planted in the Yarra – and happens to age beautifully.
yeringberg.com; tel +61 03-9739 0240; 810 Maroondah Hwy, Coldstream; visits by appointment

04 YARRA YERING

The legacy of the revered founder and winemaker Dr Bailey Carrodus abides at Yarra Yering – one of the most iconic wineries in the region. The tasting experience here is an insight into the history of the Yarra Valley and a rare opportunity to taste wines that are not so readily available, coveted as they are by collectors and loyal customers.

Dr Carrodus' house was converted into the tasting room in 2011 and it retains the comfortable vibe of a lounge room, complete with a large window giving a magnificent view of vines and the valley. There are a few options for the guided tasting and each are priced based on the wines poured. It's only an extra $10 to try them all (including the Carrodus range and a few museum releases) and it's well worth it, if only to taste three vintages of the glorious Carrodus Shiraz ($275/bottle).

In 2011, Yarra Yering took over the adjacent Warramate vineyard. Previously run by Jack and June Church and their son, David, award-winning winemaker Sarah Crowe is now overseeing production of some excellent Shiraz and Pinot Noir, alongside Chardonnay and Riesling.
yarrayering.com; tel +61 03-5964 9267; 4 Briarty Rd, Gruyere; by reservation 10am–5pm daily 💲

05 COLDSTREAM HILLS

Is it inviting payback to start a winery when you're Australia's best-known wine critic? The question certainly didn't stop James Halliday, who put his money where his mouth was and founded Coldstream Hills in 1985. After all, how hard can it be? With Andrew Fleming and Greg Jarratt in charge of the winemaking, Coldstream Hills' wines, especially the Pinot Noir, have attracted plenty of praise. In part their success has been down to the setting of the closely planted vines around a natural, north-facing amphitheatre, much as they would be in Europe. *coldstreamhills.com.au; tel +61 03-5960 7000; 29 Maddens Lane, Gruyere; 10am-5pm Fri-Mon* $

06 PIMPERNEL

Pimpernel began as a passion project for cardiologist Mark Horrigan but, as is often the case, the hobby took hold. Hard to resist when you have some of the region's great Pinot Noir being made by winemaker Damian Archibald, who knows his stuff, having worked under Dr Bailey Carrodus of Yarra Yering.

Mark was obsessed by the vineyards of Burgundy's DRC (Domaine de la Romanée-Conti) and on a visit there with his mum, she leapt the fence and borrowed a few rocks from the vineyard. Testing them back in Australia, he identified that their specific composition was similar to rocks excavated at the nearby Lilydale quarry. He set aside a half-acre of the Pinot block, dug 2m (6.5ft) down and deposited 250 tonnes of the limestone. Pinot vines were then close-planted – et voilà! DRC meets the Yarra Valley. A little extravagant, maybe, but the extraordinary results can be tasted in Pimpernel's four Pinot Noir wines from the single vineyard, each varying in style. The vineyard is dry-grown and the winemaking style is French-inspired, resulting in complex and savoury wines. The cellar door is a small room with a barrel spittoon centre stage and a couch for when you need a moment to let the magnificence of Yarra Pinot sink in. *pimpernelvineyards.com.au; tel +61 04-0701 0802; 6 Hill Rd, Coldstream; by reservation 10am-5pm Fri-Sun* $

07 MORGAN VINEYARDS

Since 2009, Morgans has been steered by owners Simon and Michele Gunther, who have renovated the cellar door and distill gin and vodka from local whey. But it was retired Welsh ex-Army captain Roger Morgan who first planted the vineyards, commenting that 'You get extremes of weather here – some years can be really hot and dry with winds from the north, but cold weather systems also roll in from the south.' That unpredictability continues in the grape that Roger chose: the enigmatic, frustrating Pinot Noir. which, he explained, likes cool, sunny places, such as Tasmania, New Zealand and the Yarra Valley. 'It's a thin-skinned, disease-prone grape, so I planted it on the east side of the north-facing vineyard where it gets the morning sun, which dries the canopy.'

The west side of the vineyard is dedicated to robust Cabernet Sauvignon, which can take the afternoon sun and, at 30 years old, are in their prime. The result is a tangy Pinot Noir and a food-friendly, mineral-rich Chardonnay. *morganvineyards.com; tel +61 04-3273 4649; 30 Davross Court, Seville; 11am-5pm Wed-Sun* $

WHERE TO STAY

HEALESVILLE HOTEL
The antique Healesville hotel, in business for some 130 years (having opened on the site of an even older hotel in 1912), is an atmospheric base for exploring the region, and has recently been treated to a sympathetic refurbishment. Rooms share bathrooms. *healesvillehotel. com.au; tel +61 03 5962 1037; 256 Maroondah Hwy, Healesville*

WHERE TO EAT

INNOCENT BYSTANDER
While you're enjoying pizza straight from the wood-fired oven, you can watch the Innocent Bystander winery at work from the split-level dining room. Founders Allison and Phil Sexton (the brewer who brought Little Creatures beer to the world) have added a cheese room, an artisan bakery and even house-roasted coffee to their cellar door. *innocentbystander.com. au; tel +61 03-5999 9222; 336 Maroondah Hwy, Healesville; Fri-Tue*

(07)

YARRA VALLEY DAIRY
Pay homage to the fromage: this is the best place to buy cheese in the area. Hard or soft, most cheeses are made on site. There's an eating area behind the counter where you can enjoy a platter of cheeses, crackers and olives. *yvd.com.au; tel +61 03 9739 1222; 70-80 McMeikans Rd, Yering; daily*

WHAT TO DO

HEALESVILLE SANCTUARY
Get up close to more than 200 species of Australian creatures, including Tasmanian devils, koalas and relaxed wombats. *zoo.org.au/healesville*

GO WILD BALLOONING
Lift off at sunrise for an hour-long flight over the vineyards followed by a gourmet breakfast and a glass of fizz. *gowildballooning.com.au*

CELEBRATIONS

There's always something happening for the viticulturally-minded in Yarra, such as the Winter Wine Festival in late June, with meals and wine pairings at local wineries. *wineyarravalley.com. au/event*

Map labels:
ROWELLA
KAYENA
SIDMOUTH
WINE
07
06
DEVIOT
MT DIRECTION
05
04
Tamar River
Pipers River
GRAVELLY BEACH
EXETER
ROSEVEARS
DILSTON
03
GRINDELWALD
LEGANA
PATERSONIA
NUNAMARA
02
St Patricks River
WAVERLEY
LAUNCESTON
Lake Trevallyn
ST LEONARDS
Meander River
TAMAR VALLEY
01
RELBIA
WHITE HILLS

[Australia]

TAMAR VALLEY

Encounter devilishly delicious Pinot Noir and outstanding local produce in the north of Tasmania on a road trip along the Tamar River.

A wine made with Pinot Noir grapes seems to inspire rapture like no other. People describe good Burgundy in almost mystical terms. In the cult wine film *Sideways* (is this the only cult wine film?), Miles attempts to explain his love of Pinot Noir: 'It's thin-skinned, temperamental, ripens early... needs constant care and attention... and it can only grow in these really specific, little, tucked-away corners of the world.' And one of those tucked-away places is the Tamar Valley in northern Tasmania, which shares a similar climate to the famed Côte d'Or in Burgundy.

If you can tear yourself away from Tasmania's other attractions – staggeringly beautiful beaches, multiday hikes through pristine wilderness, a one-of-a-kind art gallery – a weekend beside the Tamar River will introduce you to some of the world's finest Pinot Noirs and some deliciously moreish local produce;

northern Tasmania is Australia's orchard, where farmers markets are a regular feature of weekend life. The island's food scene is the match of its wine – try fresh seafood with the Tamar's white wines and its lamb with the Pinot Noirs.

The origins of Tasmanian wine lie in a vineyard just east of Launceston, once called La Provence and now known as Providence. It was planted with Pinot Noir and Chardonnay in 1956 by Jean Miguet, the son of a winemaking family. By the 1990s, wines from this part of northern Tasmania were winning international medals. Starting the tour further up the Tamar River, in tiny Relbia, means that you finish close to the Southern Ocean, for a contemplative walk along a deserted beach. 'Haunting and brilliant and thrilling and subtle...' is how Miles describes Pinot Noir in *Sideways*; it's a description that also applies to Tasmania.

GET THERE
Launceston airport, a 30min taxi or bus ride from the city, is served by most Australian cities. There's a ferry from Melbourne.

01 JOSEF CHROMY

The man behind this landmark winery is one of Australian wine's more remarkable characters. Having survived 11 years of Nazi and Soviet occupation, the penniless 19-year-old Josef Chromy left his Czech village and made his way to Australia. Over the next 40 years he built up a fortune in the butchery trade and poured the proceeds of his company's stock market float into the nascent Tasmanian wine industry, establishing Tamar Ridge in 1994 and investing in what is now Bay of Fires. Now in his 90s, Chromy has hardly slowed down, though in 2004 he handed over the task of creating his estate's eponymous wines to Jeremy Dineen, who had a geographic advantage in nurturing Chromy's

Pinot Noir vines, commenting: 'Our southerly latitude gives us the cool climate and long ripening season required by Pinot Noir. Being an island, the ocean has a huge moderating effect on Tasmania's climate so we don't get extremes of heat or cold.'

Dineen moved on from Chromy in 2021, handing over the reins to South African winemaker Ockie Myburgh, but his tenure here coincided with the evolution of Tasmanian wine. Not only is there more first-class fruit being grown today, but a new generation of younger winemakers have the determination to produce distinctive, expressive wines. *josefchromy.com.au; tel +61 03-6335 8700; 370 Relbia Rd, Relbia; tastings 10am–5pm daily* 💲🍴

02 VÉLO WINES

Cycling and wine have long been bedfellows. Indeed, in the earliest days of the Tour de France, riders would raid cafes and bars at the foot of mountains, carrying out bottles with which to fortify themselves for the tough climb ahead. Sadly, by the time Australian Olympic cyclist Michael Wilson had turned professional that practice had stopped. Wilson has now surrendered the saddle, as well as selling on the winery he founded as Legana Estates in 1966 alongside Graham Wiltshire, rebranded as Vélo in 2001. New owners Peter Bond, Ken Hudson and David Vautin have revamped the cellar door and opened an excellent on-site restaurant, Timbre Kitchen.

The standout wines from current winemaker Rod Thorpe include old-vine Cabernet Sauvignon (from some of the island's oldest Cabernet vines, planted in 1966 by Graham Wiltshire) and late-disgorged sparkling wines. *velowines.com.au; tel +61 03-6330 1582; 755 West Tamar Hwy, Legana; tastings by reservation Mon-Fri, till 5pm Sat & Sun* ✕

03 TAMAR RIDGE

Follow the blue-and-yellow signs of the Tamar Valley Wine Route to Tamar Ridge, where you can unpack a picnic on a lawn overlooking the river as it broadens. This is one of the region's larger cellar doors and was purchased from Dr Andrew Pirie, the man behind Tasmania's most successful wine brands, by the big-business Brown Brothers. Today, Tamar Ridge still produces the excellent Pirie range of sparkling wines, but the main focus is on the elegant and bold Pinot Noirs. Pirie's legacy is also reflected in the estate's cool-climate whites, including a straw-coloured, botrytis-affected Riesling dessert wine, an aromatic Sauvignon Blanc and a peachy Chardonnay. *tamarridge.com.au; tel +61 03-6330 0300; 1a Waldhorn Dr, Rosevears; 10am–5pm daily* $ ✕

04 STONEY RISE

Former cricketer Joe Holyman and his wife Lou preside over this small winery, just a twenty-minute walk from the Tamar's shore. After hanging up his wicket-keeping gloves, Joe worked in wineries in Portugal and France before returning home to restore Stoney Rise. Their 7.35 hectares (18 acres) include some of the rare Austrian white grape, Grüner Veltliner, as well as the more predictable Pinot Noir and Chardonnay. They have begun using biodynamic preparations in order to improve the health of their soil, and have given up spraying herbicides for the same reason.

They make two tiers of wine: the entry-level Stoney Rise label; and Pinot Noir and Chardonnay under the Holyman label, made with grapes from a single parcel of vines. The Holyman Pinot Noir is aged in oak *barriques*, which makes for a wine with plenty of depth and fruit.

05 The evening draws
in at Josef Chromy

06 Holm Oak views

door is a tranquil, scenic place to chill out over a glass of the excellent Maia vintage sparkling wine, or taste the Riesling and Pinot Noirs, alongside a gourmet platter of Tasmanian produce or selection of local cheeses.
smallwonderwines.com.au; tel +61 03-6394 7541; 530 Auburn Rd, Kayena; 11am–5pm Thu-Mon 💲🍴

07 HOLM OAK

Winemaker Bec Duffy and her husband Tim, a viticulturist, head up a friendly and intimate venture, named after a grove of well-established English holm oak trees originally planted to make tennis racquets, long before the days of carbon fibre. The wood didn't quite meet requirements, but the fertile soils have proved more than capable of producing winning wines – the estate-grown Pinot Noir is named The Wizard after the racquet used by Australian Wimbledon champion Jack Crawford.

The wines are all very good and quite idiosyncratic – indeed the Duffys would like to be known for down-to-earth, not super-polished but authentic wines. The cellar door sells local goodies so you can compose your own picnic to enjoy on the grounds, overlooking lush orchards and vineyards.
holmoakvineyards.com.au; tel +61 03-6394 7577; 11 West Bay Rd, Rowella; 10am–2pm Mon-Fri 💲🍴

Try it in the cellar door, set on a hill and overlooking the Tamar as it nears the ocean.
stoneyrise.com; tel +61 04-1885 3924; 96 Hendersons Ln, Gravelly Beach; 10am–5pm Thu-Mon 💲🍴

05 MOORES HILL

In 2016, Moores Hill amalgamated with fellow West Tamar vineyard Native Point, the two owner families – the Allports and the Highs – pooling resources to build a new winery and cellar door at Moores Hill and a bottling plant at Native Point. The result was Tasmania's first off-grid winery, with solar panels providing 100% of its electricity needs. There's also an electric vehicle-charging station, useful if you're looking for that sort of juice.

Going green seems to be top priority: viticulturalist Sheena High is moving towards a more sustainable way of managing the vineyard – which comprises

Chardonnay, Pinot Noir and Riesling, as well as small patches of Cabernet and Merlot – using preventative methods of controlling vine diseases and minimising chemical intervention. The sparkling Blanc de Blancs is especially recommended.
mooreshill.com.au; tel +61 03-6394 7649; 3343 W Tamar Hwy, Sidmouth; 11am–5pm daily 💲🍴

06 SMALL WONDER

Established in 2006, this small vineyard at Kayena made its name as Goaty Hill. But in mid-2022, Goaty was relaunched as Small Wonder, with the owners refocusing on regenerative farming practices, working toward organic certification and using 100% green energy on site. The new incarnation remains family owned, and the setting, with its wonderful views across the Tamar River and its valley, is as idyllic as ever. The cellar

ESSENTIAL
INFORMATION

WHERE TO STAY
RED FEATHER INN
At the ocean-end of the Tamar Valley, on the east side of the river, Red Feather Inn is one of Tasmania's best boutique hotels and also offers dinner and even cookery classes. The accommodation is in a series of historic sandstone buildings. *redfeatherinn.com.au; tel +61 03-6393 6506; 42 Main St, Hadspen*

KURRAJONG HOUSE
Owned by a Scottish-Australian couple, this well-run B&B in a handsome 1887 house near Windmill Hill Reserve offers three rooms in the main house and a self-contained cottage in the garden. Angling for a mature clientele (over 21s only), it is made exceptional through attention to detail: fresh flowers, fresh milk for in-room tea, homemade jam with breakfast. *kurrajonghouse. com.au; tel +61 03-6331 6655; cnr High & Adelaide, Launceston*

WHERE TO EAT
STILLWATER
Stillwater is set in a stylishly renovated 1840s flour mill beside the Tamar in Launceston. It serves laidback breakfasts, relaxed lunches – and then puts on the ritz for dinner, with delectable seafood, meat and vegetarian dishes. *stillwater.com.au; tel +61 03-6331 4153; 2 Bridge Rd, Ritchie's Flour Mill, Launceston; breakfast & lunch daily, dinner Tue-Sat*

INGLESIDE BAKERY CAFE
Sit in the flower-filled walled courtyard or under the high ceiling inside these former council chambers (dating

06

to 1867), where fresh-baked aromas waft from the wood oven. Expect delicious pies and pasties, a hefty ploughman's lunch and all manner of sweet treats, including Devonshire teas. bit.ly/InglesideBake; tel +61 03-6391 8682; 4 Russell St, Evandale; daily

WHAT TO DO
A terrain of undulating emerald hills covered with vineyards, orchards and stands of native forest, the Tamar Valley should be explored at a leisurely pace. On the Tamar River's eastern bank is Launceston's ocean port, Bell Bay, near George Town. The western bank is home to a string of easygoing country hamlets that are popular weekend and summer escapes for Launcestonians. The Batman Bridge unites the two shores hear Deviot. It's also worth making a trip to Evandale, south of Launceston. Walk down the main street and you'll feel like you've time-warped back a century – precisely why the entire town is National Trust-listed. Allow a few hours so you can admire its historic streetscapes, and browse a few boutiques. And if you visit on a Sunday, don't miss the Evandale Market. *tamarvalley.com.au; evandaletasmania.com*

CELEBRATIONS
In Launceston, Festivale is an annual summer party celebrating Tasmanian food, wine, beer and music, taking over the historic City Park for three days on the second weekend of February. It's a chance to try some of food-obsessed Tasmania's local produce. *festivale.com.au*

[Canada]
OKANAGAN VALLEY

The freezing winters of Okanagan Valley belie an impressive range of grape varieties grown in vineyards characterised by stunning views and complex soils.

T his trail begins not on the ground but in the air, with a 50-minute flight from Vancouver to Kelowna offering astonishing views of a landscape created by ancient glacial activity. The resulting mountains, snow, endless forests and piercing turquoise lakes are panoramic jaw-droppers, and far-removed from the kind of scenery most people associate with winegrowing.

GET THERE
Fly to Kelowna or Penticton from Vancouver in less than an hour. Car hire is available.

The Okanagan Valley has a complex geology; the glacial movement led to large deposits of silt, sand and gravel on the valley's bed and sides, resulting in a lot of sand-heavy soils in the south and rocky, sparse soils in the north, with assorted differentiations in between – all of which yield refreshingly diverse wines.

With the vineyards lying north of 49°, you might expect the cool temperatures found in Champagne or the Mosel. Many visitors are surprised that vines can be grown here, but despite the icy winters, a vast array of grape varieties can succeed, largely thanks to the hot summers. There's another benefit to the northerly location: short growing seasons are compensated for by long sunlight hours, so grapes have no problem reaching maturity. Add in the differentiation between day and night and you have wines that retain great freshness and thus zingy acidity – a signature of the Okanagan.

The wine industry and vines here are young, but growing fast; in 1984 there were 13 wineries in BC, today there are over 180 in the Okanagan alone. This means fewer rules with regards to planting (more than 230 grape varieties are sown) and wine styles, and all the more fun for wine fans.

This trail focuses first on the Northern Okanagan Valley, from Kelowna down to the cluster of award-winning wineries on the Naramata Bench, across to the other side to Summerland and Westbank, then dips south past Penticton and Kaleden. These areas are well known for cool climate grape varieties, such as Riesling, Pinot Gris, Chardonnay and Pinot Noir.

© Nalidsa / Shutterstock

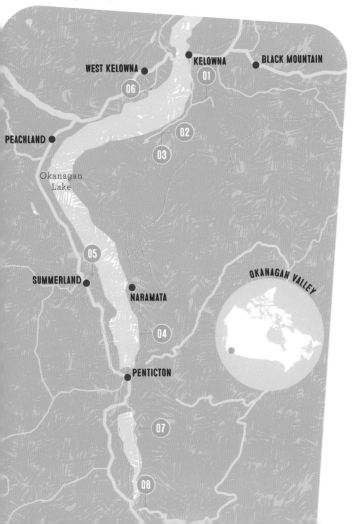

WEST KELOWNA ●
KELOWNA ●
BLACK MOUNTAIN ●
01
06
PEACHLAND ●
02
03
Okanagan Lake
05
SUMMERLAND ●
OKANAGAN VALLEY
NARAMATA ●
04
PENTICTON ●
07
08

01 Vines with a view in Kelowna

02 Quails' Gate winery

03 The pyramid at Summerhill

04 Lake fun at Quails' Gate winery

05 The tasting room at Tantalus Vineyards

06 Okanagan lavender fields

01 TANTALUS VINEYARDS

Tantalus has quite a pedigree as the oldest continuously producing vineyard in British Columbia, originally founded in 1927. It's home to some of BC's oldest plantings of Riesling, from 1978, vines which barely need irrigation, often not at all, and create very intense wines. What's more, some of the vines from this planting are vinified to create a sparkling Riesling which is utterly delicious. Only 200 cases are made so be quick to snap some up.

Pinot Noir and Chardonnay are also produced, as well as lightly sparkling, low-ABV Riesling, Pinot Noir/Meunier and Gewürztraminer/Chardonnay Piquette wines. As part of a wholehearted commitment to sustainable practice, the winery is also home to Arlo's Honey; you can buy pots of the honey in the tasting room. 'We want to achieve a sense of balance in our wines. This includes taking notions from organics and biodynamics; we take everything from our surroundings into account. We keep a 10-acre forest protected by law in the middle of our vineyards, to encourage our ecosystem,' says winemaker David Paterson.
tantalus.ca; tel +1 877-764-0078; 1670 Dehart Rd, Kelowna; daily: 10am-5pm late-May-Jul, 10am-6pm Aug to mid-Sep 💲

02 SUMMERHILL PYRAMID WINERY

Summerhill was the first winery in BC to become certified biodynamic, and has been organic since the very beginning. Here, the ethos is as much about taking care of the soils and the environment as it is about making great wines. Flowers, grass and weeds grow in abundance between the vines. Ezra Cipes, son of current proprietor and founder Stephen Cipes, says: 'Our vision of perfection does not include clean rows. The vineyard is its own ecosystem.' Gabe, Ezra's brother, creates all of the biodynamic preparations, and you'll find a beautiful little biodynamic garden on site. The focus is on fine sparkling wine, and Stephen has even created a huge pyramid for ageing the wines, a precise 8% replica of the Great Pyramid of Giza. There's also an organic, zero-waste bistro here.
summerhill.bc.ca; tel +1 250-764-8000; 4870 Chute Lake Rd, Kelowna; 10am-6pm daily 💲✕

03 MARTIN'S LANE WINERY

Built into a steep hillside, this radical six-level gravity-flow winery is breathtaking on architectural grounds alone, the building mirroring the rough, jagged and extreme Okanagan landscape. The Pinot Noir and Riesling wines are also rather special, some of the finest (and

most expensive) expressions of BC terroir, created by the exceptionally talented winemaker Shane Munn and organic viticulturist Kurt Simcic.

You can't miss the giant bust of Vincent van Gogh, missing ear to the ground, which was unveiled to mark the opening of the winery. *Project Redhead* by artist Douglas Coupland started with a global search for a van Gogh doppelgänger. Why? It turns out redheads, like Pinot Noir, both the result of genetic mutations, represent just 1.9% of their respective populations.
martinslanewinery.com; tel +1 250-707-2263; 5437 Lakeshore Rd, Kelowna; by appointment only $

04 BELLA SPARKLING WINES

Bella is a beautiful little biodynamically tended farm and winery nestled in a quiet nook next to Okanagan Lake. The winemaking approach here is one of minimal

intervention – no additives, only natural yeasts and often zero sulphur. The focus is on two grape varieties, Chardonnay and Gamay, as single-vineyard sparkling wines inspired by the Grower Champagne movement. Vinification methods take place to create both Pet Nat (naturally sparkling) and 'Trad Nat' wine, allowing the occasionally undervalued Gamay grape, in particular, to really shine.

Husband and wife proprietors Jay Drysdale and Wendy Rose named the winery after their original pet bulldog. 'Our region's like the Wild West, but our transition period has been so fast. We are getting a grasp...and understanding our sense of place; I love our diversity and micro-regions,' says Jay, adding: 'I think Gamay is really special here in BC, and I wanted to see where this little underdog grape could go.' Bella has an array of antique-glass coupes

and flutes for tasting, so take your pick and enjoy.
bellawines.ca; tel +1 778-996-1829; 4320 Gulch Rd, Naramata; visits Fri-Sun by appointment only $

05 OKANAGAN CRUSH PAD

Christine Coletta and Steve Lornie built the Okanagan Crush Pad in 2011, currently the only official custom crush pad in the area, and the place where the couple make their Freeform, Haywire, Narrative and Bizou + Yukon organic and natural wines (the latter named for their Great Pyrenees dogs). Christine and Steve quickly gained an international reputation for producing very high-quality organic, minimal intervention and terroir-driven wines, and they also experiment with vessel type; on visiting you'll be able to see egg-shaped concrete fermenters and amphorae in action. Talented Matt Dumayne is at the winemaking wheel, and there are usually skin-contact wines (aka orange wines) here to taste, too.

okanagancrushpad.com; tel +1 250-494-4445; 16576 Fosbery Rd, Summerland, BC; 11am-5pm daily (by appointment only Jan-Feb) 💲

06 QUAILS' GATE WINERY

The Stewart family put down their roots in Canada back in 1908, and purchased this property in 1956. It features the Allison House, a log cabin built in 1873, the first permanent wooden structure on the west side of Lake Okanagan, which now serves as a tasting room. The family planted their first *vinifera* vines in 1961, making them some of the oldest in the country. Nowadays, the winery focuses on Pinot Noirs, which former winemaker Nikki Callaway described as 'their own creatures', and Chardonnay, as well as Gewürztraminer, Riesling and some rarities such as a botrytis-affected (noble rot) sweet wine, plus rich reds from old Maréchal Foch vines. Quail's Gate stages events throughout the year, from cooking demos to Pinot Clones 101 classes; the Old Vines restaurant offers outstanding farm-to-table creative cuisine.

quailsgate.com; tel +1 250-769-4451; 3303 Boucherie Rd, Kelowna; tastings 10am-8pm daily 💲✖

07 PAINTED ROCK ESTATE WINERY

Husband-and-wife team John and Trish Skinner, with the help of Bordeaux-based consultant Alain Sutre, were convinced they could harness the potential of this gently sloping bench bounded by rocky banks, once the site of a huge apricot orchard. The discovery of 500-year-old pictographs gave the vineyard its name, and the couple set about planning, analysing and planting to fulfil its promise.

The vineyard has used sustainable farming methods since the end of 2010 – weeds and pests are kept at bay without harmful pesticides and larger interlopers, in the form of black bears, are deterred with a solar-powered electric perimeter fence. All the grapes are hand-harvested and processed in the winery on site, a modern and minimalistic structure with curved, reflective surfaces and a wide-open terrace overlooking Skaha Lake. Recommended drops include the smoky, herbaceous single varietal Cabernet Franc; for fans of polished Cabernet blends, the Red Icon is one of the finest of its style.

paintedrock.ca; tel +1 250-493-6809; 400 Smythe Drive, Penticton; 11am-5.30pm daily 💲

08 MEYER FAMILY VINEYARDS

Some of the most pure, terroir-driven, minimal-intervention, Burgundian-style Pinot Noir and Chardonnay are grown and crafted by the Meyer Family, as acknowledged by the winery making the top 10 in the Best Small Winery category of the 2022 National Wine Awards. The family focuses on two main vineyards, the Old Main Road on the Naramata Bench and the McLean Creek Road site in Okanagan Falls, with each wine reflecting its particular expression of soil and climate. In keeping with their small-batch, terroir-focused approach, locally sourced delicacies are available to try alongside the wines in their tasting room. If you can be tempted away from the grape, there are craft beer and cider choices too.

mfvwines.com; tel +1 250-497-8553; 4287 McLean Creek Rd, Okanagan Falls; 10am-5pm daily by reservation 💲✖

From left: courtesy of Tantalus / Lionel Trudel - trudelphotos.com; © Christopher Gardiner / Shutterstock

WHERE TO STAY

SPARKLING HILL RESORT

A luxurious health and wellness centre in Vernon, in the north of the Okanagan Valley, this hotel offers everything from an aqua meditation room to a salt steam room and even an igloo. Gaze out over panoramic views of Okanagan Lake from the infinity pool. *sparklinghill.com; tel +1 877-275-1556; 888 Sparkling Place, Vernon*

SANDY BEACH LODGE & RESORT

This historic 1940s log lodge sits on a stunning stretch of beachfront, directly on Okanagan Lake by the Naramata Bench. Rooms have private verandas looking out across the lake, and there are also 13 two-bedroom log cottages for intimate, family or group getaways. *sandybeachresort.com; tel +1 866-496-5765; 4275 Mill Rd, Naramata*

WHERE TO EAT

RAUDZ REGIONAL TABLE

With chef Rod Butters at the helm, this Kelowna hotspot dishes up locally sourced and creative food in its own Canadian style. With a 100%

Okanagan wine list, it's a great place to explore the region's wines, too. *raudz.com; tel +1 250-868-8805; 1560 Water Street, Kelowna; Tue-Sat*

BISTRO AT HILLSIDE WINERY

Beautifully set among its namesake vineyards about 5km (3 miles) from Penticton, this impressive place has great lakeside views from its various open-air decks. The menu includes upscale tacos, soups, salads, seafood and other dishes made from ingredients sourced nearby. Enjoy a glass of Mosaic, the house Bordeaux-style red. *hillsidewinery.ca tel +1 250-487-1350; 1350 Naramata Road, Penticton; Wed-Sun*

19 BISTRO @ FITZ

This waterside bistro at Fitzpatrick Vineyards offers delicious food following a strictly 'from scratch' policy, all from local producers. There's also a sparkling wine bar where you can taste the vineyard's own sparkling wine, along with well-known fizz from around the world. *19bistro.com; tel +1 778-*

479-8009; 697 Highway 97 S, Peachland; daily*

WHAT TO DO

KETTLE VALLEY RAIL TRAIL

British Columbia certainly isn't lacking in outstanding natural beauty and wildlife, including 18 volcanoes and multiple mountain ranges, as well as cougars, bears, rattlesnakes, elk and moose. You can opt to explore on two wheels along stretches of the 600km (373-mile) Kettle Valley Rail Trail. *kettlevalleyrailtrail.com*

WINE TOURS

If you're in the market for a highly knowledgeable wine-tour guide and driver, Matt and Shannon

Wentzell of Experience Wine Tours will teach you everything there is to know about British Columbia's vino. *experiencewinetours.ca*

CELEBRATIONS

There are wine-related events throughout the year in the Okanagan Valley, including the annual BC Pinot Noir celebration, held every year in mid-August and a great day out; and the Spring Okanagan Wine Festival in May. Expect creative food from top Okanagan chefs, live music and informative masterclasses – as well as, of course, bountiful Okanagan wine to taste. *thewinefestivals.com; bcpinotnoir.ca*

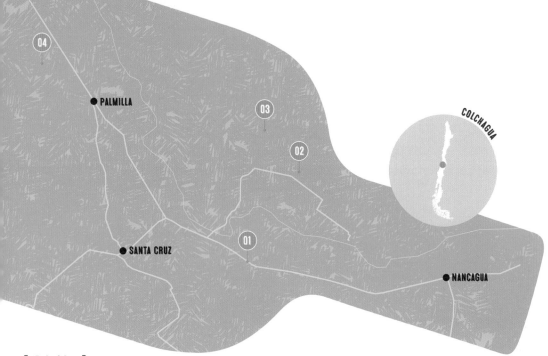

[Chile]

COLCHAGUA

Chilean wine is shaking up the wine world and the Colchagua Valley, a tranquil spot between the mountains and the Pacific Ocean, is where to surrender to its charms.

Wedged between the Andes and the Pacific Ocean, Chile has the perfect landscape and climate for growing grapes: ample sunshine, cool nights, rich soil and abundant water. Although memorable Carmenères and Sauvignon Blancs are produced in several regions, the Colchagua Valley, located just two hours' drive south of Santiago, is the country's largest and most well-known, and coming years will see continued expansion of the region into the hillsides and towards the sea.

Perhaps somewhat surprisingly, given the quantity and quality of wine made here, the Colchagua isn't overly developed for tourism. Santa Cruz, in the heart of the region, remains a relatively quiet town; local organisations such as Ruta del Vino, with a helpful office on the town's main square, assist visitors to make the most of their time. Transport can be costly and

difficult to arrange; if you want to visit several wineries, rent a car Santiago and drive down.

The tranquillity, at any rate, is part of the Colchagua Valley charm. And just because it's quiet doesn't mean it's not cutting-edge: many of the scene's pioneers are younger entrepreneurs and winemakers who've only set up their businesses in the last decade or two. The old vines are the secret: red wines produced here are world famous, consistently ranking among *Wine Enthusiast*'s lists of most exciting wines; and the region is widely considered one of the most important in all of South America. Indeed, thanks to these sophisticated wineries and the striking natural landscape, Colchagua often draws comparisons with Napa Valley. Taste the wine while looking at a map and considering a detour to the beach – you'll see that California and Chile have more in common than you expected.

GET THERE
Santiago is the nearest major airport, 172km (107 miles) from Santa Cruz. Car hire is available.

❶ VIU MANENT

Founded in 1935 by a father-son team of Catalonian immigrants to Chile, this family-owned winery is a destination in itself: in 2021, Viu Manent made it into the top 25 list of the World's Best Vineyards, drawn up by the International Wine Challenge team. That's because there's more to do than sip and swirl: in addition to tastings, there are horse-drawn carriage rides, walks and e-bike tours through the vineyards, winemaking workshops, an equestrian centre, a fair-trade boutique, a restaurant and cafe where you can balance out the wine with a strong cappuccino.

And the wines? Several are award-winners themselves, with Robert Parker and a bevy of wine experts scoring the 2021 single-vineyard Cabernet Sauvignon and Malbec 90-plus points.
viumanent.cl; tel +56 22-840 3181; Carretera del Vino km37, Cunaco; 10am-6pm Mon-Sat 💲✕

❷ MONTES

This well-respected winery started out as the passion project of a man who didn't know much about the subject. 'My only contact with wine was Sunday lunch – and that was it,' says Aurelio Montes of his lifestyle before taking his first agronomy course at university. By 1987, he says, he was eager to challenge local winemaking standards. 'Chilean wineries were not going for quality,' said Montes. 'They were happy to make an average product to sell for an average price. I wanted to make high-quality wines.'

That he did: taste the brand's signature reds at his modern winery, set into the hillside. Stay for a flame-grilled lunch with wine pairings at chef Francis Mallmann's Fuegos de Apalta restaurant, and finish with a guided hike into the hills looking over the vines.
monteswines.com; tel +56 72-281 7815; Camino a Milahue de Apalta s/n; 9am-6pm daily 💲✕

❸ VIÑA LAPOSTOLLE

Lapostolle is the most exclusive winery in the valley, and arguably in all of Chile, a level of prestige that can be explained in two words: Grand Marnier. The Marnier Lapostolle family founded and owns the brand of the world-famous liqueur, so it stands to reason that they're adept at making wine, too. Indeed, these Chilean wines, produced using French techniques, are considered some of the country's best – 'French in essence, Chilean by birth' is the tagline here.

But the family's ascent to the top was quick: they've only been making wine here since the mid-1990s. 'I couldn't imagine we could produce a wine like Clos Apalta quite that quickly,' co-founder Alexandra Marnier Lapostolle has said of her arrival on the Chilean wine scene in 1994. 'But from the beginning I knew we had great terroir and vines which were between 60 and 80 years old, and I knew we had the potential, providing we focused on quality.' The winery is set in a traditional Chilean hacienda in the town of Cunaco, a short drive from Santa Cruz; tasting and tour options include a horseback ride through the vineyards, and Lapostolle will provide complimentary transportation from Santa Cruz. *lapostolle.com; tel +56 72-2953 350; Ruta I-50, Camino San Fernando a Pichilemu, km36, Cunaquito; by reservation 10.30am-5.30pm Mon-Sat, 10.30am Sun* 💲

04 MONTGRAS

Not to worry if a horse-drawn carriage ride through the vineyards sounds too sedate for your taste: you can also zip-line over the beautiful scenery at MontGras. This friendly winery offers activities from horseback riding and hiking to mountain biking; also on offer are vineyard picnics or a meal at the on-site restaurant.

Even the wine tasting can be a hands-on opportunity here if you sign up for one of the 'make your own wine' workshops. The pioneering winemakers are known for experimenting with new technology and for their role in establishing the Colchagua Valley Wine Route to bring more tourists to the region. *Wine Enthusiast* enthuses that their Quatro Red is 'always one of Chile's best values; an overperformer year after year'. *montgras.cl; tel +56 72-282 3242; Camino a Isla de Yáquil s/n, Palmilla; 10am-4.30pm daily* 💲 🍴

01 The wine cellar at Lapostolle

02 Travel the old-fashioned way at Viu Manent

03 Grape harvesting at Lapostolle

WHERE TO STAY
HOTEL SANTA CRUZ
In the town of Santa Cruz, the Hotel Santa Cruz is elegant and central. The lovely swimming pool is the perfect place to relax. *hotelsantacruzplaza. cl; tel +56 72-220 9600; Plaza de Armas 286, Santa Cruz*

HOTEL TERRAVIÑA
Set among the vineyards of a long-running family winery, this cosy wine lodge is a travellers' favourite in the region. *terravina.cl; tel +56 98-394 3096; Camino Los Boldos s/n, Santa Cruz*

WHERE TO EAT
VINO BELLO
A gourmet Italian restaurant – the only one in town – with romantic al-fresco seating overlooking the terraced vines of the Laura Hartwig vineyard. *ristorantevinobello.com; tel +56 72-2822 755; Barreales s/n, Santa Cruz; daily*

179 PIZZERIA BAR
Excellent pizza, pasta and wines by the glass bring in a small lunch crowd to this stylish space near Plaza de Armas. *bar179.cl; tel +5672-248 6266; Besoain 179, Santa Cruz; Mon-Sat*

WHAT TO DO
Santa Cruz is home to the largest private museum in Chile, the Museo de Colchagua, offering helpful insight into the wine region's cultural context. On display are pre-Columbian artefacts, weapons, Mapuche silver, vintage cars and steam-driven machinery and winemaking equipment. *museocolchagua.cl*

CELEBRATIONS
Colchagua's annual Fiesta de la Vendimia celebrates the autumn grape harvest at the start of March. Wine flows freely at the local wineries' stands in the Plaza de Armas; highlights include traditional food, singing, dancing and the crowning of a harvest queen. Book well ahead: the quiet town sees a huge influx of visitors. *vendimiacolchagua.cl*

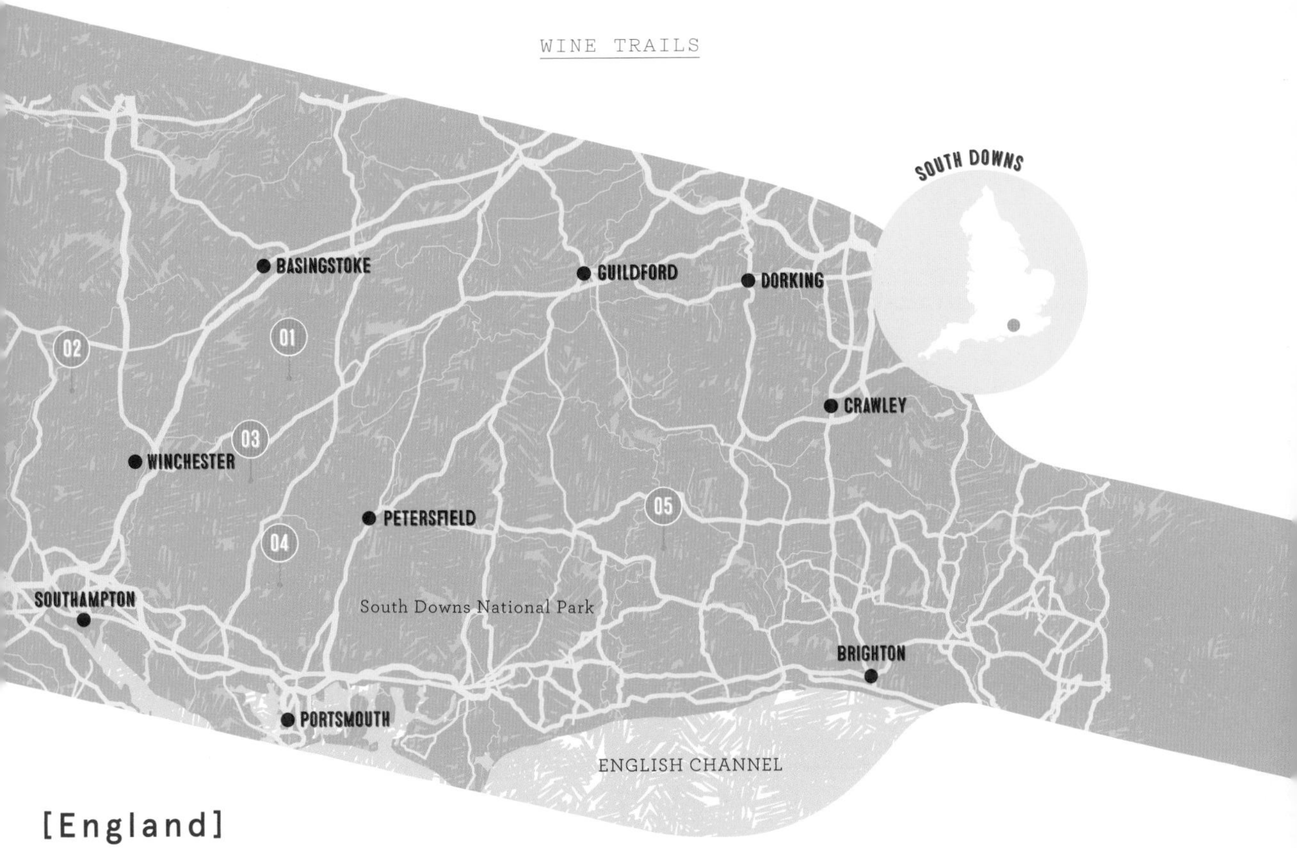

SOUTH DOWNS

- BASINGSTOKE
- GUILDFORD
- DORKING
- 02
- 01
- CRAWLEY
- WINCHESTER
- 03
- PETERSFIELD
- 05
- 04
- SOUTHAMPTON
- South Downs National Park
- BRIGHTON
- PORTSMOUTH
- ENGLISH CHANNEL

[England]

SOUTH DOWNS

It's fizzy, refined and winning awards: English white wine sparkles in the summer, the perfect time to take a tour of Southern England's vineyards.

Overhead a skylark sings in the blue sky. Green fields sweep down from a chalk ridge laced with white tracks. To the south lies the sea, to the north the counties of Hampshire and Sussex. These are England's South Downs in summer, a place of villages, hiking trails and, increasingly, vineyards. For the South Downs, now a National Park, are a narrow, 160km-long (100-mile) spine of chalk hills that run southeast all the way from Winchester, an ancient capital of England, to Eastbourne; the same seam of rock re-emerges across the Channel in Champagne country.

English wine was long a laughing stock, not least among the French, being too thin,

too sour or over-sweetened. But in the last 20 years, the South Downs region has been the source of some excellent sparkling wines. In truth, England's wineries are spread out over quite a distance, from Kent to Gloucestershire, and a tour taking in all of them would be impracticable. But there are a handful of vineyards concentrated in tranquil Hampshire (and neighbouring West Sussex) that together make a weekend exploring English wine, and some of the region's other attractions, enjoyable and something of a revelation. You'll find increasingly accomplished wines, charming country pubs, trout-filled streams and perhaps a game of cricket to watch.

GET THERE
Southampton and London Gatwick are the closest airports but the region is only an hour from London by train.

01 HATTINGLEY VALLEY

Tucked down some exceedingly narrow lanes between Basingstoke and Alresford lies one of Britain's best wineries, Hattingley Valley, which has collected considerable quantities of medals in recent years. It's a good place in which to start to understand the characteristics of English sparkling wine. What sets Hattingley apart? First, explains newly appointed head winemaker Rob MacCulloch, there's the elevation. 'We're at a relatively high altitude for England, which gives us a helpful microclimate. It's significantly more windy and comparatively frost-free here.' Then there's the chalk-based geology, with an added layer of flint. The vines of Chardonnay,

Pinot Noir, Pinot Meunier are low yielding as a result. Then there's what happens in the winery. 'Our classic flavour has a backbone of crisp, green-apple acidity,' says Rob, 'and what I have to do is keep the acidity in balance. Winemaking is about solving problems.'

The original problem of English wine was that nobody took it seriously. 'I first tasted English sparkling wine in 1997 and wondered "why are you doing this?"', laughs Rob. 'But there were a lot of plucky souls having a go.' The learning curve was steep and the proximity of Kent, Sussex and Hampshire to London meant that the better English sparkling wine got a lot of attention quite quickly. A warming climate means that the region is

not far behind Champagne now: 'our ambition is to be alongside the best of Champagne's wines,' says Rob. Except down in Hampshire you can tie in a visit to a country pub or chalk-stream fishing. *hattingleyvalley.com; tel +44 (0)1256 389 188; Wield Yard, Lower Wield, nr Alresford; weekend tours and tasting by appointment year-round* $

02 COTTONWORTH WINES

Surrounded by the clear, braided streams of the Test Valley, which flow over chalk beds and form watercress-filled meadows, and the thatched cottages of such villages as Wherwell, Cottonworth Wines' setting couldn't be more English. During the past 10 years, the Liddell

family has planted the sparkling wine grapes of Chardonnay, Pinot Noir and Pinot Meunier on south-facing slopes around their farm. But the weather can be as English as the setting. 'Our biggest challenge in the Test Valley is a short growing season in a cool climate,' says Federico Firino of Cottonworth. 'We need to be lucky enough in order to get the right weather at the right time. We are at the mercy of Mother Nature!' When everything comes together, though, there's no better way of enjoying Cottonworth's wines than with some of the local smoked trout overlooking the vineyard on a sunny afternoon. Federico believes that visiting English wineries is a great way of introducing the wine, 'but we didn't want to make it too exclusive.'

England being a new wine region means that winemakers like Hugh Liddell don't feel constrained by history or tradition. However, quality English wine already has PDO (Protected Designation of Origin) status and some believe that regions such as the South Downs may apply for a system like France's Appellation d'Origine Contrôlée (AOC). *cottonworth.co.uk; tel +44 (0)1264 860 531; Cottonworth House, Andover; tours Fri-Sat Jun-Aug* 🌑

03 RAIMES

When you pass through the hamlet of Tichborne (essentially just a pub beside the Itchen River) look for a sign on your right, next to a farm track. This is Raimes, where owners Augusta and Robert Raimes have

farmed for five generations. In 2011 they planted Chardonnay, Pinot Noir and Pinot Meunier vines on south-facing slopes and you can now taste the fruits of their labour on summer weekends at the cellar door in their farm's courtyard. Some of the sparkling wines have won awards, such as a gold medal at the International Wine Challenge in 2019 for the Classic. But for Augusta Raimes: 'The most rewarding part has been adapting to a hand-grown and hand-picked crop – and it's also a great pleasure to introduce people to English wine and see them realise how good it is.'

Although the grapes are grown along the same chalk spine that stretches to Champagne in France, some tweaking of the technique

has had to be made at Raimes. 'We establish a tall trunk to wire height which helps keep the buds away from the cold ground at springtime when there can be ground frosts.' *raimes.co.uk; tel +44 (0)1962 732 120; Grange Farm, Tichborne; tours by appointment Jul–Sep, tastings (with fee) by appointment year-round, free tastings Fri, Sat, Sun May–Sep* $

⓸ HAMBLEDON VINEYARD

Hambledon Vineyard is set in the idyllic Hampshire village of the same name: a place of hills, fields, woods and little-used flint-strewn lanes. It's been 10 years since Chardonnay vines were planted here. 'The chalk on which we grow our vines was formed on the seabed of the Paris basin some 65 million years ago,' says managing director Ian Kellett. 'The same chalk is found in the best Chardonnay areas of the Côtes

des Blancs in Champagne.' In 2015, Hambledon's Classic Cuvée beat French Champagnes in a blind tasting hosted by Noble Rot wine magazine, thanks to its scents of 'fresh sourdough, magnolia and lily with a hint of smoke'. You can taste in the new tasting room.

Sports fans may also like to visit the pitch where the first games of cricket were played, a couple of minutes' drive down the road. *hambledonvineyard.co.uk; tel +44 (0)2392 632 358; Hambledon; by appointment* $

⓺ NUTBOURNE VINEYARD

Cross the border into West Sussex to visit Nutbourne Vineyard. Nearby Nyetimber may have been in the vanguard of the English sparkling wine revolution – but it's only open to the public on select open days for a hefty fee. However, Nutbourne in Pulborough is open to all, with free-of-charge Vineyard

Trail that takes in the resident alpacas and an oak sculpture or paid-fo guided tours and picnics, all of which can conclude with a glass of chilled wine on the cellar door's verandah.

Nutbourne's white wine was the first English still wine to win a gold medal at the International Wine and Spirit Competition. The still wines use Riesling-style grapes to create fruity, aromatic flavours, typically with a hint of elderflower. The sparkling wines use Pinot Noir and Chardonnay. Discover the process with a tutored wine tasting in the vineyard during summer months.

The family-owned winery is based in a 19th-century windmill midway along the Downs. From here you can return to London or cities such as Brighton or Chichester – or just linger in the countryside for walks. *nutbournevineyards.com; tel +44 (0)1798 815 196; Gay Street, Pulborough; Mon–Sat 10–5pm*

WHERE TO STAY
HOTEL DU VIN
For city-centre accommodation and a well-crafted wine list, try the Hotel du Vin in Winchester, gateway city at the west end of the South Downs. Part of a chain that prides itself on its wine, there's another Hotel du Vin in Brighton at the opposite end of the South Downs. *hotelduvin.com*

THE ANGEL INN
In the centre of the South Downs town of Petworth, the Angel Inn offers cosy (if not cheap) accommodation close to the town's antique shops and 17th-century Petworth House, which has a remarkable art collection, wood carvings by Grinling Gibbons and a deer park designed by Capability Brown. *angelinnpetworth.co.uk; tel +44 (0)1798 344 445; Angel Street, Petworth*

WHERE TO EAT
THE HAWKLEY INN
Deep in Hampshire's steep hills (known as 'hangers'), south

of Jenkyn Place and Hattingley vineyards, this country pub serves superb lunches and local cask ales, which are best enjoyed in the large garden if the weather permits. Walk off your lunch in the woods. *hawkleyinn.co.uk; tel +44 (0)1730 827 205; Pococks Lane, Hawkley*

THE FORTE KITCHEN
Hampshire's produce stars on the breakfast and lunch menus at this stylish space in central Winchester. *thekitchenrestaurants. co.uk/fortekitchen; tel 01962 856 840; Parchment Street, Winchester*

WHAT TO DO
SOUTH DOWNS NATIONAL PARK
The South Downs have long attracted hikers, mountain bikers and horse riders. The South Downs Way trail runs, up and down, for 160km (100 miles) from Winchester to Eastbourne but is accessible at lots of points, so you can easily stretch your legs a section at a time. *southdowns.gov.uk*

LANGHAM BREWERY
Take a break from the grape with a visit to this brewery in the South Downs National Park, just west of Pulborough. Superb golden ales,

such as the summery Sundowner, are brewed here. Tours are possible and there's a shop for quick purchases. *langhambrewery.co.uk; tel +44 (0)1798 860 861; The Granary, Langham Lane, Lodsworth*

CELEBRATIONS
FIZZ FEST
Fizz Fest sees the seven members of the Vineyards of Hampshire come together for an annual celebration of sparkling wine, usually in July. Not all of the vineyards are open to the public so it's a great opportunity for some comparative tastings plus masterclasses, music and local food. *vineyardsofhampshire. co.uk/events*

HAMPSHIRE FOOD FESTIVAL
Indulge in local produce from across the county – buffalo mozzarella from Stockbridge, gin from Winchester – during this July celebration. Wine events include pop-up suppers and tasting tours. *hampshirefare.co.uk*

[France]

CHAMPAGNE

Pop! The land that produces the king of sparkling wines is a treasure trove of rolling hills, ancient cellars and traditions just waiting to be opened.

Champagne is France's great enigma: the world's most famous bubbly and an undisputed icon of Gallic glamour, yet most French people have little idea of the complex, almost mystical, secrets that go into producing Champagne.

A trip into this magical land, on Unesco's World Heritage list since 2015, is an emotional experience. You can witness perfectly cultivated vines hanging with juicy clusters of grapes that will soon begin the long transformation into the one and only Champagne. Take a pilgrimage through the centuries-old maze of cellars beneath the likes of Ruinart or Pommery that resemble holy subterranean cathedrals, or savour the simple pleasure of a smallholder *vigneron* pouring a bubbly glass of their latest vintage. Accept the sly persuasion that they may sell most of their grapes to the famous producers, but keep the best for personal production sold directly from the independent winery.

The region's bucolic vineyards stretch across gentle hills and drowsy villages that begin just an hour's drive from Paris, although wine-lovers often limit themselves to a trip to Reims. A regal city, Reims is home to the likes of Veuve Clicquot and Mumm, where incredible cellars, storing millions of bottles, are packed every day for tours. But Champagne is a complex mosaic of thousands of tiny *vignerons*, some making their own Champagne, others just supplying grapes to the luxury Champagne houses – an almost feudal relationship unchanged for centuries. So, after visiting Reims, meet these independent winemakers, who will explain the blending of Champagne's three grapes – Chardonnay, Pinot Noir and Meunier – the difference between *millésime* vintage and an NV (the anglicised non-vintage), and insider secrets like the use of the *liqueur de dosage* of cane sugar added in the final *assemblage*.

GET THERE
Charles de Gaulle is the nearest airport, 130km (81 miles) from Reims. The train from Paris to Reims takes 50min. Car hire is available.

01 REIMS

Reims is home to Champagne's own royalty, with curious visitors allowed into the hallowed cellars of the likes of Mumm and Pommery, Veuve Clicquot, Heidseck, Lanson and Taittinger. It is the perfect place to get an idea of the hidden secrets of arguably the world's most celebrated beverage, with gushing guides explaining the centuries-old alchemy that goes into its production. Each of the Grandes Maisons offers something different, but which one to choose? Taittinger stands out as being one of the rare family-owned houses, and its two-level 13th-century cellars are primarily reserved for ageing the signature vintage Comtes de Champagne, a remarkable cuvée.

The neo-Gothic castle towers of Pommery resemble a kitsch Disneyland, but this is the one must-see cellar. Madame Pommery, 140 years ago, conceived dry Brut Champagne as a counterpoint to sweet bubbly, and her 18km (11 miles) of cellars are like no others. This is where you will discover *les crayères*, some 120 awesome chalk pits dug beneath Reims in Gallo-Roman times. Madame Pommery decided these provided perfect ventilation for the maze of tunnels she built for her cellars, which today hold some 20 million bottles. *taittinger.com; vrankenpommery.com* Ⓢ

02 CHAMPAGNE GARDET

Over two-thirds of all Champagne,

including 90% exported around the world, is produced by the 290 Negociants Manipulants, the Grandes Maisons who own hardly any vines but purchase grapes at harvest. Gardet, founded in 1895, is still a relatively small maison, owning a mere 5 hectares (12 acres) of vineyards, but produces a million bottles a year using grapes it buys in from another 100 hectares (247 acres) . Visitors are received in an ornate art nouveau glass veranda filled with tropical plants. A tour of the *cuverie*, where the wine is made, and the labyrinth of cellars, takes over an hour and gives a thorough explanation of all the stages of Champagne's complex production. *champagne-gardet.com; tel +33 3 26 03 42 03; 13 rue Georges Legros,*

01 Champagne region vineyards

02 Hautvilliers, the birthplace of Champagne

03 Electric train at Mercier cellars

04 Pouring out the bubbly

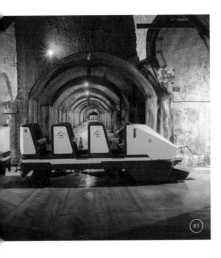

Chigny-les-Roses; by appointment Mon-Sat ⑤

⓷ CHAMPAGNE MERCIER

Lively Épernay is the genuine wine capital of Champagne, with a host of fun wine bars, gourmet restaurants and bistros. Over 100,000 visitors arrive each year at Mercier, one of the most popular Champagnes in France itself. Founder Eugene Mercier was the publicity-seeking Richard Branson of his time, building an immense wooden barrel holding 250,000 bottles of Champagne that was transported by oxen to Paris in 1900 to rival the Eiffel Tower as the star show of the Exposition Universelle. Today the barrel dominates the entrance of Mercier's outstanding cellar, where

a lift plunges visitors into an eerie maze of tunnels. A small electric train wends part of the way, and you realise how deep underground the cellar-workers are.
champagnemercier.fr; tel +33 3 26 51 22 22; 68 Ave de Champagne, Épernay; Mon-Sun ⑤

⓸ CHAMPAGNE G. TRIBAUT

Before arriving for a tasting at the friendly Tribaut family winery, take a tour of the idyllic village of Hautvilliers, known as the birthplace of Champagne. There is a rue Dom Pérignon, named after the Benedictine monk who, 300 years ago, is said to have invented the process of double fermentation that creates Champagne's unique bubbles. Ghislain and Marie-José

Tribaut, along with their daughter and grandson, love to welcome wine tourists. 'I am a Récoltant Manipulant,' explains Ghislain, 'someone who cultivates and harvests their grapes, and can then sell them to a Négociant Manipulant – Grandes Maisons like Krug and Taittinger. But personally, I keep them all for myself, enough to produce 200,000 bottles of our own Champagne.' After tasting Marie-José's delicious *gougères* (light puff pastry filled with Gruyère), paired with a dry Rosé Brut, many visitors end up coming back here to help out during the grape harvest.
champagne.g.tribaut.com; tel +33 3 26 59 40 57; 88 rue d'Eguisheim, Hautvillers; daily ⑤

05 Pannier's 12th-
century cellars

06 Notre-Dame
cathedral, Reims

05 CHAMPAGNE ASPASIE

Paul-Vincent Ariston is an artisan *vigneron* who bubbles with as much enthusiasm as his Champagne. His family have been making wine for five generations, and it's well worth visiting the cellar below his 400-year-old stone farmhouse, where Paul-Vincent proudly shows a huge wooden grape press, ancient but functioning, then explains the *dégorgement*, when sediment is frozen in the neck of the bottle and spectacularly popped out before final bottling. Try the Brut de Fut, aged in oak barrels, while his unique cuvée, Brut Cépages d'Antan, has none of the usual Champagne grapes but, rather, three rare varieties – Le Petit Meslier, L'Arbanne and Pinot Blanc – that were grown here centuries before Champagne was popularised worldwide.
champagneaspasie.com; tel +33 3 26 97 43 46; 4 Grande Rue, Brouillet; by appointment Mon-Sat 💲

06 CHAMPAGNE PANNIER

Pannier is one of Champagne's better-known cooperatives, a Coopérative de Manipulation to use the official title. It features a breathtaking 2.5km-long (1.5-mile) labyrinth of cellars, dug down 30m (98ft) beneath the earth, which date back to the 12th century when they were excavated to build churches. A small group of 11 *vignerons* formed the original cooperative in 1974, which has since mushroomed into a vast winery representing 400 growers. Although it produces millions of bottles a year, the cooperative keeps Pannier separate as its prestige brand, blending the local Meunier grape with Chardonnay and Pinot Noir grown in vineyards from the faraway Côte des Blancs and Montagne de Reims.
champagnepannier.com; tel +33 3 23 69 51 30; 23 rue Roger Catillon, Château-Thierry; Mon-Sat 💲

07 CHAMPAGNE FALLET DART

Just an hour's drive from Paris, this part of the agricultural Marne valley was only incorporated into the exclusive members-only club of the Champagne appellation in 1937. Paul and Adrien Dart are dynamic young winemakers, and although the estate is medium-sized, stretching over 18 hectares (44 acres), it still has something like one million bottles ageing in its cellar. Be sure to taste the Clos du Mont, a blend of vintages from a vineyard dating from the 7th century. Dart is also proud of the domaine's Ratafia, a luscious aperitif, and an elegant Fine de Champagne, aged in barrels like a Cognac.
champagne-fallet-dart.fr; tel +33 3 23 82 01 73; 2 rue des Clos du Mont, Drachy, Charly sur Marne; Mon-Sat

WHERE TO STAY

LES CRAYÈRES
Built by the family of Madame Pommery, this grand château, sumptuously furnished and with a two-star Michelin restaurant, offers the full Champagne experience. *lescrayeres.com; tel +33 3 26 24 90 00; 64 Blvd Henry Vasnier, Reims*

PARVA DOMUS
Claude and Ginette Rimaire pamper guests in their cosy home on Avenue de Champagne, which Churchill named 'the world's most drinkable address'. Hearty breakfasts and a glass of Champagne on arrival are included. *parvadomusrimaire. com; tel +33 6 73 25 66 00; 27 Ave de Champagne, Épernay*

WHERE TO EAT

LA GRILLADE GOURMANDE
A favourite restaurant where *vignerons* rub shoulders with owners of the Grandes Maisons. Try the hearth-grilled meat or delicate dishes such

as pigeon stuffed with foie gras. *lagrilladegourmande. com; tel +33 3 26 55 44 22; 16 rue de Reims, Épernay; Tue-Sat*

AU 36
A perfect spot for food and Champagne pairing, this designer bar serves plates of local specialities – creamy Chaource cheese, Reims ham, smoky lentils and pink macarons – served with three different Champagnes. *au36.net; tel +33 3 26 51 58 37; 36 rue Dom Pérignon, Hautvillers; daily*

LA CAVE À CHAMPAGNE
'The Champagne Cellar' is well regarded by locals for its humble *champenoise* cuisine (snail-and-pig's-trotter casserole, fillet of beef in Pinot Noir), served in a warm, traditional atmosphere. Pair these dishes with inexpensive regional Champagnes and wines. *cave-champagne.fr; tel +33 3 26 32 20 51; 16 rue Gambetta, Épernay; Thu-Mon*

WHAT TO DO
Notre-Dame de Reims is a must-see 800-year-old Gothic cathedral, and the historic venue for the coronation of the kings of France. Its interior is adorned with intricate stained-glass windows. *cathedrale-reims.fr*

CELEBRATIONS
Épernay celebrates Habits de Lumière for three days in mid-December, when Champagne flows amid fireworks, light shows and street theatre. *habitsdelumiere. epernay.fr*

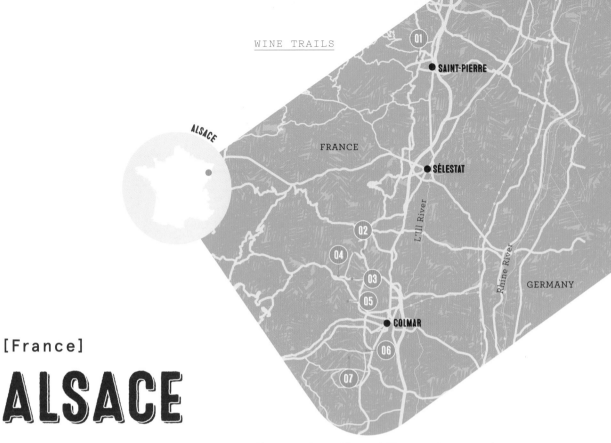

SAINT-PIERRE

ALSACE

FRANCE

SÉLESTAT

01

02

04

03

05

COLMAR

06

07

L'Ill River

Rhine River

GERMANY

[France]

ALSACE

Take a trip through the picturesque villages of northeast France to sample distinctive white wines among traditional, half-timbered wineries.

Winemaking in Alsace has had its ups and downs throughout a long history, which begins with the Romans planting the first grapes. In the Middle Ages, records show 160 villages growing vines; by the 16th century, they were making some of the most prized wines in Europe. Then came 300 years of war, phylloxera and political ping-pong, with the territory passed back and forth between France and Germany. A renaissance has taken place over the last 50-odd years, seeing a significant increase in quality, and today Alsace is in the vanguard of the movement towards organic cultivation. The picture-perfect vine-clad hillsides here are the ultimate terroir for white wines, with Pinot Noir the only red among the seven official grape varieties. Each village, each winemaker, creates a complex patchwork of interpretations of Riesling, Gewürztraminer, Pinot Blanc and Gris, Muscat and Sylvaner.

Nowhere in France can compare when it comes to the welcome given to wine tourists. Alsace was one of the first regions to organise its own Route du Vin, some 60 years ago, and today local *vignerons* are constantly coming up with new ideas to attract wine-lovers: bike tours and marathon races through the vines; food and wine fairs; a procession honouring Alsace's iconic Gewürztraminer past the fairy-tale half-timbered houses of Bergheim (a strong candidate for the most beautiful village in France); and night-time illuminations of medieval churches as bottles of bubbly Crémant are popped in celebration. And throughout Alsace there is a long tradition of winemakers opening up their rustic houses as welcoming *chambres d'hôtes*. Rather than a formal tasting, guests are often privileged to sit down with the winemaker for a relaxed session trying some favourite vintages; a long aperitif that often continues over dinner in a local bistro.

GET THERE
EuroAirport Basel Mulhouse Freiburg is the nearest major airport, 99km (62 miles) from Mittelbergheim. Car hire is available.

01 DOMAINE ALBERT SELTZ

Albert Seltz is a 16th-generation winemaker and Alsace's champion of the humble Sylvaner, which he describes as 'the grape no one wants to talk about and prefers to imagine does not exist'. Sylvaner is often overlooked compared to the likes of Riesling, and Seltz went on a crusade to make French officialdom recognise the Sylvaner vines around here as a Grand Cru. Visitors can sit back as Albert takes them through a dozen of his sensational Sylvaner vintages, from the wonderfully drinkable Sylvaner de Mittelbergheim through, perhaps, to a seductive 2013 'Sono Contento' Vieilles Vignes, which he poetically describes: 'Look at the colour, a dull gold that is autumn. Smell the nose; now imagine that with sautéed wild trout.'
albert-seltz.fr; tel +33 3 88 08 91 77; 21 rue Principale, Mittelbergheim; daily by appointment ⓢ

02 DOMAINE BECKER

An old barn of the Beckers' rambling winery has been converted into a giant *winstub* (traditional Alsatian wine lounge), with an ambience more like a jolly pub than a sophisticated wine bar. In addition to her own organic wines, Martine Becker also promotes local specialities: organic honey and jam, distinctive Alsace pottery. Martine is a mine of legendary village tales: 'Can you imagine that during WWII over 150 of the villagers used to sleep down in our cellar at night to avoid bombs – and Papa said they also drank a lot of our stock to avoid the occupying German army getting it!'
vinsbecker.com; tel +33 3 89 47 90 16; 4 Rte d'Ostheim, Zellenberg; Apr-Dec daily, or by appointment ⓢ

03 DOMAINE PAUL BLANCK ET FILS

Sitting in the rustic wood-panelled tasting room of Domaine Blanck's 16th-century cellar, surrounded by vast oak casks painted with traditional Alsatian scenes, it's quickly apparent that Philippe

Blanck is an expert at explaining the complex world of Alsace wines, from a simple Sylvaner to a Grand Cru Pinot Gris. Philippe offers advice that is appropriate for all Alsace cellar guests: 'Visitors here should do three things: see our fabulous vineyard landscapes, try the wine with the winemaker himself, then ask him where to eat, as our wines are best when you taste Alsatian cuisine at the same time.' blanck.com; tel +33 3 89 78 23 56; 32 Grand'Rue, Kientzheim; Mon-Sat 💲

04 DOMAINE WEINBACH

The Route du Vin that runs into Kaysersberg, another idyllic Alsatian village, is marked by a long stone wall protecting an ancient vineyard and Capuchin monastery, now a grand mansion and winery, where Catherine Faller and her sons Eddy and Théo make a sensational selection of wines. Behind the wall is the timeworn Capuchin monastery where monks planted the surrounding 5-hectare (12-acre) Clos des Capucins in 1612. The monks were evicted during the French revolution and Catherine's grandfather bought the property in 1898.

While tasting vintages such as the complex, concentrated Pinot Gris Altenbourg 2018 or a luscious late-harvest Gewürztraminer, Catherine is full of suggestions for food pairings. 'Can't you imagine this Muscat with fresh asparagus, the Pinot Blanc with a cheese soufflé,' she enthuses, 'or our full-bodied Pinot Noir S de Schlossberg alongside a succulent leg of lamb?' domaineweinbach.com; tel +33 3 89 47 13 21; 25 Route du Vin, Kaysersberg; Mon-Sat by appointment 💲

05 VIGNOBLE KLUR

The Klur family have created a paradise getaway for lovers of 'eco' wine. While Clément Klur and his daughter Elisa produce an outstanding selection of biodynamic wines, they have also transformed the family mansion into a bohemian B&B, offering wine courses, traditional Alsatian cooking

are standing among the vines that produce our Riesling Grand Cru Eichberg – Hill of Oaks – you absorb this incredible history and heritage.' *emile-beyer.fr; tel +33 3 89 41 40 45; 7 place du Château, Eguisheim; Mon–Sat by appointment* 🟢

07 GÉRARD SCHUELLER

This 500-year-old winery has no tasting room, just a rickety table wobbling with a dozen half-opened bottles. It's squeezed between steel vats and barrels, and a workspace where labels are stuck – by hand – onto magnums of the highly original Bulle de Bild, a sparkling Gewürztraminer blended with 10% Riesling grape juice, which provocative Monsieur Schueller refuses to call a Crémant. It turns out that he often falls foul of the authorities with his unorthodox 'natural wines' failing to pass official tasting tests. 'I like to leave my wines open when tasting just to see whether there is an effect of oxidisation. But I'm not scared, and they only seem to get better the longer they are open,' he explains. And this is borne out when the tasting begins, as he digs out delights such as bottle opened two weeks ago of a wonderful lush, dark-amber 2008 Riesling Grand Cru.
Tel +33 3 89 49 31 54; 1 rue des 3 Châteaux, Husseren les Châteaux; Mon–Fri by appointment

classes and even poetry readings. The grounds extend over vegetable gardens, ponds, a sauna and the Tack & Glou jewellery studio; walking tours are organised through the stunning terraced vineyard looking out over Katzenthal (the 'Valley of the Cats'). The Klurs are innovative in the cellar, too, refusing to add any sulphites, so the whole range here is now classed as *natur* (natural), including a striking orange wine blending Gewürztraminer with Muscat grapes.
klur.net; tel +33 3 89 80 94 29; 105 rue des Trois Epis, Katzenthal; Mon–Sat by appointment 🟢

06 MAISON EMILE BEYER

Visitors flock to enchanting Eguisheim, unchanged since the Middle Ages, gathering in the town square to stare up at the iconic storks' nests balancing atop the church steeple. One of the traditional, brightly coloured half-timbered houses on the square has been the winemaking home of the Beyer family since 1580. Today they have a modern winery on the outskirts of town, but tastings are held here in the cobbled courtyard. As is the case all over Alsace, be prepared for a marathon session, as the Beyers produce some 30 different wines on their 16-hectare (40-acre) organic estate. Try a surprisingly mineral Pinot Gris or the full-bodied oak-aged Pinot Noir, though the stars of the show are the Grand Cru Rieslings. The estate is now run by 14th-generation winemaker Christan Beyer alongside his wife, Valérie; Christian notes that 'Records exist that grapes were first grown on these rolling hillsides by the Romans, and I believe when you

WHERE TO STAY
CLOS FROEHN
Guests are pampered at Martine and Alphonse Aubrey's 17th-century cottage, which overlooks the vineyards. At breakfast, Alphonse (formerly the village baker) dispenses cakes and pastries. *clos-froehn.com; tel +33 3 89 47 95 68; 46 rue du Schlossberg, Zellenberg*

SYLVIE FAHRER
The rooms are simple at this reasonably priced B&B, but breakfast is in a grand half-timbered salon. Evening wine tastings are held in a converted barn filled with barrels and tractors. *fahrer-sylvie.com; tel +33 3 89 73 00 40; 24 Route du Vin, Saint-Hippolyte*

WHERE TO EAT
FERME-AUBERGE DU KAHLENWASEN
High above the wine village of Turkheim, enjoy panoramic views and hearty home cooking that makes use of wonderful fresh farm produce: smoked meat; potatoes fried with bacon; Munster cheese made just that morning. *facebook.com/Kahlenwasen; tel +33 3 89 77 32 49; Luttenbach-près-Munster; daily*

CAVEAU MORAKOPF
You won't see many tourists in this snug, welcoming bistro, but locals tuck into enormous portions of *jambonneau* (crispy pork knuckle) or Val d'Orbey trout with almonds. *caveaumorakopf.fr; tel +33 3 89 27 05 10; 7 rue des Trois Épis, Niedermorschwihr; Tue-Sun*

BRASSERIE L'AUBERGE
Colmar is the wine capital of Alsace, and this atmospheric century-old brasserie is a temple to traditional cuisine, serving up steaming plates of tangy *choucroute* (sauerkraut dressed with sausages). *grand-hotel-bristol.com/en/restaurants/brasserie-lauberge; tel +33 3 89 23 17 57; 7 place de la Gare, Colmar; Mon-Sat*

WHAT TO DO
BALLONS DES VOSGES
This national park is a paradise for nature-lovers, with a rolling range of pine-clad peaks, lush valleys and tranquil lakes. During summer it's popular for hang-gliding, rambling, canoeing and, above all, cycling: the park is often featured during the Tour de France. In winter, visitors come for the superlative cross-country skiing, as well as small, family-friendly downhill resorts. *parc-ballons-vosges.fr*

CELEBRATIONS
Molsheim is home to a memorable weekend festival in June, which includes a half-marathon run through the vineyards. *marathon-alsace.com*

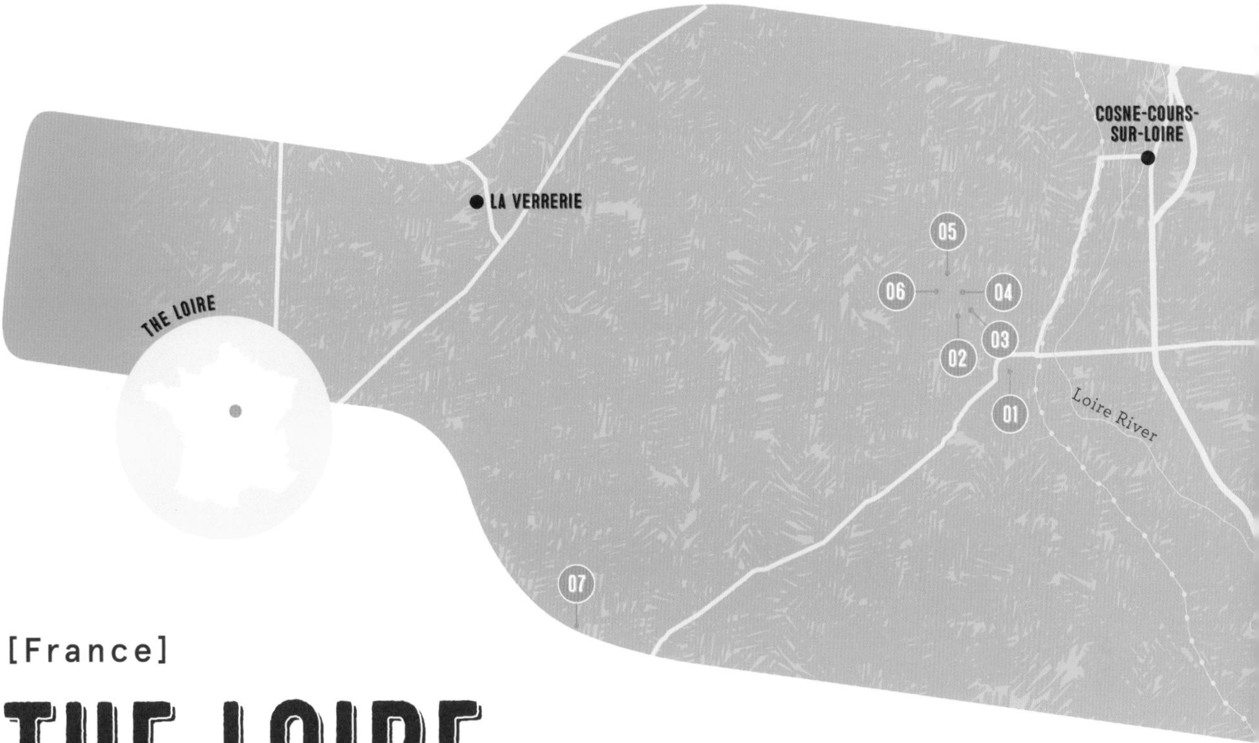
COSNE-COURS-SUR-LOIRE
LA VERRERIE
05
06
04
03
02
01
Loire River
THE LOIRE
07

[France]

THE LOIRE

Take your time and explore the crisp white wines and fairy-tale châteaux of the languid Loire River in central France by boat, bicycle or car.

The Loire is the longest river in France, and along its banks some of the nation's most famous and varied wines are cultivated: the sharp white Muscadet and Anjou; sparkling Vouvray; and the fresh tannins expressed in the Cabernet Franc grape of Chinon and Saumur. And just 200km (124 miles) from Paris are the remarkable vineyards of Sancerre, from which distinctive Sauvignon has become one of the world's best-loved wines. The grand medieval town of Sancerre sits majestically atop a vine-clad hill overlooking the dozen villages that cover the appellation. The first reference to wines from Sancerre date back to 583 CE, when Gregory of Tours mentioned the vintages here. Up until the phylloxera epidemic of 1886, the majority of production was actually red wine – Pinot Noir – and it was only when the vines were replanted that the decision was made to change to the now-famous Sauvignon Blanc.

GET THERE

Paris Charles de Gaulle is the nearest major airport, 226km (140 miles) from Sancerre. Car hire is available.

Few people who tour the Loire's state-of-the-art cellars realise that just one generation ago there was a great deal of poverty here, with *vignerons* struggling to sell a little-known and little-respected wine, and only surviving by raising goats and producing Crottin de Chevignol cheeses; the brutal frosts of 2021, which impacted production for many Loire vineyards, served as a reminder of how vulnerable winemakers here are to the vagaries of the elements. Sancerre owes its present fame and success to the young generation of vintners who took their wines to Paris after the end of WWII, opening wine bars, convincing the capital that Sancerre was a fashionable wine and becoming early exponents of wine tourism by encouraging Parisians to visit Sancerre, see the vineyards and buy direct from the winemaker. Wine tourists still get a very special welcome – and now the whole world seems to have fallen in love with Sancerre.

01 DOMAINE ALPHONSE MELLOT

For 19 generations, as far back as 1513, the Mellot family has been making wines here. This incredible history is apparent as you wander through their 15th-century cellars beneath the streets of Sancerre. Tasting the wines, though, alerts you to the advances of modern winemaking. The latest Alphonse, known as Junior, has made this 50-hectare (123-acre) vineyard biodynamic, limiting each vine to just four to six bunches of grapes at harvest, and sending quality soaring. The cornerstone, La Moussière, is a classic flinty Sancerre, while the barrel-aged Cuvée Edmund has a richness of flavour and subtle aroma that is rare for a Sauvignon. And Generation XIX is a spectacular Pinot Noir, meriting comparison with great Burgundy vintages rather than Sancerre Rouge.
mellot.com; tel +33 2 48 54 07 41; rue Porte César, Sancerre; Mon-Sat by appointment

02 DOMAINE FIRMIN DEZAT

The Dezat family were pioneers of Sancerre's philosophy to sell directly to the public through estate visits, and the family has a well-deserved reputation for producing outstanding wines. Their signature Sauvignon Blanc is always aged in steel vats, while the excellent Pinot Noir matures in three- to five-year-old barrels, with a Cuvée Spéciale from 50-year-old vines in new oak, perfect if you are patient enough to lay down the wine for a few years. Though the 2021 frosts hit the Dezat vineyards hard, severely limiting their production that year, the family have big bounceback plans, with a new range of wines (and a spanking new website) in the pipeline. Book a tasting to discover how their reinvention has been realised.
dezat.fr; tel +33 2 48 79 47 80; rue des Tonneliers, Chaudoux, Verdigny; Mon-Sat by appointment

03 DOMAINE PAUL CHERRIER

Stéphane Cherrier is a young *vigneron* with a lot of respect for the past. A proud portrait of his grandfather in WWI uniform hangs in the tasting room here, and Stéphane recounts how, 'my grandmother used to raise goats to make cheese, which often saved families from poverty when there was a bad harvest or before Sancerre became such a popular wine.' Some of the family's vines grow on the flat in *argilo-calcaire* (limestone and clay) soil, while

tending the vines and precariously hand-picking during the harvest. Pierrot, as this domaine's young *vigneron* is known, does not need much persuasion to take visitors up to the top of his two prize vineyards: Les Culs de Beaujeu and Les Monts Damnés (the 'cursed mountains'). You'll need a head for heights, as the vineyard drops off like the edge of a cliff. Back in the cellar, the exceptional wines are perfectly paired with the famous Crottin de Chavignol goat's cheese. *Tel +33 2 48 54 24 57; Le Bourg, Chavignol; Mon–Fri by appointment*

06 DOMAINE PASCAL ET NICOLAS REVERDY

Follow a winding road through scenic vineyards to the tiny hamlet of Maimbray, whose 40 inhabitants include 10 winemaking families. The *famille* Reverdy is one such dynasty: Pascal Reverdy is helped by his two sons, both committed to becoming *vignerons*. Don't be surprised if he begins a dégustation by pouring his fresh, fruity Pinot Noir: 'I feel the Sancerre Blanc is too aromatic to taste first, as afterwards the rosé and red may appear bland.' This used to be a working farm, and the wine cellar resembles a museum, filled with ancient farming tools, while the cosy tasting room looks like the family dining room, with a long wooden table, kitchen and wood-fired stove.

those on the slope are marked by the more distinctive *terre blanche* (clay, limestone and oyster shells); it is these two soil types that really typify the wines of Sancerre. While Stéphane's sharp, acidic Sauvignon is aged in steel vats, he is also working to develop the complex Cuvée Philippa in wooden barrels. *Tel +33 2 48 79 37 28; Chemin Matifat, Chaudoux, Verdigny; by appointment*

04 DOMAINE VINCENT GAUDRY

Vincent Gaudry is an artisan winemaker whose ancient cellar may be in the village of Chambre, but the 11-hectare (27-acre) organic-certified vineyard is spread out in parcels across the communes of Sury-en-Vaux, Saint-Satur, Verdigny and Sancerre, 'because I want grapes growing on the key different

soils in the region,' explains Vincent, 'flinty silex, *caillotte* [pebbly] and *argilo-calcaire* [clay and limestone]'. His wines are explosive, especially Constellation du Scorpion, a Sauvignon made from a parcel of 100% silex. 'I want to continue the unique characteristics we have with our wine,' he says, 'to respect our elders who have made Sancerre famous all over the world, and not change for change's sake.' *bit.ly/vincentgaudry; tel +33 2 48 79 49 25; Petite Chambre, Sury-en-Vaux; Mon–Fri by appointment*

05 DOMAINE MARTIN

Of all the villages surrounding Sancerre, Chavignol is the most picturesque, its medieval houses tightly enclosed by two steep hillsides crisscrossed with vineyards. The slopes are incredibly difficult to work, both in terms of

04 Central Sancerre

05 Sancerre townscape

06 Vineyards, Sancerre

Paul-Henry Pellé welcomes visitors to his state-of-the-art cellar and may whisk them off in his battered old army jeep for a tour

bit.ly/Reverdy; tel +33 2 48 79 37 31; Maimbray, Sury-en-Vaux; Mon-Tue & Thu-Sat by appointment

⑦ DOMAINE PELLÉ

The sprawling Pellé vineyard spreads across Sancerre into the adjoining appellation of Menetou-Salon. There are many reasons this is a must-visit winery. It provides the perfect opportunity to judge the Sauvignon Blanc and Pinot Noir from Menetou-Salon, so long the poor cousin to Sancerre, but now the rising star. Paul-Henry Pellé welcomes visitors to the state-of-the-art cellar and, at the drop of a hat, will whisk you off in his battered old army jeep for a tour of the surrounding vineyards. And be prepared to taste a lot of wines, too, as Paul-Henry vinifies each *clos* of vines separately and often bottles them as individual cuvées, showing how the soil can completely change a wine. 'Yes, I have a lot of different cuvées,' he says, 'but that is what is exciting about making wines – otherwise I would just get fed up.'
henry-pelle.com; tel +33 2 48 64 42 48; Morogues; Mon-Fri

WHERE TO STAY
MOULIN DES VRILLÈRES
Winemaker B&Bs are rare in the Sancerre region, but visitors here get a warm welcome from Christian and Karine Lauverjat, who provide a full tour of their cellar and a tasting. *sancerre-online.com; tel +33 2 48 79 38 28; Sury-en-Vaux*

LA CÔTE DES MONT DAMNÉS
Jean-Marc Bourgeois is the son of one of the most famous Sancerre winemakers, but chose to become a chef before returning home to renovate an old hotel. Today, his guests can relax in designer rooms and dine on refined tasting menus in his gourmet restaurant. *montsdamnes.com; tel +33 2 48 54 01 72; place de l'Orme, Chavignol*

WHERE TO EAT
RESTAURANT LA TOUR
This restaurant showcases the many talents of chef Baptiste Fournier. Don't miss the *pigeonneau de St*

Quentin (pigeon served with grapes and wild mushrooms). *latoursancerre.fr; tel +33 2 48 54 00 81; 31 Nouvelle Place, Sancerre; Tue-Sat*

AU P'TIT GOÛTER
A brilliant village bistro with wines from more than 50 local Sancerre producers – the ideal accompaniment to both Crottin de Chavignol cheese, made by the owner's son; and another local speciality, a *friture* of tiny deep-fried fish caught in the Loire. *bit.ly/ptitgouter; tel +33 2 48 54 01 66; Le Bourg, Chavignol; daily*

WHAT TO DO
Sancerre overlooks the mighty Loire River, so for a healthy break from wine tasting, go hiking or cycling along its banks, rent a canoe or, at the sand flats of the village of Saint-Satur, sunbathe at the water's edge (though beware of currents). *loirevalley-france.co.uk*

CELEBRATIONS
Get the lowdown on wine-related festivities in the area at the Maison de Sancerre; the Facebook page details regular events at local vineyards. *facebook.com/ maisondsancerre; tel 02 48 54 11 35; 3 rue du Méridien, Sancerre*

Map labels: DIJON, 01, 02, VOSNE-ROMANÉE, NUITS-ST-GEORGES, 03, 04, BEAUNE, 05, POMMARD, 06, 07, BURGUNDY

[France]

BURGUNDY

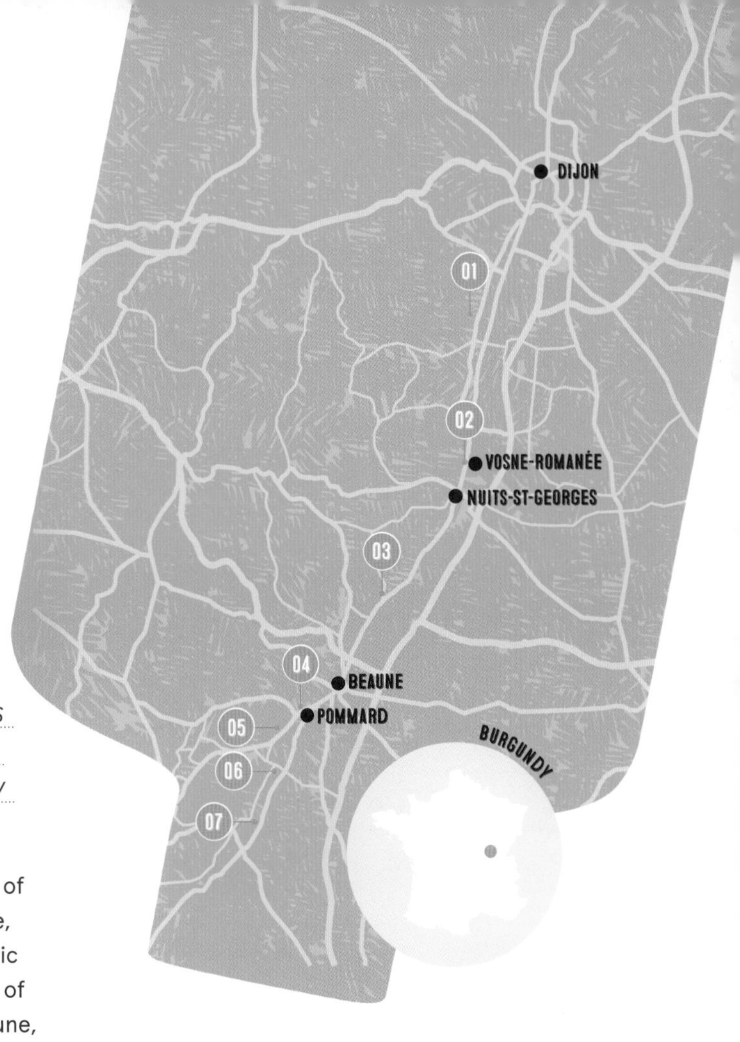

It's easy to feel daunted by Burgundy's reputation, but don't – the locals love to share the secrets of their legendary Pinot Noir with visitors.

Burgundy stretches as far as the vineyards of Chablis, Mâcon and the Côte Chalonnaise, but the quintessential heart of this historic winemaking region is the 80km (50-mile) stretch of road along the Côtes de Nuits and Côtes de Beaune, from Dijon down to Santenay. The illustrious vineyards that line both sides of La Côte d'Or, or Gold Coast, as it is known, produce probably the most famous wines in the world. This essentially monoculture terroir of painstakingly manicured vines provides the perfect interpretation of Pinot Noir and Chardonnay, grapes that may be grown all over the world but which attain unassailable peaks here in Burgundy.

The taste, colour and aroma of a Burgundy Pinot Noir varies according to its village of origin (even according to each parcel of vines), but it is always marked by an evocative fruity flavour, balanced acidity and a signature touch of minerality. In fact, the name of the grape is never written on the label of a Burgundy wine, just the vineyard, known as a *climat*, along with the official classification of appellation – either 'Village', 'Premier Cru' or the ultimate accolade, a 'Grand Cru'.

Despite producing some of the world's most celebrated wines for over 2000 years, most Burgundy winemakers, whose families have often owned their vineyards for centuries, are down-to-earth and welcoming. This friendly reception is appreciated: tasting wines here can feel a little intimidating, due to both the incredibly high quality and the incredibly high prices. But once you sit down at a rough wooden table in a rustic cellar with a cheerful *vigneron*, gently swirling a glass of subtly coloured Pommard or golden-hued Montrachet, it is impossible not to succumb to the Burgundy charm. It's a million miles from the glitzy world of a three-star Michelin restaurant, where the same vintage is being carefully poured by a smartly dressed sommelier.

GET THERE
Geneva is the nearest major airport, 269km (167 miles) from Fixin. Car hire is available. The train from Paris to Dijon takes 1hr 33min.

01 DOMAINE JOLIET PÈRE ET FILS

Fixin (pronounced 'Fissin') is just outside Dijon at the beginning of La Route des Grands Crus. As the sleepy village does not actually boast a Grand Cru, it's often bypassed as enthusiasts speed on to the mythical vineyards of Chambolle and Vougeot. But Bénigne Joliet makes exceptional red wines, and his tiny domaine is pretty much unchanged since the time of its construction in 1142 by Benedictine monks. Sitting in the immense vaulted wine cellar, complete with a medieval wooden press, Bénigne explains how this magical place inspires him. 'Every morning when I come in to check the barrels I imagine the scene a thousand years ago: the monks dressed in their habits, going out to work in the vines, no phones, no computers. I feel privileged to make wine here.'
domainejoliet.fr; tel +33 6 23 25 08 45; Manoir de la Perrière, Fixin; Mon-Sat by appointment $

02 DOMAINE RION

Vosne-Romanée looks like just another tranquil Burgundy village. But behind almost every anonymous gate lie some of the world's most famous vineyards: Romanée-Conti, La Tâche, Richebourg. Dating back to at least the 11th century, these wines are, quite simply, priceless. Not surprisingly, few of these famous names are open for visits, but the Rion family can claim a long heritage as residents, even if today their cellars are on the busy road linking Beaune with Dijon. 'My father decided back in the 1950s that it was just not practical to be based in the village', explains fifth-generation *vigneronne*, Armelle Rion. 'Small producers like us had to wash our barrels out on the pavement, and delivering the grapes during harvest was a nightmare. Here we have plenty of room to both make and age our wine, as well as receiving visitors to taste our Vosne Romanée, Clos de Vougeot and Chambolle Musigny.' All tastings are accompanied by truffle-laced morsels.
domainerion.fr; tel +33 3 80 61 05 31; 8 Rte Nationale,

*Vosne-Romanée; Mon-Sat by
appointment* 💲🍴

03 DOMAINE CAPITAIN-GAGNEROT

One of the oddities of Burgundy is
that with so many domaines owning
small parcels, it is by no means
assured that the best wines come
from a cellar actually in the village
that bears the name of a Grand
Cru. This is certainly the case for
Aloxe-Corton, an utterly idyllic
hamlet with a fairy-tale castle. Few
tourists stop off in busy adjacent
Ladoix, and the Domaine Capitain-
Gagnerot sits on the trunk road
to Dijon. But visitors are warmly
welcomed to try the excellent
selection of Corton Grands Crus,
including an outstanding white
Corton-Charlemagne, as well as
the less-renowned but complex
Premier Cru of Ladoix itself.
*capitain-gagnerot.com;
tel +33 3 80 26 41 36; 38 Rte de
Dijon, Ladoix-Serrigny; Mon-Sat
by appointment*

04 THIERRY VIOLOT-GUILLEMARD

They say in the village of Pommard
that Thierry Violot-Guillemard is
more deeply rooted here than
one of his vines. Certainly, a
tasting in his tiny cellar, or a stay
in the family's B&B, is the perfect
introduction to the ingrained
hospitality of a typical Burgundy
vigneron. His 6-hectare (15-acre)
organic estate spreads over Volnay,
Beaune, Monthélie and Meursault,
but Thierry is defined by his
incomparable interpretation of
Pinot Noir in Pommard. 'Our most
important work is always in the
vineyard, with as little intervention
in the cellar as possible,' he
philosophises, 'and then, the wine
must be left alone to age.'
*violot-guillemard.fr;
tel +33 3 80 22 49 98; 7 rue
Sainte-Marguerite, Pommard;
Mon-Sat by appointment*

05 DOMAINE GLANTENAY PIERRE ET FILS

With its commanding church and
solemn war memorial, Volnay seems
an austere village. But there is
nothing austere about the elegant
wines presented in the homely
tasting room of the Glantenay

family. Pierre Glantenay has handed the reins to his children, Guillaume and Sarah, who have built a dazzling modern cellar. 'I am committing myself to the domaine for a very long time with this kind of financial investment,' Guillame says, 'but we have such a unique terroir that with the new cellar I really believe I can make even more exceptional wines than my father.'
domaineglantenay.com; tel +33 3 80 21 61 82; 3 rue de la Barre, Volnay; Tue-Sat by appointment

06 DOMAINE YVES BOYER MARTENOT

With its grand château-like town hall covered with zigzagging coloured roof tiles, Meursault is one of Burgundy's famed destinations. Vincent Boyer is a down-to-earth winemaker, producing a selection of

distinctively mineral Premier Crus: 'Our vines are mostly very old, many over 90 years, which means low yields but high quality. I have been moving towards organic for the last few years, all but eliminating the use of chemicals, but I won't yet sign up for the inflexibility of certification.'
boyer-martenot.com; tel +33 3 80 21 26 25; 17 place de L'Europe, Meursault; Apr-Nov Tue-Sat, Dec-Mar Mon-Fri

07 DOMAINE JEAN CHARTRON

The most famous name in Burgundy for white wine is Montrachet. Five Grands Crus are concentrated around Chassagne-Montrachet and Puligny-Montrachet villages. Visiting the modern winery of Jean-Michel Chartron, he dips the tasting pipette into a barrel and describes

what it's like to make what is often known as the world's greatest wine: 'I don't feel that I own my vines, but rather that I am a guardian for the centuries of workers who have toiled the land before and the future generations. My name on the bottle is not important.' After wandering through these historic vineyards, most people can't resist buying at least one bottle, regardless of the expense. A 10-year-old Bâtard-Montrachet, say, with its intense aromas and flavours of apple, almonds and spices, is perfect to savour over a romantic meal at home, accompanying perhaps scallops or lobster.
bourgogne-chartron.com; tel +33 3 80 21 99 19; Grand Rue, Puligny-Montrachet; Easter-Nov Thu-Sun 10am-noon & 2-6pm; Aug & Dec-Easter by appointment

WHERE TO STAY
CHÂTEAU DE GILLY
A fairy-tale castle near the iconic Clos de Vougeot and vineyards of Romanée-Conti. Four-poster beds and a 14th-century vaulted dining room await. *chateau-gilly.com; tel +33 3 80 62 89 98; Gilly-les-Citeaux, Vougeot*

CHAMBRES D'HÔTES DE L'ORMERALE
The winemaking Fouquerand family run a simple cottage B&B in this delightful village. Be sure to sample the local bubbly, Crémant de Bourgogne. *domaine-denisfouquerand.com; tel +33 3 80 21 88 62; rue de l'Orme, La Rochepot*

CHÂTEAU DE MELIN
A romantic château B&B with a verdant park and lake. Most evenings, in the medieval cellar, Arnaud Derats hosts a tasting of his wines, which originate from small parcels from Meursault to Chambolle-Musigny. *chateaudemelin.com; tel +33 3 80 21 21 19;*

Hameau de Melin, Auxey-Duresses

WHERE TO EAT
RESTAURANT LE CHARLEMAGNE
Encircled by vineyards, Le Charlemagne resembles a zen temple, and Michelin-starred chef Laurent Peugeot surprises with a fusion of terroir tastes with Japanese flavours. *lecharlemagne.fr; tel +33 3 80 21 51 45; Rte de Vergelesses, Pernand-Vergelesses; dinner Thu-Mon, lunch Sat & Sun*

LA BISTRO D'OLIVIER
Respected *vigneron* Olivier Leflaive has transformed Puligny-Montrachet with his hotel and restaurant, its menu tailored for wine pairings. *olivier-leflaive.com; tel +33 3 80 21 37 65; place du Monument, Puligny-Montrachet; Tue-Sat*

BOISROUGE
Feast on roast suckling pig with crunchy cabbage at chef Philippe Delacourcelle's gourmet venue, where you can also stay the night or sign up for a cookery course.

boisrouge.fr; tel +33 3 80 34 30 56; 4bis rue du Petit Paris, Flagey-Echézeaux; Tue-Sat

WHAT TO DO
Intermingle boating, cycling and wine tasting via a barge cruise along Burgundy's historic canal. *burgundy-canal.com*

CELEBRATIONS
On the third Sunday in November, the Hospices de Beaune holds its world-famous charity wine auction, as it has done since 1851. *hospices-beaune.com*

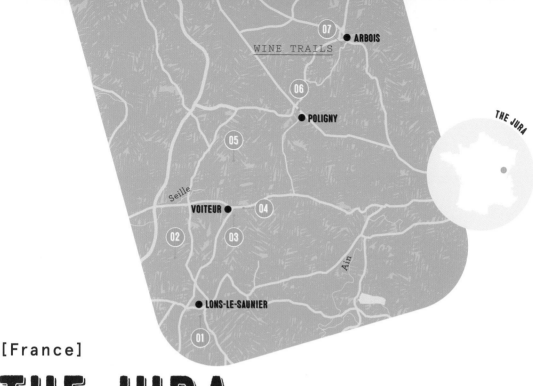

07 ● ARBOIS

06

● POLIGNY

05

Seille

VOITEUR ●   04

02   03

THE JURA

Ain

● LONS-LE-SAUNIER

01

[France]

THE JURA

This oft-overlooked region tucked away on the Swiss border, quietly making wine for centuries, holds some quirky surprises for even experienced wine-tourers.

Wine has been made in the mountainous Jura for well over a thousand years. But it is only recently that this corner of France has begun to make a name for itself in the world of wine. The region has a rich biodiversity of lush valleys and thick forests, with vineyards adjacent to agricultural and grazing land. The majority of grapes cultivated are little-known indigenous varieties, from delicate light reds – Trousseau, Poulsard – to the remarkable Savagnin, which makes a white wine perfect for long ageing. A new generation of *vignerons* are making their mark here, using modern winemaking techniques alongside the Jura's traditional method.

And nothing quite prepares you for a tasting of the extraordinary Vin Jaune. No one is left undecided about Vin Jaune, so be prepared to love it or hate it. While the distinctive aroma immediately seems different from other wines – a mix of walnuts, hazelnuts and exotic spices – the taste is altogether something else, incredibly dry yet somehow fruity and nutty at the same time. The wine is a brilliant cooking ingredient, with all Jura households stocking a bottle to add to dishes such as chicken with morel mushrooms. It's also an ideal pairing with the Jura's tart Comté cheese. Made purely from Savagnin grapes, Vin Jaune is barrel-aged for six years, but with a pocket of air left open; its oxidising effect is limited as the maturing wine is covered by a natural *voile*, a film of yeast, in the same way Spanish sherry is produced in Jerez.

Wine tourism is still in its early days in the Jura, but that makes for an even more refreshing welcome when travellers turn up to taste in a little-known backwoods domaine. For now, these young Jura *vignerons* are concentrating all their efforts on winemaking, though many are already converting parts of their rambling stone farms into holiday homes.

GET THERE
Geneva is the nearest major airport, 143km (89 miles) from Montaigu. Car hire is available.

01 DOMAINE PIGNIER

A tasting at this historic domaine is the perfect introduction to the Jura. Ask Marie-Florence Pignier, a seventh-generation *vigneronne*, to take you down for a tour of the astonishing 13th-century cellar. The vast, high, vaulted barrel-chamber resembles a cathedral, so it's not surprising to learn that this was formerly a monastery, founded in 1250 by *vigneron*-monks who planted the original vineyard. The wines produced today are organic and highly contemporary, and certain cuvées are *naturel*, with no sulphite added. Don't miss the Vin Jaune either, which Marie-Florence proudly claims is 'the ultimate wine for ageing, even if you want to wait a century!'

domaine-pignier.com; tel +33 3 84 24 24 30; 11 place Rouget de Lisle, Montaigu; by appointment Mon-Sat

02 DOMAINE VANDELLE

Étoile sits in a bucolic valley encircled by a series of rolling hills covered with vineyards and woods. 'Pretty much each hill and its vines is owned by a different village *vigneron*,' recounts Philippe Vandelle, 'and each of us make wines with a different personality due to the variations of soil and exposure to the sun.' The Vandelles came to the Jura over two centuries ago from Belgium, and a cousin still owns the grand Château de l'Étoile winery. Philippe has converted a stone labourer's

cottage into a snug tasting room, and it is a surprise to learn that 30% of his production is devoted to Crémant du Jura, made following the classic Champenoise method. *vinsphilippevandelle.com; tel +33 3 84 86 49 57; 186 rue Bouillod, L'Étoile; Mon-Sat*

03 FRUITIÈRE DE VOITEUR

As you drive out of Voiteur, you can't miss the massive and spectacular limestone outcrop with Château-Chalon balancing on its summit to the left of the road, while opposite is an imposing modern winery. 'A Jura *fruitière* has nothing to do with fruits,' explains Bertrand Delannay, the director here, 'but is rather an agricultural cooperative devoted to one of the region's two

01 Château-Chalon

02 Village views from Château-Chalon

03 European bee-eaters in the Jura

specialities – wine or cheese.' There are a challenging 14 wines to taste, with eminently affordable prices and a lot of variety. 'Many Jura *vignerons* specialise only in barrel-aged wines as that is the tradition here, but we try to offer some easier-to-drink alternatives too, such as a young floral Chardonnay aged in steel vats.'
fvv.fr; tel +33 3 84 85 21 29; 60 rue de Nevy, Voiteur; daily

04 DOMAINE CREDOZ

Medieval Château-Chalon, classified as one of France's most beautiful villages, looks down on a crisscross patchwork of vineyards, including 9 hectares (22 acres) cultivated by Jean-Claude Credoz, an innovative *viticulteur* (winemaker). His excellent

sparkling Crémant is sold out a year in advance, while enthusiasts come just to taste his Macvin, the unique Jura aperitif that he makes from the must (juice) of Savagnin grapes, and a distilled Marc (made with pulped skin and seeds) aged for four years in oak. Working essentially old vines, some over 80 years, and ageing from three to seven years in ancient barrels, his white wines – Chardonnay, Savagnin and Vin Jaune – are elegant and subtle on initial tasting, but with all the grape's delicate expression coming out in what Jean-Claude lovingly describes as the *longueur* of the aftertaste.
domaine-credoz.fr; tel +33 3 84 44 64 91; 3 rue des Chèvres, Château-Chalon; Mon-Thu by appointment

05 LES DOLOMIES

Céline and Steve Gormally only founded their domaine in 2008. 'There is a great feeling of solidarity here,' Céline explains. 'I immediately sought organic certification...and when I first started, I was able to rent parcels of wonderful 70-year-old vines at a fair-trade price from an agricultural association.' To lessen the financial burden of establishing the vineyard, the Gormallys ran a kind of club under the AMAP model (a French scheme designed to support small-scale farmers), in which some 70 local residents ordered wine for the forthcoming vintage but paid a year in advance. Today, Les Dolomies' whites are bottled by individual parcels of vines, tended biodynamically; the

Pinot Noir is surprisingly full-bodied for the Jura. Ask to try naturally fermented Tout Pet bubbly, too. *les-dolomies.com; tel +33 6 87 03 39 98; 40 rue de l'Asile, Passenans; by appointment*

06 DOMAINE BADOZ

Bernard Badoz launched the Percée du Vin Jaune festival in 1977, where every *vigneron* in the Jura presents their wines, and which launched this little-known region on to the world wine map. Visitors arrive at this modern boutique where they can taste Comté cheeses from a cousin's farm, organic honey and regional charcuterie such as smoky Morteau sausage. Bernard's son, Benoit, who runs the organic estate today, has created a new range of special cuvées; 'Edouard' is Chardonnay

aged in barrels made from wood in the forest above Poligny, while 'Arrogance', which he modestly named for himself, sees a crisp, acidic Savagnin aged normally rather than oxidised with the traditional *voile* of yeast used for Vin Jaune. *domaine-badoz.fr; tel +33 3 84 37 18 00; 19 place des Déportés, Poligny; daily* ✕

07 DOMAINE RIJCKAERT

Arbois is the lively winemaking capital of the Jura, but the winery of dynamic *vigneron* Florent Rouve is hidden just outside town in a sleepy hamlet. Florent is always renovating and innovating, so there is no sign outside his ancient farmhouse and no proper tasting room, but that doesn't detract from the joy of discovering his artisan vintages.

He is a white-wine fanatic, working almost exclusively with Chardonnay and Savagnin (there's only one red, the Arbois La Rouge). Informal but animated tastings take place down in a 17th-century vaulted cellar that is mouldy, cold and humid – perfect conditions, according to Florent, to age using the traditional *voile* method. 'I press the juice, bring it down into the barrels and begin ageing on the lie. Then wait. It really isn't complicated to make good wine, you just need patience,' he says with a wry smile. *rijckaert.fr; tel +33 3 71 41 00 06; Villette-les-Arbois; daily by appointment* Ⓢ

04 Domaine Credoz

05 Salins-les-Bains

WHERE TO STAY

LE RELAIS DE LA PERLE
Nathalie Estavoyer welcomes travellers to her beautifully restored *maison de vigneron*, organising wine tastings and even a hot-air balloon trip high above the vineyards. *lerelaisdelaperle.fr; tel +33 3 84 25 95 52; 184 Rte de Voiteur, Le Vernois*

LE DORTOIR DES MOINES
The magnificent Romanesque abbey of Baume-les-Messieurs is already one of the Jura's most spectacular sights. Stay in one of its private apartments, now transformed into magical accommodation. *dortoir-des-moines. info; tel +33 6 33 21 21 46; L'Abbaye, Baume-les-Messieurs*

WHERE TO EAT

CHEZ JANINE
Now under new ownership, with a retro feel and hearty *plats* of local specialities, many laced with a splash of Jura wine. *facebook.com/ ChezJanineNev;*

tel +33 3 84 48 43 78; 771 Rte de la Vallée, Nevy-sur-Seille; Tue-Sat

LA FINETTE TAVERNE D'ARBOIS
A rustic wooden chalet in Jura's winemaking capital. Feast on regional specialities such as succulent slow-cooked chicken in Vin Jaune. *finette.fr; tel +33 3 84 66 06 78; 22 Ave Louis Pasteur, Arbois; daily*

LE BISTROT DE PORT LESNEY
With red-checked tablecloths and a zinc bar, this classic bistro oozes Gallic charm, and chef Julien Zangiacomi prepares traditional dishes including local-cheese platters and frogs' legs in a parsley sauce. *bistrotdeportlesney. com; tel +33 3 84 37 83 27; place du 8 Mai 1945, Port-Lesney; daily*

WHAT TO DO
Visit the subterranean salt mines of the Unesco World Heritage-listed Salins-les-Bains. *salinesdesalins.com*

CELEBRATIONS
Every year, on the first weekend of February, a different village hosts La Percée du Vin Jaune, toasting the new vintage. *percee-du-vin-jaune. com*

05

[France]

BORDEAUX

Discover another, more accessible side to world-famous Bordeaux: in the saddle, in the trees or up in the air.

Premier Cru classé; Left Bank, Right Bank; €8000 cases of Château Margaux: the world of Bordeaux wine can seem an intimidating, confusing and, yes, expensive place. For one thing, France's largest Appellation d'Origine Contrôlée (AOC) comprises several subregions, each very different. On the Right Bank of the Dordogne River lie Saint-Émilion and Pomerol. On the Left Bank of the Garonne River, which flows through the city of Bordeaux and meets the Dordogne in the vast Gironde estuary, is the Médoc, home to Margaux and other hallowed names.

But one region of Bordeaux has made a special effort to be more accessible than its neighbours: Graves and Sauternes, upriver of Bordeaux on the Left (south) Bank of the Garonne. During the last 10 years, wineries along the Graves and Sauternes wine route have introduced ever more novel ways of tasting and learning about the region and its unique wines: visitors can cycle to châteaux, go canoeing, take sightseeing flights from vineyards and taste wines in treehouses.

This trail begins and ends in the dynamic university city of Bordeaux, whose fortunes have ebbed and flowed like the broad Garonne that bisects it. Grapes were first grown here during the region's Roman period when Burdigala was an import/export hub and there are still vineyards within the city

GET THERE
Bordeaux has an international airport on its outskirts (take bus 1 to the centre for €1) and is 2hr from Paris by train.

limits. Come the 12th century, Eleanor of Aquitaine's marriage to Henry II in 1152 enabled Aquitaine to become England's sole supplier of wine. In the 16th century, the Dutch encouraged the Bordelais to expand; by the 18th century, wine merchant families such as the Lurtons and the Bartons ushered in Bordeaux's next golden age, building many of its most beautiful châteaux.

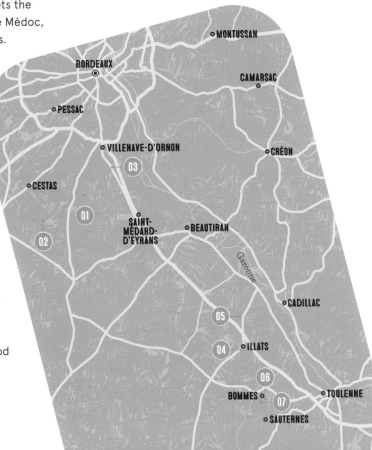

01 CHÂTEAU LARRIVET HAUT-BRION

Rouse your taste buds with a chocolate-and-wine tasting at Château Larrivet Haut-Brion, a few minutes' drive south of Bordeaux in the Graves region's Pessac-Léognan appellation. Elsewhere on this trail you'll try dry reds in Graves and sweet whites in Sauternes; red wines at Larrivet Haut-Brion are paired with single-origin chocolates from Bordeaux's Chocolaterie Saunion. Unlike the five prestigious 'First Growth' châteaux (Pauillac's Lafite, Latour and Mouton, and Graves' Margaux and Haut-Brion), which received their designation in 1855, the 19th-century Larrivet Haut-Brion isn't one of Bordeaux's Premier Crus and so, according to the château's manager of wine tourism Alexandra Monfort, is free to be more experimental. For example, white wines are fermented in giant concrete eggs. Red wines, however, remain in French oak barrels for six to 18 months. 'The collaboration between a cooper and a winemaker is crucial,' says Alexandra. 'A light toast imparts flavours of vanilla and cinnamon and a darker toast brings stronger flavours such as tobacco.'

The owners, the Gervoson family, host chocolate-egg hunts in the château's Jardin d'Ivresse around Easter time. *larrivethautbrion.fr; tel +33 5 56 64 75 51; 84 Avenue de Cadaujac, Léognan; daily by appointment* 💲

02 CHÂTEAU DE LÉOGNAN

The emblem on the bottles of Château de Léognan's Cabernet Sauvignon and Merlot blend depicts a phoenix, a symbol borrowed from the chapel in the grounds of this country house. It's an appropriate choice: since purchasing this beautiful rural property on the west side of Léognan in 2006, Philippe and Chantal Miecaze have restored its every corner. The main house now features several B&B suites, and a restaurant, Le Manège, occupies the tree-shaded former horse-training ring.

Château de Léognan is part of the Pessac-Léognan appellation, which was founded by André Lurton in 1987 and is the only Bordeaux appellation outside Médoc to have a Premier Cru and to be part of a city. According to Chantal Miecaze, Bordeaux wine has a natural advantage: 'The soil in Graves is well-drained because it used to be an estuary,' she explains. 'Before settling on its final course, the Garonne River meandered from the Pyrenees to the Atlantic, bringing

01 The Garonne at
Bordeaux

02 Take to the skies
above Château Venus

03 Wine tours by bike
at Château Bardins

gravel down from the mountains.
The gravel is great for grapes: water
drains quickly so the vines have to
make more of an effort to seek it,
and the pebbles reflect the sun,
lengthening the day for grapes to
ripen.' You can sample the wine over
lunch or at a tasting.
*chateauleognan.fr; tel +33 5 56
64 14 96; 88 Chemin du Barp,
Léognan; Mon-Sat by appointment*
$ ✕

⑬ CHÂTEAU BARDINS

At the next stop, Château Bardins,
Pascale Larroche and fifth-
generation owner Stella Puel
offer a very active approach to
discovering Graves' wines. Formerly
a farm and still enjoying a pastoral
setting, Château Bardins has been
producing wine since WWII, in
addition to honey, preserves, crops
and raising livestock. Visitors can
take an hour's bicycle ride around
the locale with Pascale.

'We take in 10 châteaux in
10km [6 miles],' she says. 'That's
only possible in Bordeaux where
vineyards are so close together.'
Along the way Pascale explains why
the ground is good for vines: 'they
only get a little to eat and drink –
their roots need to go down 7m
[23ft] sometimes to find water –

and annual *épamprage*, or pruning,
stops them wasting energy growing
shoots that won't fruit.' While the
vines may go hungry, there's no
need for visitors to: Stella is happy
for people to bring picnics to enjoy
in the château's wooded grounds,
especially if you buy some of the
organic wine.
*chateaubardins.fr; tel +33 5 56
30 78 01; Chemin de la Matole,
Cadaujac; by appointment* $

⑭ CHÂTEAU JOUVENTE

Head southeast down the
backroads to Château Jouvente,
in the centre of Illats, where you'll
find some of the best-value red
wine in Graves. This is a small,
newish winery owned by Benjamin
Gutmann, who contracts the
winemaking out to Oliver Bernadet.
You can taste three to four wines
on a free 30-minute tour or book a

longer visit – with quiz questions for
families – which shows how the wine
is produced before you taste it.
The white is a classic Graves – fruity
but elegant: 'peach and pineapple
from the Semillon and citrus from
the Sauvignon,' says Benjamin.
The red is a characterful blend of
Petit Verdot, Merlot and Cabernet
Sauvignon and at €19 it's a bargain.
*chateau-jouvente.fr; tel +33 5 56
62 49 69; 93 Le Bourg, Illats; Mon-
Fri, by appointment Sat-Sun* $

⑮ CHÂTEAU VENUS

Bumping down a grassy runway
between rows of vines in a truly
tiny two-seater plane is an exciting
way to start your tour of Château
Venus. Once airborne, pilot – and
winemaker – Bertrand Amart will
take you on a looping 20-minute
circuit of Sauternes and Graves;
longer flights up to Saint-Émilion

04 Bordeaux's Cité du Vin museum

05 Interactive displays inside the Cité du Vin

in summer and autumn brings fog to the surrounding vineyards, which is good for causing the botrytis fungus on the grapes that we need to make Sauternes.' This 'noble rot' dehydrates the grapes and adds a honeyed flavour. *chateau-sigalas-rabaud.com; tel +33 5 57 31 07 45; Bommes; daily by appointment* 💲✕

⑦ CHÂTEAU DE RAYNE VIGNEAU

At Château de Rayne Vigneau, one of the 1855 Grand Cru classé châteaux, winemaker and managing director Vincent Labergère is set on updating Sauternes to modern tastes. 'The 19th century was a golden age here,' he says. 'Then Rayne Vigneau's fame slipped away.' Investment from new owners has reignited ambition. 'I wanted to make a more thirst-quenching, versatile wine,' explains Vincent, 'so we brought a new freshness to the wine. We're looking for more acidity and less sugar now.' Similarly, he is intent on introducing the wine and the region through new experiences: you can take a bike tour, taste the wines in a treehouse, blend your own wines or be a grape-picker for a day (followed by dinner with the winemaker). *raynevigneau.fr; tel +33 5 56 76 64 05; 4 Le Vigneau, Bommes; by appointment daily, closed Sun Dec-Mar* 💲✕

and Pomerol or all the way to Le Bassin d'Arcachon, weekend beach retreat for the Bordelais, are also possible (prices range from €79 to €139, depending on the route). Even on the short flight you can see all the way to the Dune of Pilat on the coast and get a good understanding of the geography of the Garonne. And on the half-day Toutes Options itinerary (€399), you'll combine all seven flights on offer. Bertrand started flying lessons at the age of 18. His other passion is winemaking – he worked with his wife Emmanuelle in Napa and Barossa before returning to start Château Venus. They produce sustainably farmed red wine that is designed to be both fruity and immediate; 30-minute tastings are free, but there are longer tour and tasting combos too. *chateauvenus.com; tel +33 6 03 17 91 39; 3 Pertigues Lieu dit Brouquet, Illats; Mon-Sat* 💲

⑥ CHÂTEAU SIGALAS RABAUD

Château Sigalas Rabaud is in the heart of Sauternes, the region where France's most famous dessert wine is produced. A near neighbour across the fields, Château Yquem, is opening up to the public, but it costs from €84 to €300 for a private tasting there. Sigalas Rabaud is a more accessible option, thanks to owner and director Laure de Lambert Compeyrot, the sixth generation of her family to run the property. She has opened B&B suites overlooking the vines and offers a range of tastings, from 30-minute 'discovery' visits to a leisurely tour with tastings paired with gourmet treats. Laure explains why this pocket of land is perfect for creating golden, sweet Sauternes: 'The Ciron River that flows nearby is fed from a spring and is very cold. The temperature difference

WHERE TO STAY
DOMAINE ECÔTELIA
A fun spot for families: choose from yurts, log cabins, safari-style lodges and even spacious tree houses. Each has abundant space and there's also a swimming pool and other areas to explore. Breakfasts are provided each morning and healthy meals are available at other times. *domaine-ecotelia.com; +33 5 56 65 35 38; 5 Lieu dit Tauzin, Le Nizan*

MERCURE BORDEAUX CHATEAU CHARTRONS HOTEL
This hotel in the former wine merchant district of Bordeaux offers decent-value accommodation close to the Cité du Vin, the riverside attractions and the restaurants of Bordeaux's old town. *accorhotels.com; +33 5 56 43 15 00; 81 Cours Saint-Louis, Bordeaux*

WHERE TO EAT
LE PETITE GUINGETTE
This hip open-air tapas bar serves local wines, beers and snacks from a shack in a Sauternes

courtyard from spring to autumn. It's a relaxed local favourite, where vineyard owners and workers socialise. Check the Facebook page for details of upcoming musical performances. *lapetiteguinguette.com; 2 Chemin de Pasquette, Sauternes; Thu-Mon*

HÔTEL-RESTAURANT LALIQUE
At the other end of the spectrum, with two Michelin stars and a spectacular setting overlooking terraced vines, this stately restaurant in Premier Cru classé Château Lafaurie-Peyraguey is the place to indulge in exquisitely crafted four- or five-course menus. Wine tastings and

accommodation are also on offer. *lafauriepeyragueylalique. com; tel +33 5 24 22 80 11; Lieu dit Peyraguey, Bommes; hours vary*

WHAT TO DO
CHÂTEAU DE ROQUETAILLADE
Take a vineyard breather with a history lesson from Sébastien de Baritault at Mazères' Château de Roquetaillade, which has been passed down through his family for 800 years. It was based on an 8th-century stronghold then rebuilt in the 14th century following the design of Welsh castles. Although the exterior is fortified, the interior was restored by French architect Viollet-le-Duc in the 19th century and is a

fascinating display of Arts and Crafts design inspired by the Gothic Revival work of William Morris and William Burges. *roquetaillade.eu*

CITÉ DU VIN
The Cité du Vin offers a cultural context to the world of wine with temporary exhibitions and a permanent floor of excellent interactive displays, plus restaurants, a wine cellar, a library and a top-floor viewing gallery – all housed in a dramatic building. Arrive by boat to get a sense of the wealth generated by Bordeaux's wine trade as you pass the 19th-century waterfront mansions. *laciteduvin.com; infotbm.com*

CELEBRATIONS
BORDEAUX FÊTE LE VIN
Every two years this four-day June festival, dedicated to the wines of Bordeaux and Aquitaine, takes over the city's riverfront with performances, tastings, workshops and food. *bordeaux-wine-festival. com*

WINE TRAILS

THE RHÔNE

01 VIENNE
ST-ÉTIENNE

Rhône

Drac

02 **03**
04 VALENCE

05

06 MONTÉLIMAR

Ardèche

07 GRIGNAN

Rhône

VAISON-LA-ROMAINE

[France]
THE RHÔNE

From a phenomenal region of France, with snowy mountains in its north and broad, hot valleys to the south, come blockbuster red wines that will dazzle your palate.

The wine region of the Rhône Valley stretches from just below Lyon, past Avignon and right down through the south, where the mighty river meets the Mediterranean. Grapes have been grown here for more than 2000 years and there is a tremendous variety of wines to discover as you travel the length of the valley.

The northern Rhône, from Vienne down to Valence, boasts spectacular scenery, with the river's steep banks covered by terraced vineyards producing some of France's most famous wines: the intense Syrah of Côte-Rôtie, Cornas and Hermitage; and the elegant Condrieu made from the complex Viognier grape. Below Valence the landscapes become more Provençal, and Syrah is grown alongside Grenache, Mourvèdre and Carignan. These grapes are often blended, which can produce the potent and celebrated Châteauneuf-du-Pape, as well as up-and-

coming appellations such as Gigondas, Vacqueyras and Rasteau, or Côtes du Rhône, the classic wine served in every French bistro. Travellers will quickly discover that winemakers in the northern Rhône tend to be more traditional. But once the road heads south of Valence – where plots of vines are much cheaper – a new generation of younger *vignerons* is moving in, eager to experiment, especially with natural wines, which are sweeping the fashionable wine bars of European cities.

Wine tourism has become a well-organised art in the Rhône, with visitors offered tempting places to stay on many domaines, while restaurants have woken up to the wonderful opportunities of wine pairings: a sharp white Crozes-Hermitage with local cheeses such as creamy Saint-Félicien and tangy Picodon; the flinty Saint-Péray accompanying salt-baked line-fished sea bass; and a robust Cornas perfect with a lean fillet of wild venison and forest berries.

GET THERE
Lyon is the nearest major airport, 49km (30 miles) from Chavanay. The train from Paris to Lyon takes 2hr. Car hire is available.

01 DOMAINE DU MONTEILLET

Stéphane Montez is one of those classic larger-than-life French winemakers. His state-of-the-art cellar, perched high above the Rhône, is a lively rendezvous where local winemakers, wine merchants, chefs and curious tourists bustle in and out all day to taste his splendid wines. Be sure to go to the back of the tasting room, as a glass wall lets you peek into a barrel cellar carved into the rock face. Stéphane is a 10th-generation winemaker, with vines in the two most prestigious Rhône appellations, the red Côte-Rôtie and white Condrieu. He explains how, till the early 1980s, 'Condrieu was just known as "Viognier", as this was our own native grape, for centuries grown only here. Today, the whole world seems to be planting Viognier, from Australia to California and Chile, but it only becomes a great wine here.' *montez.fr; tel +33 4 74 87 24 57; 7 Le Montelier, Chavanay; Mon-Sat by appointment* 💲

02 CAVE DE TAIN

Founded in 1933, the Cave de Tain has 300 *associés vignerons*, covering 1000 hectares (2471 acres) of vines, with a reputation that sees critics nominate it as France's top winemaking cooperative. Although it produces a staggering five million bottles a year, membership is restricted to winemakers within a radius of roughly 15km (9 miles), and Tain is one of the rare cooperatives to own its own domaine. These precious vines include highly prized parcels that make it the second-largest owner of Hermitage, which is the name not only of the appellation, but also of the hill that looms over its cellar. A visit here includes a tour of the ultra-modern cellars, a €10 million investment that ranges from a barrel room of 2000 *barriques* (wine barrels made of new oak) to the modern technology of cement 'hippos' used for single-parcel vinification. *cavedetain.com; tel +33 4 75 08 20 87; 22 Rte de Larnage, Tain-l'Hermitage; May-Aug daily, Sep-Apr Sat-Sun and by appointment* 💲

03 DOMAINE COURBIS

Driving into medieval Châteaubourg, you can't miss a huge mural

'Today, the whole world seems to be planting Viognier, from Australia to California and Chile, but it only becomes a great wine here'

-Stéphane Montez, winemaker

'advertising the St Joseph and Cornas wines made by the Courbis brothers, Laurent and Dominique. They can trace their family roots here back to the 16th century, though their modern cellar makes use of all the latest technology.

The vineyards of St Joseph stretch for about 50km (31 miles) along the Rhône, and both the red and white vintages produced at Courbis are reasonably priced and need little further ageing. The Syrah is peppery and rich, while the white Marsanne is incredibly mineral, which is no surprise if you drive up to the Les Royes vineyard and see the barren, rocky limestone that the vines shoot up from.
vins-courbis-rhone.com; tel +33 4 75 81 81 60; Rte de Saint-Romain, Châteaubourg; Mon-Fri, Sat by appointment

04 DOMAINE ALAIN VOGE

Alain Voge, who died in 2020, was a highly respected figure in the recent history of Cornas, which has metamorphosed from a little-known wine into a genuine contender for the title of the top Rhône wine, with steep prices to match. In 2004, Voge handed over the running of his estate to Alberic Mazoyer, formerly from Chapoutier, who moved it to 100% organic and biodynamic winemaking, a rare achievement in this part of the Rhône Valley. After 14 years, Mazoyer bestowed the reins to Lionel Frasse and current winemaker Laurent Martin, who continue to build on Voge's legacy.

unstable, slightly oxidised or a little fizzy but, when perfectly made, will surprise even the most expert taster. Siblings Gérald and Jocelyne Oustric inherited an estate whose grapes used to go straight to the village cooperative. Gérald, however, was intent on making and bottling his own unique wines. In his murky cellar, an ancient stone cottage in picturesque Valvignères, be sure to taste the Cuvée Charbonnières, a distinctive interpretation of Chardonnay, aged for one year in steel vats followed by two years in old wooden barrels. *Tel +33 4 75 52 51 02; Valvignères; Mon-Sat by appointment*

07 MAS DE LIBIAN

As the Rhône heads south below Valence and Montélimar, the winemakers are young, unconventional and pushing boundaries. In dreamy Saint-Marcel d'Ardèche, the Mas de Libian is a matriarchial family of *vigneronnes* whose estate of venerable bush vines dates back to 1670. Hélène Thibon, together with her mother and sisters, produces certified organic and biodynamic wines, and ploughs the soil using horses. Their most popular cuvée is Vin de Pétanque, a blend of Grenache and Syrah that's eminently drinkable on a steamy summer evening. *masdelibian.com; tel +33 4 75 04 66 22; Quartier Libian, Saint-Marcel d'Ardeche; Mon-Fri by appointment*

In Voge's own words: 'Just drive up to the walled terraces of the Cornas vineyard and you will see that our work is just as much that of a builder, spending months each year restoring and repairing the walls that keep the vineyard together. These walls date back to Roman times and we often dig up artefacts and fossils. This is why the wine is relatively expensive, because we have to invest so much financially.' *alain-voge.com; tel +33 4 75 40 32 04; 4 Impasse de l'Équerre, Cornas; Mon-Fri by appointment*

05 DOMAINE DU TUNNEL

Sitting in the comfy leather armchairs of his tasting boutique on Saint-Péray's high street, affable *vigneron* Stéphane Robert asks if many winemakers can claim their cellar is housed in a genuine 19th-century train tunnel. He began making wine in his parents' garage,

then persuaded the town hall to sell him an abandoned tunnel. Visiting his tunnel today is a spectacular experience, a 150m-long (492ft) cellar carved into the hillside, where he vinifies, stores barrels for ageing and receives guests for special tastings, by appointment – well worth the small fee. Stéphane produces individual, high-calibre wines of little-known white Saint-Péray and intense Cornas vintages, some from vines over 100 years old. *domaine-du-tunnel.fr; tel +33 4 75 80 04 66; 20 rue de la République, Saint-Péray; tasting room Mon-Sat by appointment* $

06 LE MAZEL

This corner of the southern Rhône is something of a Holy Land for crusaders of the natural wine movement, with a band of New Age *vignerons* making zero-sulphite wines that may sometimes be

WHERE TO STAY
LA GERINE
Perched high above the Rhône, with a relaxing pool and spectacular views, this comfortable B&B is surrounded by the terraced vineyards of Côte-Rôtie. *lagerine.com; tel +33 4 74 56 03 46; 2 Côte de la Gerine, Ampuis*

HOTEL
MICHEL CHABRAN
An old-fashioned but charming inn on the Rte Nationale 7, which travels down to the south of France. It's run by a Michelin-starred chef. *chabran.com; tel +33 4 75 84 60 09; 29 Ave du 45ème Parallèle, Pont de l'Isère*

DOMAINE NOTRE
DAME DE COUSIGNAC
Winemaker Raphaël Pommier and his American wife, Rachel, welcome guests to a rustic farmhouse, hosting tastings of their organic wines most evenings. *domainedecousignac. fr; tel +33 4 75 54 61 41; Quartier Cousignac, Bourg-Saint-Andéol*

WHERE TO EAT
AUBERGE MONNET
This romantic restaurant on an island in the Rhône serves regional specialities, such as frogs' legs, stuffed pig's trotters, tasty cheeses and charcuterie. Eric, the welcoming owner, has a brilliant selection of wines sold by the glass. *facebook.com/ aubergemonnet; tel +33 4 75 84 57 80; 3 place du Petit Puits, La Roche-de-Glun; Thu-Tue*

LA TOUR CASSÉE
A cosy village bistro that mixes traditional Ardèche favourites (hearty cabbage soup) with exotic recipes such as a tagine of duck confit with dates and quince – and an excellent list of natural wines. *bit.ly/TourCasse; tel +33 4 75 52 45 32; Valvignères; Mon-Sat*

LA FARIGOULE
Overlooking a vineyard, this old-fashioned auberge is perfect for kicking back over a chilled Côtes du Rhône rosé accompanied by a delicious *caillette*, the local take on meatloaf, or a salad starring warm goat's cheese. *auberge-lafarigoule. com; tel +33 4 75 04 02 60; Bidon; daily*

WHAT TO DO
From Vallon Pont d'Arc, you can head off for the day on a scenic guided canoe trip along the Ardèche River, during which you will weave through spectacular gorges and glide under the Pont d'Arc. *en.ardeche-guide.com*

CELEBRATIONS
Two wonderful festivals are hosted at different ends of the Rhône: Jazz à Vienne for two weeks from the end of June; and Avignon's Theatrical Festival) running through the month of July. *jazzavienne.com; festival-avignon.com*

[France]
LANGUEDOC

Craggy cliffs and wooded valleys greet visitors to this dynamic wine region, fast becoming one of France's most exciting.

Some of the most interesting and innovative wines in France are emerging from the vast Languedoc-Roussillon region, which covers much of the south from the Spanish border up to the vineyards of Provence and the Côte d'Azur. A third of France's wine is produced here, but for years the region suffered from poor quality and over-production. Not any more. The winery scene has changed dramatically, with a flood of new appellations, the huge popularity of Vin de Pays wines, and advances in both vineyard and cellar. Dynamic young *vignerons* are drawn here, not to contribute to the old system of the winemaking cooperative, but to set up their own small vineyards, often organic and biodynamic. There are new regional stars: intense reds from Pic St-Loup and La Clape, where many *vignerons* are experimenting with ageing wines in terracotta

GET THERE
Toulouse is the nearest major airport. The train from Paris to Narbonne takes 4hr. Car hire is available.

jars, as in Roman times; the bubbly Blanquette de Limoux; and crisp white Picpoul de Pinet, perfect with local oysters. And one patch, the Corbières, wedged between Montpellier and Perpignan, remains under the radar, waiting to be discovered.

The sheer variety of the landscapes here is spectacular, with vineyards pressing up against the Mediterranean along the flamingo-filled lagoons of Peyriac-de-Mer, through dramatic limestone hills and valleys where visitors can stay in *chambres d'hôtes* in isolated medieval hamlets, right up to the wild mountain castles built by the Cathar tribes during the 12th century in the foothills of the Pyrenees. Locating a restaurant in this rugged corner is not always easy, but when you do, you'll find the Grenache, Syrah and Carignan reds from Corbières are sturdy, spicy and robust, and perfect with the region's hearty cuisine.

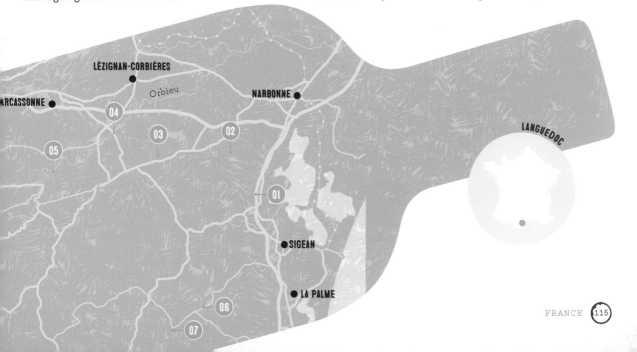

LÉZIGNAN-CORBIÈRES
Orbieu
NARBONNE
CARCASSONNE
LANGUEDOC
04
03
02
05
01
SIGEAN
LA PALME
06
07

01 CHÂTEAU FABRE-CORDON

Amandine Fabre-Cordon is typical of the numerous passionate young women earning respect as independent *vigneronnes* in the Corbières today. She took over her father's estate in 2011, after learning her craft in New Zealand and California. The terroir here is known as Corbières Méditerannée, as the sea is just 3km (1.9 miles) away at the picturesque fishing village of Peyriac. She makes an especially strong selection of white and rosé organic wines – Grenache Blanc, Viognier and Vermentino. Other dynamic female winemakers to check out nearby are Cécile Bonnafous (domaine-esperou.fr) and Fanny Tisseyre (domainegraindefanny.com).

chateaufabrecordon.fr; tel +33 6 87 84 15 46; L'Oustal Nau, Peyriac-de-Mer; Mon-Sat by appointment

02 ABBAYE DE FONTFROIDE

This magnificent medieval abbey is the perfect place to get a feel for the history and winemaking heritage of the Corbières. Fontfroide was founded in 1093 by monks, who immediately planted vines to provide wine for religious services. At its peak, these Cistercians controlled thousands of hectares. Abandoned at the end of the 19th century, the abbey was bought by the Fayet family in 1908, and although 40% of production goes to the local cooperative, they are producing some fine wines in their nearby modern cellar, especially a dry Muscat and Spiritualis, a velvety blend of Syrah and Mourvè. The tour round the abbey (entry fee applies) and its wonderful gardens followed by a tasting is simply unforgettable.

fontfroide.com; tel +33 4 68 45 50 72; Rte Départemantale 613, Narbonne; daily ✕

03 CHÂTEAU LES OLLIEUX ROMANIS

As its name implies, this vast estate in the heart of the Boutenac Cru (a tiny but high-quality appellation within Corbières) has roots going back to Roman times, and today with 150 hectares (370 acres) of vines the château is one of the

Laurent and Sylvie Bachevillier are typical of the new generation of young *vignerons* choosing the Corbières as the ideal place to set up a winery

largest private domaines. But there is a very warm, human welcome provided by the enthusiastic team of *vignerons* that surround the owner, Pierre Bories. This is a still old-fashioned farm, with donkeys wandering about, sheep and goats grazing and chickens ranging around freely. Pierre's parents made the crucial decision not to pull up and plant new vines in the 1980s, meaning he inherited a tremendous selection of vines, some 120 years old, growing in a mix of red clay and sandstone. You can tour the estate on foot via a series of walking trails, or visit the tasting room to sample the wines; Bories has also opened a restaurant, La Touketa, overlooking the vines.

ollieuxromanis.com; tel +33 4 68 43 35 20; Rte Départementale 613, Montséret; daily 🍴

04 DOMAINE LEDOGAR

The Ledogar family have been making wine in Ferrals for many generations, closely associated with the local winemaking cooperative until the arrival of uncompromising brothers Xavier, Mathieu and Benoit. They are what could be termed 'natural wine fundamentalists', and since 1997 have created a sprawling 22-hectare (54-acre) vineyard, producing wines that are 100% organic, working the vines around a lunar calendar, with no sulphur and with a hand-picked harvest. More than a dozen different grape varieties are cultivated – not just classic Carignan and Grenache but Mourvèdre, Maccabeu and Merselan too. There is a small tasting room in the centre of Ferrals, where discussions can get passionate.

Tel +33 6 81 06 14 51; place de la République, Ferrals-les-Corbières; daily by appointment

05 A glass at Château
Les Ollieux Romanis

06 Château de
Peyrepertuse

saintecroixvins.com; tel +33 6 85 67 63 88; 7 Ave des Corbières, Fraïssé-des-Corbières; daily by appointment

07 CASTELMAURE

This historic winemaking cooperative dominates an isolated hamlet of 150 souls, lost in the wild, windswept Cathar mountains. Intrepid visitors receive a fantastic welcome in the surprisingly modern tasting room and sample some extraordinary wines. You can't escape the culture of the winemaking cooperative in the Corbières, a system that historically has given *vignerons* financial security but has hardly garnered a reputation for quality wines. Not here in Castelmaure, though. Founded in 1921, the cooperative has around 60 participants – all are characters, but none more so than Patrick Marien, who has served as Castelmaure's president for some 30 years. Antoine Robert, one of the newer winemakers, constantly experiments – ageing in the bottle rather than barrels, using the old method of cement vats, keeping dosages of sulphite low and devising strikingly creative labels. Each wine is a surprise, from the uncomplicated La Buvette, 'our *vin de soif*' (easy to drink when you're thirsty), to the barrel-aged N°3 Corbières. *castelmaure.com; tel +33 4 68 45 91 83; 4 Rte des Canelles, Embres-et-Castelmaure; daily*

05 DOMAINE LES CASCADES

Laurent and Sylvie Bachevillier are typical of the new generation of young *vignerons* choosing the Corbières as the ideal place to set up a winery, and have also opened a charming three-room B&B and eco-gîte adjacent to the cellar.

Their domaine revolves around the concept of biodiversity, producing not only organic wine but vegetables, saffron, truffles and olive oil too. Instead of using chemical insecticides, Laurent takes out their two donkeys and three fearsome Hungarian sheep to graze among the vines. The couple's wines will take you by surprise, especially Cuvée S, a natural wine, 100% Grenache with no sulphite added.
domainelescascades.fr; tel +33 6 88 21 84 99; 4bis Ave des Corbières, Ribaute; daily by appointment

06 DOMAINE SAINTE-CROIX

The landscape changes as you climb into the dramatic jagged mountains of Hautes Corbières. There is very little agriculture, villages are few and far between, and ancient vines grow in a patchwork of small parcels on a variety of different soils – limestone, clay, schist, volcanic. It was this diversity that attracted adventurous English winemakers Jon and Elizabeth Bowen to settle here some 15 years ago. In the cellar, Jon works primarily with steel tanks, occasionally using old barrels to age, 'just to give an idea of the wood, nothing more'. These organic wines immediately have a strong identity, especially *mono-cépage* cuvées using ancient indigenous grapes like Aramon, Terret Gris and Grenache Noir. This is very much an anarchic, garage winery, with Jon setting up bottles and glasses on an old wooden barrel as a tasting table.

de la Mairie, Villesèque-
des-Corbières; Wed-Sun

CHEZ BEBELLE
Narbonne's historic
covered market heaves
at lunchtime as crowds
teem around the stall
of ex-rugby star Gilles
Belzons, who theatrically
shouts orders over a
megaphone while grilling
his delicious steaks and
sausages.
*chez-bebelle.fr;
tel +33 6 85 40 09 01;
Halles de Narbonne,
1 Blvd Dr Ferroul,
Narbonne; Tue-Sun*

WHERE TO STAY
CHÂTEAU DE L'HORTE
Run by a winemaker, this
B&B is set in a grandiose
18th-century château
with the four bedrooms
located over the vast
chai (barrel room).
There's a pool along
with a garden terrace
for barbecues; on-site
tastings are available, as
are local tours.
*chateaudelhorte.com;
tel +33 6 42 02 74 69;
Rte d'Escales,
Montbrun-des-
Corbières*

CHÂTEAU DE LASTOURS
Lastours combines
a state-of-the-art
winery, giant outdoor
contemporary
sculptures, a restaurant
and 12 B&B rooms in
discrete cottages.
*chateaudelastours.com;
tel +33 4 68 48 64 74;
Portel-des-Corbières*

WHERE TO EAT
O VIEUX TONNEAUX
Peyriac is famous for
its wetland lagoons
and flamingos, and the
daily menus at this cosy

bistro feature plenty of
locally sourced fish and
seafood. Regular live
music, too.
*bit.ly/VieuxTonneaux;
tel +33 4 68 48 39 54;
3 place de la Mairie,
Peyriac-de-Mer; daily*

PLACE DU MARCHÉ
Rub shoulders with
vignerons in this lively
gourmet bistro where
Eric Delalande serves
the likes of duck grilled
with wild garrigue herbs.
*bit.ly/placemarches; tel
+33 4 68 70 09 13; 8 Ave*

WHAT TO DO
The Corbières mountains
are marked by awesome
clifftop Cathar castles,
dating from the 12th-
century religious wars.
Follow the route of the
châteaux – and don't
miss the precariously
situated Château de
Peyrepertuse.
payscathare.org

CELEBRATIONS
The small town of
Conilhac gets taken over
for a month-long jazz
festival each November.
jazzconilhac.fr

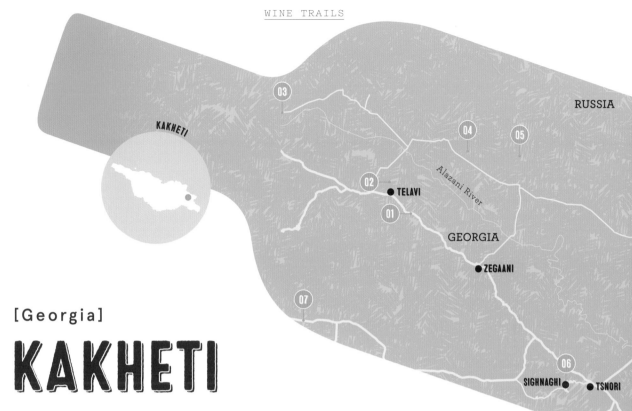

RUSSIA

KAKHETI

03

04

05

Alazani River

02

01 ● TELAVI

GEORGIA

● ZEGAANI

07

06

SIGHNAGHI ● ● TSNORI

[Georgia]

KAKHETI

In this ancient, mountainous land, a youthful spirit and world-class traditional wines reward grape-loving travellers with a taste for the unknown.

Vineyard-hopping in Georgia is a journey to wine's earliest origins. An 8000-year-old clay wine jar unearthed here in 2017 is the oldest-known relic of winemaking. Put another way, by the time the ancient Greeks were stomping their first grapes, the Georgians had been at it for millennia.

Traditional Georgian winemaking has changed surprisingly little since antiquity: grapes are harvested by hand and foot-pressed in *satsnakheli*, hollowed-out tree trunks. The juice flows into underground *kvevri* clay pots, where it ferments and matures with minimal intervention. The following spring, the wine is clear, aromatic and ready for clinking at *supras*, Georgian feasts known for their elaborate toasts. *Kvevri* wines are so laborious that they account for only around 10% of the country's wine production, but a new generation of winemakers hopes to turn that ratio on its head.

The most storied Georgian wine region is Kakheti, two hours' drive east of Tbilisi, where 80% of the country's wine originates. Its best 'whites' are prized for the grippy tannin and amber hue resulting from extended contact between grape juice and skins. But Kakhetian wines are far from homogeneous, thanks to the region's diverse terrain, distinctive grape varieties and innovative winemakers.

The Gombori mountains roughly split Kakheti into Inner and Outer zones. Perched on a Gombori escarpment, Sighnaghi is a popular base, with wineries lining its cobblestoned streets; out in the countryside, there are château-style resorts and countless guesthouses. But Kakheti's most thrilling wines are often found in villagers' backyards, not in sleek tasting rooms. Take time for leisurely meals, impromptu polyphonic singing, chats with winemakers and unsolicited shots of chacha (120-proof grape spirit).

GET THERE
Tbilisi International Airport, 100km (62 miles) from Sighnaghi, services the region. Car hire is available.

① TOGONIDZE'S WINE CELLAR

At first glance, Togonidze's Wine Cellar could be mistaken for an art commune, with its walls adorned with abstract paintings and tables covered in colourful doodles, but down in the cellar, artist-turned-winemaker Gia Togonidze makes some of the region's most rave-worthy *kvevri* wine. A whiff of his Mtsvane will almost knock you off your chair with its forceful nose of overripe apricots and toasted walnuts, while his Saperavi features earthier notes like mushrooms and coffee. It'd be remiss not to stay for dinner – Togonidze's wife, Lika, is a local celebrity for her modern riffs on Georgian dishes like aubergine *pkhali*, a traditional vegetable-walnut spread that she enriches with caramelised onions. *facebook.com/togonidzeswine; tel +995 591 22 95 94; Shalauri, Telavi; daily by appointment* 🛈 ✕

② MARANI RUISPIRI

Ruispiri has quickly achieved cult status in the natural wine world for its commitment to biodynamic winemaking, which goes beyond conventional organic farming to incorporate mystical practices like burying manure-filled cow horns in the vineyard, and planting and harvesting according to the cycles of the moon – and the only 'pesticides' used on the vines are herbal teas and lavender. The winery has an enjoyably eco, Burning Man-esque vibe with rainbow-painted sheds, abandoned wooden pallets and a graffitied jalopy parked out front. The wines, however, are elegant and precise, a testament, perhaps, to winemaker Georges Aladashvili's Swiss training. Sample the red Rkatsiteli, a virtually unheard-of varietal redolent of caramel-dipped apples. Farm-to-table meals overlooking the vines can be arranged by advance booking. *ruispiris-marani.com; tel +995 557 51 11 55; 12 Napareuli, Ruispiri, Telavi; daily by appointment* 🛈 ✕

③ LAGAZI WINE CELLAR

Shota Lagazidze is one of Georgia's most promising young winemakers, a bearded back-to-the-lander who left a career in tourism to pursue

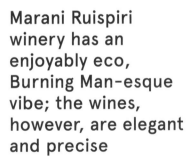

Marani Ruispiri winery has an enjoyably eco, Burning Man-esque vibe; the wines, however, are elegant and precise

ancestral winemaking. Lucky us – his musky Rkatsiteli (amber) and rose-scented Saperavi (red) are so enchanting you'll want to snap up as many as you can; with his annual production clocking in at around 2000 bottles, you just might clear him out. In addition to tastings, Shota and his family can whip up

a feast of soup dumplings, cheese bread, stews and salads from their native Tusheti, the remote mountainous corner of Kakheti known for its snowbound villages and prehistoric, pagan-influenced culture. Shota, a proud Tush, will happily regale you with fascinating stories from his homeland between toasts. *facebook.com/LagaziWineCellar; tel +995 551 94 02 17; Zemo Alvani, Akhmetis Raoni; daily by appointment* 💲 ✗

04 ARTANULI GVINO

This 'estate', best known for its lusty Saperavi, is something of a boho hang-out for agriculturalist epicureans. It's tempting to linger here all day, sipping wine

under the trees and geeking out with seasoned winemaker Kakha Berishvili to the soundtrack of the rushing Didkhevi River. Berishvili's daughter, Keti, is now making wine of her own under the Gogo Wine label; her Corazón Partido, a Rkatsiteli mono-varietal fermented on its skins for two months, has a punchy maraschino cherry finish. *facebook.com/artanuligvino; tel +995 599 18 11 01; Artana Village, Telavi; daily by appointment recommended* 💲 ✗

05 CHUBINI WINE CELLAR

It's worth visiting this buzzy winery for its Eden-like setting alone, hemmed in by the Greater Caucasus mountains on one side and the Gombori range on the

other. You can take in both from a picnic table in the front yard, where husband-and-wife team Tornike and Likuna pour generous tastes of *kvevri*-aged Rkatsiteli and Saperavi. The former gets its floral headiness from the addition of Chinuri, a grape from the Kartli region seldom seen in these parts. Call ahead to book a full-on Georgian *supra* lovingly prepared by the young couple. *facebook.com/chubiniwine; tel +995 591 03 02 94; Shilda, Kvareli; tastings daily, meals by reservation* 💲✖

06 OKRO'S WINES

John Okruashvili heads up this winery, which was instrumental in reviving *kvevri* winemaking in the early 2000s. Okruashvili's multilayered Rkatsiteli has turned many wine critics' heads over the years, but the current vintages of Kisi (a little-known, gorgeously honeyed grape) and Saperavi (the region's inky standby red) are equally standout. All of Okruashvili's wines are sulphur dioxide- and additive-free and fermented in *kvevri*, and they're available at several price points. Of course, they taste best when sampled over a meal at the winery's top-floor restaurant, where the balcony looks out over the terracotta rooftops of Sighnaghi towards Azerbaijan. *bit.ly/Okros; tel +995 599 54 20 14; 7 Chavchavadze Str, Sighnaghi; daily 25*

07 JUSO'S WINERY

If your schedule is too tight for an overnight in Kakheti, you can still get a taste of Georgian wine country at Juso's, situated an hour outside Tbilisi in the Soviet time-warpy town of Sagarejo. Juso's small team presides over a fledgling 17-*kvevri* cellar where award-winning Rkatsiteli and Saperavi ferment underground with no additives or industrial yeasts, as well as their trademark Kostaphé. Sidekicks to the wine usually include pickled *jonjoli* (bladdernut blossoms) and *guda*, a crumbly ewe's-milk cheese aged in sheepskin. With a few hours' notice, winemaker Lasha Khvedelidze can also throw together a traditional Kakhetian barbecue starring *mtsvadi*, kebabs stacked with hunks of local pork and singed to crackly perfection over grapevine embers. *facebook.com/jusoswinery; tel +995 595 55 88 57; 24 Gulisashvili Str, Sagarejo; daily by appointment* 💲✖

WHERE TO STAY
GUESTHOUSING
Hotels abound in Kakheti, but staying with a local family ('guesthousing') can be the best way to go. Georgian comfort food, personal recommendations and affordable driver services are frequent perks; so is homemade wine. Search for Kakheti on booking.com for a rundown of what's available, or ask at any local winery.

TWINS WINE CELLAR
Eight standard and four upgraded rooms occupy the top floor of Twins Wine Cellar, distinguished by its sky-high *kvevri*, perhaps the largest in the world. Wake up to crowing roosters and sweeping vineyard views backed by the Caucasus mountains.
cellar.ge; tel +995 599 33 38 84; Napareuli

RADISSON COLLECTION HOTEL TSINANDALI ESTATE
Kakheti finally has a world-class luxury hotel in the Tsinandali Estate, in the heart of Georgia's

wine country. Pamper yourself with high-thread-count linens and rooftop sunbathing (and cocktailing) by the pool.
radissonhotels.com; tel +995 350 27 77 00; Tsinandali

WHERE TO EAT
PHEASANT'S TEARS
Chef Gia Rokashvili's creative winery kitchen hinges on foraged vegetables, fresh herbs and local meats. Wine pairings are a must. In summer, the private outdoor patio, equally suited to intimate diners and large groups, provides spectacular views and, often, spontaneous and joyful live music.

pheasantstears.com; tel +995 355 23 15 56; Baratashvili Str, Sighnaghi; daily

KAKHETIAN HOUSE VAKIRELEBI
Zakro and Eka Demetrashvili, owners of this little paradise just outside Sighnaghi, greet all guests with the same phrase: 'Make yourself at home.' After sipping a *piala* (clay bowl) of Zakro's homemade wine, let Eka show you how to make *churchkhela*, a walnut-grape-juice confection. Then enjoy a Kakhetian feast.
facebook.com/ vakirelebi; tel +995 555 77 78 55; Vakiri, Sighnaghi; daily

WHAT TO DO
MONASTERY OF ST NINO AT BODBE
Close to Sighnaghi, this is one of Georgia's most sacred churches. It was built in the 9th century CE and houses an active convent and the tomb and relics of St Nino, who brought Christianity to Georgia wielding a cross of grapevines bound with her own hair.

INTER GEORGIA TRAVEL
Wine-lovers seeking local experiences should link up with Kartlos Chabashvili, Tbilisi-based guide and owner of Inter Georgia Travel. A native Kakhetian, he knows everyone who's anyone here and is a terrific translator to boot.
intergeorgia.travel

CELEBRATIONS
Each May, Georgian winemakers flaunt their best bottles at Tbilisi's New Wine Festival, while the mid-May Zero Compromise Natural Wine Fair features only natural wine and draws an eclectic crowd of in-the-know oenophiles. *nwa.ge*

[Germany]

MOSEL

Vertigo-inducing vineyards, meandering river bends, unparalleled variations on the theme of Riesling and even Pinot Noir: thrill-seekers will feel right at home in the Mosel.

Few wine regions are as dramatic as the Mosel. Named after the river that takes 237km (147 miles) of looping bends to cover the linear 96km (60-mile) distance from Trier to Koblenz, it is Germany's Riesling canyon. It's a region of superlatives encompassing the steepest vineyards, the narrowest valleys, the most breathtaking Rieslings and a string of diverse villages that, to the initiated, read like a wine list: Leiwen, Piesport, Braunberg, Bernkastel, Graach, Wehlen, Traben-Trarbach and Enkirch. But that is just the Mosel – two of its tributaries, Saar and Ruwer, are also subsumed under this region's name.

The three river valleys are quite distinct, and wine fans can compare tasting notes from the fruit-driven Rieslings of the Mosel with the more austere but equally thrilling wines from Ruwer and Saar. The landscapes differ, too: the Saar is wilder and more spacious; the Ruwer tiny and impressive; and the Mosel valley is the most storied. Driving along the river is a must: the road runs right along the bank past countless world-famous vineyards, their names proclaimed in white lettering from afar. Locals have a hard time of it, stuck behind the awestruck tourists creeping slowly along the winding roads, craning their necks to marvel at the steepness of the terrain. But this is an indispensable part of the trip, as the unfolding vistas explain why the spectrum of wine styles is so wide: steepness, altitude, aspect, relative distance from the river all have a bearing on the finished wine, which comes in endless permutations here. Add viticultural differences like planting density and harvest points to this, as well as individual winemaking decisions, and the mind starts to boggle. Tasting your way through the resulting abundance of styles is one of the great pleasures of a visit.

GET THERE
Frankfurt-Hahn is the closest German airport, but Luxembourg Airport is also about a 1hr drive from the region.

01 WEINGUT HEYMANN-LÖWENSTEIN

This tasting room here allows for a real flavour experience of the Lower Mosel, the last stretch of the river before it runs into the Rhine at Koblenz. Owners Cornelia and Reinhard Löwenstein were pioneers of authentic Mosel styles when they started out in the 1980s. Today, under the helm of their daughter Sarah, all the Rieslings produced here are fermented with wild yeast in old oak *Fuder* barrels. The differences in slate between their chief sites, the Röttgen and three Uhlen parcels, are beautifully clear. Their winery, a distinctive cube-shaped edifice, is emblazoned with fetching metal lettering that quotes the German translation of Pablo Neruda's poem *Ode to Wine*. *hl.wine; tel +49 2606 1919, Bahnhofstr 10, Winningen; Fri–Sat & by appointment* 💲

02 WEINGUT MELSHEIMER

This estate has been in the same family for five generations, run organically since 1995 and awarded biodynamic certification in 2013. But that alone would not make it outstanding. What makes it special is winemaker Torsten Melsheimer's unconventional approach: try the Vade Retro Riesling made without added sulphur, the bone-dry Sekt and the vivid, delicious Pet Nat. This is the Mosel, but not as you know it. *melsheimer-riesling.de; tel +49 6542 2422; Dorfstr 21, Reil; by appointment* 💲

03 IMMICH-BATTERIEBERG

The wine labels at Immich-Batterieberg show little angels firing a cannon with a Riesling-bottle-shaped barrel – a reference to the creation of the vineyards in the 19th century by blasting away the rocks with dynamite. Try the impressively pure Rieslings of sinuous elegance, handcrafted organically by Gernot Kollmann. If you're lucky, you will find the companionable Gernot himself in the tasting room. If so, you are in for a wonderful chat. *batterieberg.com; tel +49 6541 815 907; Im Alten Tal 2, Enkirch; by appointment*

04 WEINGUT SELBACH-OSTER

On most days, you can drop into this light-filled *Vinothek* (wine store)

In the same family for five generations, Torsten Melsheimer's estate is special due to his unconventional approach. This is the Mosel, but not as you know it

without an appointment. Do not let the contemporary architecture deceive you; this estate is famed for its nuanced interpretations of classic Kabinett, that most light-footed of Riesling styles. There is a charge for tasting, but it's worth it for the expert explanations you'll receive from your host. Try comparing the separately vinified parcels of old and age-old vines from the same vineyard – an educational treat. *selbach-oster.de; +49 6532 2081; Uferallee 23, Zeltingen; Mon-Sat, Sun by appointment* 🕓

05 MARKUS MOLITOR

Taste world-class Riesling and fine Mosel-grown Pinot Noir in the *Vinothek* (wine store) of this 19th-century winery. The setting is beautiful, and the wines exquisite, still made by Markus Molitor himself, now one of the largest yet most exacting producers in the Mosel. *markusmolitor.com; tel +49 6532 9540 059; Haus Klosterberg, Bernkastel-Wehlen; by appointment*

06 WEINGUT NIK WEIS SANKT URBANS-HOF

One of the Mosel's top estates, where you can taste Rieslings from both the Mosel and Saar valleys, comparing the wines side by side. All are brilliantly executed, textbook examples for the region, and cover the full spectrum from dry to sweet. Thanks to this estate, which also runs a wine nursery and propagates cuttings from ancient Riesling vines across the region, much of the

05 Nik Weis of
Weingut Nik Weis
Sankt Urbans-Hof

06 Exploring the
Mosel by bike

07 Leiwen

08 Cochem Castle,
overlooking the Mosel

Mosel's original genetic diversity has been preserved.
nikweis.com; tel +49 6507 93770; Urbanusstr 16, Leiwen; Mon-Sat, Sun by appointment 💲

07 VAN VOLXEM

This estate, revived in 1999 by Roman Niewodniczanski, has only one aim: to roduce historically faithful, dry Saar Riesling as it was made in its Belle Époque heyday. This has been achieved with thrilling results. Everything from affordable entry-level varieties to age-worthy, single-site wines comes highly recommended. Its modern winery is bedded into the Saar landscape; visit the *Vinothek* or book a tasting.
vanvolxem.com; tel +49 6501 802 2915; Zum Schlossberg 347, Wiltingen; Tue-Sun 💲

08 WEINGUT PETER LAUER

There are two good reasons to visit this winery: Sekt lovers will find long-aged, late-disgorged Riesling Sekts of exquisite quality, while lovers of traditional Prädikat styles (Kabinett, Spätlese, Auslese) will find exacting, show-stopping wines. Florian Lauer, the estate's fifth-generation winemaker, has a clear philosophy and his wines enjoy (deserved) cult status in New York wine bars. There's also a hotel and winery restaurant.
lauer-ayl.de; tel +49 6581 3031; Trierer Str 49, Ayl; by appointment Mon-Fri 🍴

ESSENTIAL
INFORMATION

WHERE TO STAY
JUGENDSTILHOTEL BELLEVUE
A real relic from a bygone age, this hotel offers 35 rooms lovingly restored in the Jugendstil (art nouveau) style. Period detail is combined with modern comfort. *bellevue-hotel.de; tel +49 6541 7030; An der Mosel 11, Traben-Trarbach*

SCHLOSS LIESER
After years or painstaking restoration, this sumptuous Mosel palace opened its doors to visitors in 2019. Find true splendour in a truly fabulous setting. *marriott.com; tel +49 6531 986 990; Moselstr 33, Lieser*

GÄSTEHAUS CANTZHEIM
On a quiet side-arm of the Saar, at the foot of the Kanzemer Altenberg vineyard, this contemporary guesthouse in a baroque building has been finished to the highest standards. The hosts also make wine and hold various events.

gaestehaus-cantzheim. de; tel +49 6501 607 6635; Weinstr 4, Kanzem an der Saar

WHERE TO EAT
ZELTINGER HOF
Seasonal, regional food and a great wine menu are at the heart of this operation. If you go in spring, you might see the landlord peeling basketfuls of white asparagus in a sunny spot on the street. There are rooms, too. *zeltinger-hof.de; tel +49 6532 93820; Kurfürstenstr 76, Zeltingen-Rachtig; daily*

DIE GRAIFEN: WEINE, LEBEN, ESSEN
Inside and out, the restaurant at Die Graifen exudes ambience and hospitality. Seasonal menus cater for both casual diners, with its tapas-style plates, and dinner guests looking for more substantial dishes. *graifen.de; tel +49 6541 811 075; Wolfer Weg 11, Traben-Trarbach; Mon-Sat*

RÜSSEL'S LANDHAUS
Situated in the hills above the Mosel, this establishment offers a choice between fine dining in the main building (Landhaus) or rustic, local specialities in the Hasenpfeffer restaurant. *ruessels-landhaus.de; tel +49 6509 91400; Büdlicherbrück 1, Naurath/Wald; Fri-Mon*

WHAT TO DO
Strike out on foot or take to the water to get a real feel for the local landscape. The Moselsteig is a long-distance hiking trail that runs the entire length of the river in 24 stages. The tourist office also offers guides to various well-posted hiking and cycling tracks. Hiring canoes or signing up for a guided canoe tour are also fun ways to see the sights from the water. *moselsteig.de; mosel-kanutours.de*

CELEBRATIONS
Don't miss two well-organised wine events: Mythos Mosel in mid- to late May and Saar Riesling Summer in late August. Both mobilise the entire region over a weekend of tastings and parties. Tickets include free travel on shuttle buses, which serve the tasting stops at various estates. Sample top wines, find new favourites and make friends with an international, Riesling-loving crowd. *mythos-mosel.de; saar-riesling-sommer.de*

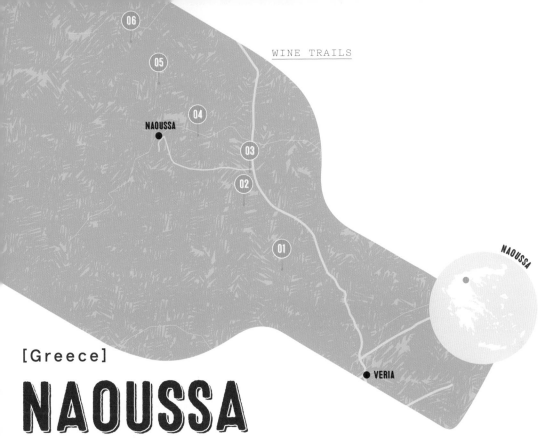

[Greece]

NAOUSSA

Verdant and wild, Naoussa's cool hills attract as many outdoor enthusiasts as they do wine-lovers, who come for a taste of Greece's best red wines.

Drive only an hour west of Thessaloniki and you'll find yourself cosseted in the forested hills of the Vermio Mountains. The streams and waterfalls that course down the deep-green slopes once made the region a powerhouse in the silk trade, with Naoussa at its centre; today, they feed the vines responsible for the country's most exalted red wines.

Those wines are made from just one grape, Xinomavro (pronounced kse-no-mav-ro). The name means 'sour-black', though it's not actually sour nor particularly deeply coloured. In fact, its wines are most typically aromatic and perfumed, with plummy fruit filigreed with notes of thyme, saffron, liquorice and sun-dried tomato. Xinomavro is often compared to Nebbiolo for its powerful tannins, acidity and ability to age for decades; the variety also earns comparisons to Pinot Noir for its delicate, detailed flavours.

It also shares a reluctance to travel, a magic synergy with place: as Nebbiolo is to Piedmont, and Pinot Noir is to Burgundy, so Xinomavro is to Naoussa. In fact, in 1971 Naoussa was the first modern winegrowing area in Greece to be recognised for top-quality wine, thus setting a standard for subsequent regulations across the country. If you want to taste great Xinomavro, it's worth the trip to enjoy it in situ.

The best way to approach Naoussa is from Thessaloniki. Driving west across the plain of Imathia, the Vermio Mountains form a high, green crescent against the sky. Follow narrow, twisty mountain roads up to Naoussa's city park and gaze out over the plains to the east and south. You can see why Naoussa became a crossroads of culture and identity, and take in the wild beauty of a lush winegrowing landscape that's one of Greece's national treasures.

GET THERE
Thessaloniki airport is 93km (58 miles) from Naoussa. Trains run five times a day and take just over 1hr; double that for the bus trip.

01 THYMIOPOULOS VINEYARDS

Apostolos Thymiopoulos is one of the most talked-about winemakers in the Naoussa region. In 2004, he began to help his father bottle wines from vineyards his family had cultivated for generations. Now at the helm of the estate, he works in the vineyards and winery with as little intervention as possible. His wines speak of the vineyards' purity as well as the warmth and rich soils of Trifolos, in the lower altitudes southeast of town. Bottlings range from the fresh, fruit-forward Young Vines Xinomavro to the full-throttle Earth & Sky, intended for long ageing. He also makes one of the best pink wines in Greece, the earthy, savoury Rosé de Xinomavro.

thymiopoulosvineyards.gr; tel +30 23310 93604; Trilofos, Imathia; by appointment 💲

02 BOUTARI WINERY

For decades, Naoussa wine was synonymous with Boutari, the first winery to bottle a Xinomavro commercially (in 1879). By buying grapes from farmers all over the countryside, the family was instrumental in keeping the grape-growing tradition alive in a region that's had its share of political unrest. The family-run company has grown to include wineries all over Greece, but its heart remains in Naoussa. The winery itself is a local landmark: it has one of the largest cellars for ageing wines, with a collection of bottles going back decades. Visits include a multimedia display that tells the story of the region and its wine, a tour of the facilities and tastings of the wines paired with local food. Boutari's Naoussa Grande Reserve remains its flagship wine; also look for the 1879, which is harvested from a single outstanding vineyard in Trifolos.

boutari.gr; tel +30 23320 41666; Stenimachos, Naoussa; by appointment 💲🍴

03 TSANTALI

Another storied Greek estate, with roots running back to 1890, Tsantali bears a relation to Boutari, with multiple holdings throughout the country, a huge array of wines and a stake in the continued vitality of

01 Tasting at
Dalamára winery

02 Greek salad

03 Dalamára vineyards

04 Winemaker Kostis
Dalamára

05 Keeping vine leaves
for future use at Argatia

06 The town of
Naoussa

the Xinomavro varietal in Naoussa. Tsantali not only owns vineyards here, but also has contracts with a host of local growers, helping to keep its traditional methods alive and viable. There are only two Xinomavro bottlings here, Naoussa and Naoussa Reserve, yet their delicate, floral character deserve a visit and tasting.

Visiting Tsantali, it can feel like you're on a rooftop of the ancient world. At your feet, dark gnarled vines rise up to frame a dozen shades of blue. Beneath you, a ring of old hilltops roll toward the distance in a series of waves before merging with the sky.
tsantali.com; tel +30 23320 41461; 59200 Naoussa (railway station); by appointment

❹ DALAMÁRA WINERY

Located on the eastern foothills of Mt Vermio, just outside the town of Naoussa, this historic, organic estate is currently run by Kostis Dalamára, the sixth generation of the family to grow vines here. Although Kostis studied in Burgundy and has made wine in California, France and Spain, he returned home on the strength of his conviction that Xinomavro is an outstanding grape. He tends his vines as his father did, without chemicals or fertilisers; the oldest date back 100 years. Take time to walk through the vineyards, listening to the chickens cluck in the family's kitchen garden; afterwards, take a quick tour of the winery before adjourning to the cosy, stone-

walled space that serves as its tasting room. The star wine here is the oak-aged Paliokalias Naoussa Xinomavro, which balances its rich body with delicate spice scents. Beyond this, of special interest are the 'cellar offerings', or 'confidential cuvées': experimental bottlings of blends, clones and single vineyards offered only at the winery.
bit.ly/Dalamara; tel +30 23320 28321; Epar. Od. Naoussa-Kato Vermiou 31, Naoussa; by appointment

❺ KIR-YIANNI

Kir-Yianni means 'Sir John'; in Greek, the greeting connotes a special warmth and cordiality. The 'John' here is Yiannis Boutari, of

the famous Boutari winemaking family, who split off from the family business in 1996, taking some vineyards with which to build his own brand. Based in Yianakohori, at one of the highest altitudes in Naoussa, the estate has since become one of the region's most famous, recognisable by the picturesque 200-year-old stone lookout tower in the midst of the vines. In part, the estate's fame has to do with Yiannis himself, who's deeply involved in politics and conservation (he runs a wildlife reserve in nearby Nymphaio, and has served several terms as the mayor of Thessaloniki). But the winery is also an extension of his sense of responsibility to the region: here, working with his sons Stelios and Mihalis, he's created one of Naoussa's most forward-looking estates, the vineyards dedicated

to researching the area's full potential with wine. Kir-Yianni offers a dizzying number of bottlings, including Xinomavro in sparkling, rosé and red versions, as well as in blends with Merlot and Syrah. The tasting-room experience here can be lengthy, yet is terrifically enjoyable and intimate. And don't miss the sublime views: at 300m (1000ft) in altitude, you can see clear across the treetops to the town of Naoussa.
kiryianni.gr; tel +30 23320 51100; Yianakohori, Naoussa; by appointment Tue-Sun 💲

06 ARGATIA

Few people know the vineyards of Naoussa as intimately as Haroula Spinthiropoulou and her husband, Panagiotis Georgiadis. Haroula is one of the most respected agronomists in Greece, a sought-after consultant

who has worked with many of the region's top producers; Panagiotis was the director of The Wine Roads of Northern Greece, an organisation dedicated to promoting wine tourism in Naoussa. Together with their son, Christofer, they run this small winery out of the bottom of their house in Rodochori, a high, forested area on the northwest edge of the appellation. A visit with them is like getting a masterclass in Naoussa's wines, only with warm, open friends as teachers rather than stuffy professionals. Xinomavro predominates, which Haroula makes in a delicate, layered style. She also grows a range of lesser-known grapes, such as Negoska and Mavrodaphne, which she works into fascinating blends.
argatia.gr; tel +30 69762 69759; Rodochori, Imathia; by appointment Tue-Sun

WHERE TO STAY
PALEA POLI
In the heart of Naoussa's Old City, this stone mansion houses a collection of luxe rooms and suites, all surprisingly affordable given the elegant decor and exceptionally good breakfast. The hotel also hosts a great restaurant with an extensive array of local bottles.
paleapoli.gr; tel +30 23320 52520; Vassileos Konstantinou 32, Naoussa

SFENDAMOS WOOD VILLAGE
Sfendamos rents out six rustic-chic chalets in the Vermio Mountains, fitted out with fireplaces and balconies; the main chalet functions as a gathering place where guests can dine on traditional dishes. There's plenty of Xinomavro on the wine list, too.
sfendamos.gr; tel +30 23320 44844; Pigadia, Naoussa

WHERE TO EAT
OINOMAGEIREMATA
The name says it all,

translating roughly as 'wine and cooking place'. Just off the town's main square, this cosy space excels at the region's traditional cuisine, including fish that owner Dimitris Tavoularis catches himself. His wine list is one of the town's best, reasonably priced and deep in vintages.
Tel +30 23320 23576; 1 Dragoumi Stefanou, Naoussa; Tue-Sun

12 GRADA
A short drive south of Naoussa, 12 Grada stands as one of the region's finest watering holes. The food ranges from simple to fancy, but it's always great, drawing in a steady stream of locals – including winemakers.
facebook.com/12grada; tel +30 23311 00112; Sofou 11, Veroia; Tue-Sun

WHAT TO DO
POLYCENTRIC MUSEUM OF AIGAI
It's well worth the detour to Vergina to check out the archaeological ruins of Aigai, the first capital of the Kingdom of Macedonia. Now a Unesco World Heritage Site, the ruins, including a lavish palace and extensive necropolis of ancient royals, give a fascinating window into the prestige and power that the area once enjoyed.
aigai.gr

RIVER ARAPITSA
A short drive from Naoussa, take a walk along the storied Arapitsa, the ancient natural border between the plains of Imathia and the Vermio Mountains. In summer, green forests and waterfalls provide a backdrop for meditation on historical forces that have shaped this region.

3-5 PIGADIA
Naoussa offers some of the best skiing in Greece. The slopes of 3-5 Pigadia range from beginner level to steep black diamonds and off-piste areas. During the summer, you can explore the area by mountain bike.
bit.ly/35Pigadia

CELEBRATIONS
Carnival is Naoussa's largest celebration: 12 days of springtime festivities capped off with a costume parade, and abundant chances to enjoy Xinomavro. The city also stages 'Wine and Culture' events during the September to November harvest.
visitnaoussa.gr

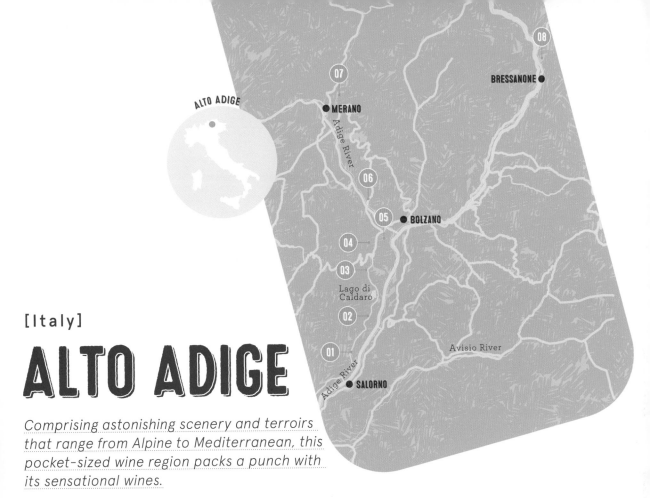

[Italy]
ALTO ADIGE

Comprising astonishing scenery and terroirs that range from Alpine to Mediterranean, this pocket-sized wine region packs a punch with its sensational wines.

The Italian Tyrol state of Alto Adige stretches up as far as the Alpine frontier with Austria, holding a unique semi-autonomous status. Village names are expressed in both Italian and German – from Bolzano (Bozen) in the south up to Bressanone (Brixen) in the north. Even though the region begins roughly just an hour up the *autostrada* from Verona, locals here will greet you with a cheery *Grüss Gott* instead of *ciao*, and rather than pasta and tiramisu, the favourite dishes are *canederli* (bread dumplings) and apple strudel.

The native Rhaetian tribes of Alto Adige were making wine and storing it in barrels long before the Romans arrived but, until recently, cooperative cantinas opted for low-quality, bulk production. Not today, though. You will find some of Italy's finest whites here: Pinot Bianco, Pinot Grigio, Chardonnay, Sauvignon and Gewürztraminer. Two indigenous reds

deserve to be better known: the light, drinkable Vernatsch and intense Lagrein, and some cuvées of Pinot Nero Riserva can rival even those of Burgundy.

The scenery on Alto Adige's historic wine trail (Strada del Vino; suedtiroler-weinstrasse.it) is outrageously beautiful. It passes through the base of steep glacial valleys planted with thousands of fruit trees, while both sides are covered by a geometric maze of crisscrossing vineyards. This is one of the oldest wine trails in Italy, started back in 1964, and it comprehensively covers the whole of the region. No matter how lost wine enthusiasts may get, there is always the distinctive sign of the Strada del Vino to point them in the right direction. Throughout the year, the association organises walking, biking and horse-riding trips through the vineyards, as well as gastronomic celebrations in winemaking villages.

GET THERE
Venice Marco Polo is the nearest major airport, 250km (155 miles) from Magrè. Car hire is available.

01 Alpine scenery in Alto Adige

02 Cantina Tramin

03 Vegetarian cuisine at Alois Lageder's Paradeis restaurant

04 Tasting at Alois Lageder winery

01 ALOIS LAGEDER

Driving into Alto Adige from the neighbouring Trentino region, the first obligatory stop-off is the cantina of Alois Lageder, a pioneer winemaker. Way back in 1995 Alois created a revolutionary cantina, powered by solar energy; today, the family's own 55 hectares (135 acres) are both organic and biodynamic, while over 50% of the 80 smallholders they buy grapes from have converted too. Tastings are held at Paradeis, a rambling 15th-century manor, with the Paradeis restaurant serving mainly vegetarian organic cuisine. Deciding what to select from the extensive list of 35 different wines is quite a task, but be sure to ask for the Löwengang, an impeccable Chardonnay; and Lagrein Lindenburg, a fruity red made from a native grape.
aloislageder.eu; tel +39 0471 809 580; Via Casòn Hirschprunn 1, Magrè; Mon-Sat 💲🍴

02 CANTINA TRAMIN

The sign at the entrance to the enchanting village of Tramin proudly states that this is 'home' of the world's Gewürztraminers, the aromatic grape that has been grown here for a thousand years and is now found all over the globe. At the outskirts of town right on the Strada del Vino, you can't miss the dramatic avant-garde winery of the *cantina sociale* (cooperative association), resembling a maze-like green cube with a panoramic glass tasting room. The cantina sold most of its wine *sfuso* (in bulk) until Willi Sturtz was appointed winemaker in 1992. He began to raise the quality in the vineyards and cut yields. The cantina now produces some 1.8 million bottles of high-quality wines annually. While both the Pinot Grigio and Müller-Thurgau are surprising, the special Gewürztraminer Nussbaumer Cru is simply exceptional.
cantinatramin.it; tel +39 0471 096 633; Strada del Vino 144, Tramin; by appointment Mon-Sat 💲

03 KLOSTERHOF

Guests arriving at the *weingut* (estate) winery of Oskar Andergassen can be sure of a

(04)

warm welcome from this jolly *vignaiolo* (winegrower) and his family. He is one of the new generation of small producers who have stopped selling grapes, choosing instead to make his own vintages from a perfectly positioned 4-hectare (10 acre) vineyard situated high above Lake Caldaro. Oskar concentrates on Pinot Bianco, Vernatsch and Pinot Nero, all very distinctive. The Pinot Bianco is aged in acacia-wood barrels, while the Vernatsch comes from ancient vines cultivated in the traditional pergola system.

Klosterhof is not just a cantina but a comfortable Tyrolean hotel too, with a vineyard pool and a cosy *weinstube* (wine bar), the perfect place to try plates of home-cured speck and delicious mountain cheeses.
klosterhof.it; tel +39 0471 961 046; Prey-Klavenz 40, Caldaro; by appointment Tue, Fri & Sat 💲✖

04 CANTINA COLTERENZIO

Wherever you are in Alto Adige, it's impossible to miss the distinctive black tower that marks the wines of the Colterenzio's *cantina sociale*. At any time of day there's a steady stream of wine enthusiasts filling the tasting room of this contemporary winery, which has a range that stretches from affordable, sharp Chardonnay and Pinot Grigio through to vintages such as Cornelius, a tremendous Merlot-Cabernet blend honoured by the

coveted Tre Bicchieri, Italy's top wine award. The *cooperativa* was founded in 1960 by just 28 small vintners; today there are 300 *soci* (members).
colterenzio.it; tel +39 0471 664 246; Strada del Vino 8, Cornaiano; Mon-Sat 💲

05 STROBLHOF

The date 1664 is carved into the entrance of Stroblhof, and *vignaiolo* Andreas Nicolussi-Leck explains, 'Wine has always been produced at our *maso*, to go with the meat produce of the farm. A plate of speck is not complete without a glass of Vernatsch – this is what everyday life is all about here.' Today, guests staying at Stroblhof have a much more luxurious time, pampered with a wellness spa and freshwater lake pool; there's also an upscale restaurant and a garden terrace serving breakfast and light lunch.

The soil here is a mixture of volcanic and chalk, which produces a sharply acidic, mineral Pinot Bianco – which Andreas ages in large barrels – as well as a tannic Pinot Nero that stays 18 months in small *barriques*.
stroblhof.it; tel +39 0471 662 250; Via Pigano 25, Appiano; by appointment daily 💲✖

06 CANTINA TERLANO

Terlano is the story of a far-sighted winemaker, Sebastian Stocker, who transformed this relatively small, conservative *cooperativa* into quite possibly the leading cantina in all of

05 Cloisters at Abbazia di Novacella

06 Novacella wines

07 Abbazia di Novacella collegiate church

Alto Adige. Stocker was convinced that Terlan's microclimate – hot days, cool nights – combined with the porphyr volcanic soil was perfect for ageing white wines. For many years the *soci* would have none of this, preferring to sell the wine young. So every year, beginning back in 1955, Stocker stashed a couple of hundred bottles of each wine in the cellar's hidden nooks and crannies. When he finally revealed all, the *soci* were furious – until they tasted how wonderfully the wines had aged.

Stocker's successor, Rudi Kofler, has continued to make award-winning yet affordable wines. Be sure to book ahead for a visit to the futuristic cellar.
cantina-terlano.com; tel +39 0471 257 135; Via Silberleiten 7, Terlano; shop Mon-Sat, tours by appointment

07 INNERLEITER

The narrow lane up to Innerleiter zigzags through a series of hair-raising bends, emerging at a romantic *gasthaus* (hotel) with breathtaking views across the snowcapped Alps. Karl Pichler cultivates just 1.7 hectares (4 acres) of vines encircling the hotel. He has built a modern cantina and works alone without a wine consultant, making some bold decisions, such as to totally abandon cork in favour of screw-tops. 'Many hotels here have vineyards like us,' he says, 'but they are always separate, and I wanted to bring the cantina and hotel together. So you can sit down in our tasting room, try the chef's pairing snacks with each glass, and see the barrel room through a glass wall.'
innerleiterhof.it; tel +39 0473 946 000; Via Leiter 8, Scena; Wed-Mon 🏷✕

08 ABBAZIA DI NOVACELLA

Even if this was not the home of some of the finest wines in Alto Adige, it would still be worth the detour to discover this magnificent Augustinian monastery, with its baroque chapels and ornate library. It has been cultivating vines since its foundation in 1142. The Abbazia lies just outside Bressanone, and its white-wine vineyards rise up to almost 1000m (3280ft). Red wines come from another monastery near Bolzano, but in the Abbazia be sure to taste fruity, mineral Sylvaner, Müller-Thurgau, Veltliner and the full-bodied Kerner, a curious cross of Riesling and Vernatsch. And don't miss the aromatic Moscato Rosa, which could easily be called rose-petal wine.
abbazianovacella.it; tel +39 0472 836 189; Via Abbazia 1, Varna; Mon-Sat 🏷✕

WHERE TO STAY

GASTHAUS KRAIDLHOF
Two spacious, slickly
designed apartments in
a farmhouse surrounded
by orchards and
vines, with a glorious
infinity pool in the
Mediterranean gardens.
*kraidlhof.com; tel +39
0471 880 258; Hofstatt 2,
Kurtatsch*

DER WEINMESSER
Christian Kohlgruber
is a wine fanatic and
sommelier. His luxurious
hotel revolves around
wine, from trips to the
vineyard to tastings in the
cellar and vinotherapy in
the spa.
*weinmesser.com;
tel +39 0473 945 660;
Via Scena 41, Scena*

GASTHOF HALLER
At the edge of bustling
Bressanone, this Alpine
chalet is a haven of
peace where you can
almost touch the owner's
vineyard from your
window. Meals are served
in a snug wood-panelled
weinstube.
*byhaller.com; tel +39
0472 834 601; Via dei
Vigneti 68, Bressanone*

WHERE TO EAT

PFEFFERLECHNER
This unique cantina has
a dining room that looks
directly into a stable
with resident horses and
cows. There's a beer
garden, a microbrewery
and a copper alembic
that's used to distil
grappa.
*pfefferlechner.it;
tel +39 0473 562 521;
Via San Martino 4, Lana;
Thu-Sun*

HOPFEN & CO
In the heart of medieval
Bolzano, this 150-year-
old osteria is the perfect
place to sample such
classic Tyrolean dishes as
roast pig's knuckle and
sauerkraut.
*boznerbier.it; tel +39
0471 300 788; Piazza
Erbe 17, Bolzano; daily*

WHAT TO DO

Spend a day at Merano's
historic thermal baths
(Terme Merano) with its
pools, sauna and spa.
*termemerano.it; tel +39
0473 252 000; Piazza
Terme 9, Merano*

CELEBRATIONS

Merano's wine and
food festival is held in
November; Egna hosts
Pinot Nero Days in
May; and in April/May
the annual asparagus
season is celebrated
with wine pairings in
Terlan. Törggelen season
in cantinas begins at the
end of September, when
you can taste partly
fermented grape juice
that's served alongside
freshly roasted sweet
chestnuts.
meranowinefestival.com

07

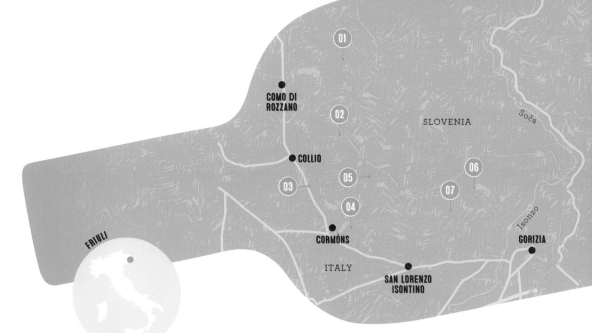

01

02

SLOVENIA

Soča

COMO DI
ROZZANO

COLLIO

05

06

03

07

04

FRIULI

CORMÒNS

Isonzo

ITALY

GORIZIA

SAN LORENZO
ISONTINO

[Italy]

FRIULI

In little-visited northeast Italy, snowy mountains and fertile plains are reflected in the variety of wines, from intense reds to fragrantly sweet whites.

The rugged Friuli region stretches up from the Adriatic shores to the Alps, forming a wedge between Italy's border with Eastern and Central Europe. Vineyards spread along the flat plains of the Piave, Italy's 'sacred river' (where rough Raboso wine was a great favourite of Ernest Hemingway) to the Carso, a rocky peninsula running up towards Trieste, where cantinas are often hewn into underground caves. Inland, the Collio Orientale – the eastern hills around the ancient town of Cividale – are famous for fascinating reds with such intense local grapes as Refosco and Pignolo, but the jewel in Friuli's crown is the Collio, a 50km (31 mile) necklace of hills.

The clay and sandstone soil here produces some of the finest white wines in Italy: fruity indigenous grapes such as Ribolla Gialla; the unique Picolit, late-harvested for a luscious dessert wine rivalling Sauternes; and the local favourite, Friulano, once known as Tokai, though today this name can only be used by Hungary's famed sweet wine.

Many Collio winegrowers have opened up their estates as B&Bs, inviting guests to whizz around the vineyards on signature bright-yellow Collio Vespas, and as Friuli remains off the heavily beaten track, you are sure of a warm welcome. The same is true of eating out; all over the countryside there are rustic *agriturismi* (farmstays) that open at weekends and offer traditional Friulian fare, more influenced by Central European cuisine than Italian. Plump gnocchi stuffed with susina plums is perfect with a sharp Friulano; and the more characteristic Ribolla Gialla goes well with juicy baby squid sautéed with slightly bitter red radicchio. A popular dish is Friuli's rich goulash stew; to accompany it, it's worth opening a bottle of one of the region's stellar reds, Livio Felluga's Sossó, a potent combination of Merlot and Refosco.

GET THERE
Trieste-Friuli Venezia Giulia is the nearest major airport, 30km (19 miles) from Dolegna del Collio. Car hire is available.

① VENICA & VENICA

Just before you drive into the sleepy village of Dolegna, a small sign on the right directs you down a narrow route that leads to one of the Collio's most important wineries. Venica & Venica refers to two brothers, Gianni and Giorgio, who have turned the small vineyard founded by their grandfather some 80 years ago into a slick, modern estate spanning 37 hectares (90 acres). The wine not to miss here is Ronco Bernizza, a surprising, steely Chardonnay that's perfect with *spaghetti alle vongole* (spaghetti with clams), or with the cheese platters offered with tastings. *venica.it; tel +39 0481 61264; Località Cerò 8, Dolegna del Collio; by appointment Mon-Sat* 💲

② CRASTIN

Crastin is the tiniest hamlet imaginable, with a single ancient farmhouse where Sergio Collarig cultivates a 10-hectare (25 acre) property. He is a rough-and-ready *contadino*, what might romantically be termed a peasant farmer, aided by his sister Vilma. Together they have progressed from producing *vino sfuso* (wine sold in bulk) to creating a small garage cellar yielding not just the Friulano and Ribolla Gialla whites that Collio is so famous for, but also full-bodied Merlot and Cabernet Franc aged in oak barrels. Each weekend they open up as an *agriturismo*, with Vilma preparing generous plates of ham, sausages and cheeses while Sergio opens bottles for tastings.

vinicrastin.it; tel +39 0481 630 310; Località Crastin 2, Ruttars; Sat-Sun & by appointment 💲✕

③ LIVIO FELLUGA

This historic family winery sets the benchmark for excellence in both the Collio and adjoining Collio Orientale vineyards, its vast estate covering a total of 160 hectares (395 acres). The founding father of the estate, Livio Felluga, who passed away in 2016 at the age of 102, declared that, 'There were many doubters when I started clearing forest land and planting vines here 60 years ago, but history told me that wine had been produced here for centuries and I was sure that this was the perfect place for white grapes like Friulano,

01 Autumnal Friuli
vineyards

02 Picking crew,
Venica & Venica

03 Ripening on
the vine

04 Livio Felluga estate

'I grow wonderful grapes. I just do the minimal fine-tuning in my cantina so as not to spoil the grapes and let them make their own magic'

– Paolo Caccese, winemaker

Sauvignon and Pinot Grigio and our indigenous red Refosco.' The family have also taken over the Abbazia di Rosazzo, a magnificent frescoed abbey surrounded by vineyards, where monks began making wine a thousand years ago; it now serves as an atmospheric venue for their wine tastings.

liviofelluga.it; tel +39 0481 60052; Abbazia di Rosazzo, Piazza Abbazia 5, Località Rosazzo, Manzano; by appointment Mon-Sat 💲

04 PAOLO CACCESE

The hamlet of Pradis stretches over a series of rolling vine-clad hills whose sole inhabitants are a dozen *viticoltori*, all making exceptional wines. Paolo Caccese's cantina sits atop the highest hill, surrounded by his 6-hectare (15-acre) vineyard. Paolo is a genuine eccentric, dressed like a country gentleman, and resembling more the lawyer that he trained to be than a producer of a clutch of elegant wines. His classic Friulano and Malvasia are delicious, but ask

to try such oddities as the fruity Müller-Thurgau, the aromatic, rose-scented Traminer and the honeyed Veronica dessert wine made with Verduzzo grapes. He defiantly ignores trends and fashions, still uses old-fashioned cement vats, and explains, 'I grow wonderful grapes here on a rich soil in an incredible position on the hillside, so I just do the minimal fine-tuning in my cantina so as not to spoil the grapes and let them make their own magic.'
paolocaccese.it; tel +39 348 797 2993; Località Pradis 6, Cormòns; daily by appointment

05 RENATO KEBER

The meandering road that leads out of Cormòns towards

Ø5 A tasting at Venica
& Venica

06 The Abbazia di
Rosazzo at Livio Felluga

San Floriano is marked on both sides by the Collio's distinctive winemaker signs, and at Zegla, a narrow lane leads you to the domain of Renato Keber, a one-of-kind *vignaiolo*. A quiet and unassuming man, Renato has built a swanky tasting room that affords panoramic views over his vineyards, where he loves surprising visitors with his spectacular wines.

Renato waits seven years before bringing out each of his Merlot and Cabernet vintages, but also follows the same philosophy with his whites – so it can come as quite a shock when he opens, say, a 2008 Pinot Grigio or a 2007 Sauvignon. 'My wines are marathon wines,' he jokes, 'and it is best to wait at least until you get to the 20km mark!' *renatokeber.com; tel +39 0481 639 844; Località Zegla 15, Cormòns; daily by appointment* 🛈

06 AZIENDA AGRICOLA FRANCO TERPIN

Franco Terpin is an anti-establishment artisan winemaker, the guru of a small group of natural, no-sulphite wine producers. Certified organic, and favouring long maceration, natural yeast and absolutely no chemicals, Franco's wine spends a year in the barrel, another year in steel vats, then three years ageing in the bottle. He produces 90% white wines on the small estate, which includes vines across the border in Slovenia. They have a quite incredible orange colour, known here as *vini arancioni*.

Franco tells his visitors: 'My wines are natural and, quite frankly, they are the only kind of wines I drink now – I can't stand a Chardonnay that has a banana aroma or the classic cat's pee of Sauvignon – these are chemically induced. With my wines you can drink a few bottles, party till 3am, and have absolutely no hangover the next morning.' *bit.ly/FrancoTerpin; tel +39 346 330 4134; Località Valerisce 6/A, San Floriano del Collio; daily by appointment*

07 GRADIS'CIUTTA

The Princic family have been cultivating grapes in the Collio and in nearby Slovenia since 1780, though today's modern winery was officially founded in 1997 when winemaker Robert Princic persuaded his parents, Zorko and Ivanka, to expand their working farm to include a serious vineyard. Robert also served as President of the Consorzio, representing all of the Collio winemakers, until stepping down in 2019.

His own crisp, mineral wines include a still and sparkling Ribolla Gialla, while his Chardonnay is one of the finest in the region. Visitors are assured of a warm welcome, whether from Robert, explaining all the technical aspects of his barrel-ageing, or Mamma Ivanka slicing up thick chunks of salami produced on the farm; the estate also has guest rooms and apartments. *gradisciutta.eu; tel +39 0481 390 237; Località Giasbana 32/A, San Floriano del Collio; Mon-Sat* 🛈

WHERE TO STAY
BORGO SAN DANIELE
Mauro and Alessandra Mauri make outstanding wines and have created a designer B&B with a pool adjacent to their cantina. *borgosandaniele.it; tel 0481 60552; Via San Daniele 28, Cormòns*

AZIENDA AGRICOLA PICECH
Roberto and Alessia Picech rent out three rooms in their farmhouse winery, with stunning terraces overlooking vine-blanketed hills. Breakfast is served in the family's own kitchen, where wine tastings are held in the evenings. *picech.it; tel +39 0481 60347; Località Pradis 11, Cormòns*

WHERE TO EAT
TRATTORIA AL CACCIATORE DELLA SUBIDA
This once-rustic trattoria has been transformed by the Sirk family into an elegant Michelin-starred restaurant offering locally sourced set menus paired with regional wines.

lasubida.it; tel +39 0481 60531; Via Subida 52, Cormòns; Thu-Mon

AGRITURISMO STEKAR
A working farm and vineyard that Sonia Stekar opens as a restaurant every weekend (and Wed-Fri for dinner, but call ahead to check), serving up goulash, award-winning salamis, pumpkin gnocchi and out-of-this-world apple strudel. *bit.ly/AgriStekar; tel +39 0481 391 929; Località Giasbana 25, San Floriano del Collio*

ENOTECA REGIONALE DI CORMÒNS
This pulsating wine bar offers the chance to mingle with local *vignaiolo*, sample some of the 100 wines available by the glass and nibble on generous plates of locally sourced meats and cheeses. *enotecadicormons.com; tel +39 0481 630 371; Piazza XXIV Maggio 21, Cormòns; Wed-Mon*

WHAT TO DO
From the ancient Roman town of Cividale del Friuli, you can explore the wooded valley along the fast-flowing Natisone River, perfect for hiking, mountain-biking and trout-fishing – and not short of appealingly rustic trattorias, either.

CELEBRATIONS
Each September, Gorizia celebrates Gusti di Frontiera, a food and wine festival, while at the end of October the Jazz & Wine festival has a roster of musicians performing in cellars in and around Cormòns. *bit.ly/GoriziaGustiF; controtempo.org*

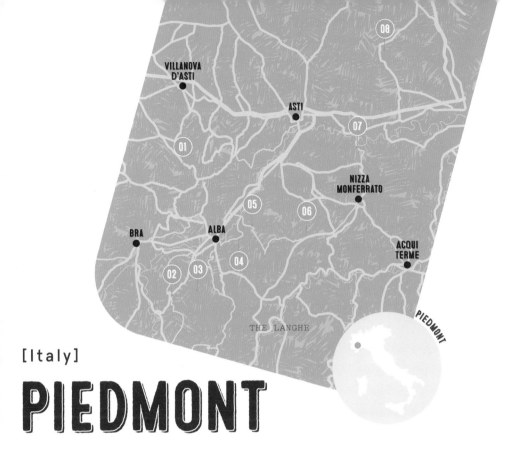

The Langhe

PIEDMONT

[Italy]
PIEDMONT

Dive into deep, delicious Barolo and Barbaresco red wines in this famously food-loving quarter of northern Italy, before checking out the local truffles.

N o region in Italy quite compares to Piedmont's combination of fine wines, gastronomy and beautiful countryside, lying at the foot of the Alps. It would be quite easy to spend a whole trip just wandering through the picture-postcard vineyards and celebrated cantinas of the Langhe, whose hills produce some of the world's greatest, most structured red wines, Barolo and Barbaresco, as well as Nebbiolo, Barbera and Dolcetto. The vineyard landscape is unique and so perfect that, in 2014, it achieved the ultimate honour of being added to the exclusive list of Unesco World Heritage Sites.

But it's worth exploring further to discover the surprising Grignolino and Freisa of the Monferrato region, which are made from native grapes, as well as the delicately sweet Moscato and bubbly Spumante produced around Asti and Canelli.

Meanwhile, a new generation of young *viticoltori* (winegrowers) are breathing life into the rural countryside of the Roero, just across the river from the Langhe, with their Arneis and Favorita – both fresh, aromatic whites. Stay in a rustic *agriturismo* where food-lovers can splash out on the ultimate gourmet extravagance of aromatic white truffles, or enjoy simple handmade pasta known as *plin*, which is stuffed and pinched together.

This is one of the most developed parts of Italy for wine tourism, with numerous winemaker B&Bs and splendid regional *enoteche* (wine shops), where dozens of different wineries are presented in a single tasting. Visitors will quickly realise that the Piedmontesi are reserved people, very proud of their own culture and language. They may not fall over at first to ingratiate themselves with tourists, but you'll soon discover just how hospitable and friendly they are.

GET THERE
Turin-Caselle is the nearest major airport, 73km (45 miles) from Montà. Car hire is available.

01 MICHELE TALIANO

The Tanaro River divides the Barolo and Barbaresco vineyards of the Langhe from Roero, a more biodiverse landscape encompassing farm and woodlands too. Today, a new generation of Roero *viticoltori* are pushing boundaries and producing some exceptional Barbera and Nebbiolo wines. It's when it comes to white wines that the Roero terroir comes into its own, making a serious reputation for the crisp, acidic Arneis and more fragrant Favorita.

Accompany Ezio Taliani on a tour of the vineyard and you embark on an adventure safari on rutted tracks through dense forest before coming out at a breathtaking vista of graphic crisscrossing vines. Make sure you

ask him to open a bottle of the intensely aromatic sparkling Birbet, made from Brachetto del Roero, a native grape that is fast disappearing. *talianomichele.com; tel +39 0173 976 100; Corso Manzoni 24, Montà; daily by appointment* $

02 CANTINA MASCARELLO BARTOLO

Maria Teresa Mascarello may not have a website to her name, but visitors are certainly made to feel welcome at her tiny cantina in the heart of the medieval wine town of Barolo. The winemakers around here are divided into modernists, who favour single vineyard cuvées, aged in small French barrique barrels, and traditionalists who insist on blending different parcels of vines and using

huge Slavonian oak casks. Maria Teresa is definitely a traditionalist: she's a fierce defender of Barolo's historic identity, making wines of intense purity and finesse. Working a small 5-hectare (12-acre) estate of prime Nebbiolo vines, she is a far cry from the typical red-faced Piemontese *viticoltore* – a pixie-like figure who looks miniscule as she walks past the towering wooden vats in her cantina.
Tel +39 0173 56125; Via Roma 15, Barolo; Mon, Tue & Fri by appointment

03 PAOLO MANZONE

Serralunga is a spectacular amphitheatre of vineyards, and Paolo Manzone's cascina (farmhouse, cellar and *agriturismo*) is hidden away

No region in Italy quite compares to Piedmont's combination of fine wines, gastronomy and beautiful countryside

down a zigzag dirt track. A lengthy tasting session with Paolo is the perfect opportunity to understand the complex world of Barolo. He is an innovative *viticoltore*, forever experimenting but never abandoning the traditions surrounding Barolo's unique grape, Nebbiolo. It has been grown here for some seven centuries, and takes its name from the mist that often descends on the vineyards in autumn.

Paolo makes two very different Barolo – the traditional Serralunga, which is aged in large, old oak barrels; and the more modern Meriame, using smaller, new French barrels. He describes his crisp, fresh Dolcetto d'Alba as 'a wine I make for my father – not elegant but rustic, drinkable, like the wine that he sold in demijohns'.
barolomeriame.com; tel +39 0173 613 113; Località Meriame 1, Serralunga d'Alba; daily by appointment ⑤

⑭ CA' DEL BAIO

Three generations work together in this idyllic winery nestling in a valley of vineyards. This is classic Barbaresco country, a wine that historically has been the 'little brother' of Barolo – but when you taste this family's vintages, you will discover it can reach equally great heights. The winemaking is in the hands of three dynamic sisters, Paola, Valentina and Federica, who recount 'when our great-grandfather bought the land in 1900, everyone thought he was mad, that it was just worthless woodlands. But he always believed in the potential of the soil and began planting vines.' Don't miss the eminently drinkable Dolcetto – 'great with a pizza,' says Paola with a grin.
cadelbaio.com; tel +39 0173 638 219; Via Ferrere Sottano 33, Treiso; Mon-Fri by appointment ⑤

05 Carlo Santopietro
of Il Mongetto

06 Twilight over Turin

05 CANTINA DEL GLICINE

Adriana Marzi is a delightfully eccentric woman, but very serious about the award-winning Barbaresco she produces from this small 6-hectare (15-acre) estate. Before the tasting, Adriana takes you through a forbidding blood-red door that leads down to the cantina, what the Piemontese call 'Il Crutin', a natural grotto that is then hollowed out and extended into a maze of cool cellars. This one dates back to 1582, and is like walking into a scene from *The Lord of the Rings*, with mushrooms, gobbled up by snails, growing over the damp walls, dark corners stacked with ancient wooden barrels, and alcoves filled with dusty bottles laid down to age. Beware that Adriana always insists visitors try her famous fiery grappa. *cantinadelglicine.it; tel +39 0173 67215; Via Giulio Cesare 1, Neive; Thu-Mon* 💲

06 CANTINE COPPO

The words Asti and Spumante have been famous for more than 150 years as the symbol of Italian sparkling wine. The story of Spumante began in Piedmont, near to the town of Asti in medieval Canelli, at the house of Gancia. The cellars of this world-renowned winery have recently re-opened to visitors, but there are a host of other spectacular cellars, known as the underground Cathedrals of Canelli, that also welcome wine-lovers. Founded in 1892, the family-run Cantine Coppo has one of the most evocative of these, hewn into Canelli's hills and recognised as a Unesco World Heritage Site. It stores over a million bottles of Spumante, which is made using the same grapes as Champagne – Chardonnay and Pinot Nero – and the historic *metodo classico* process to add bubbles. Be sure to taste its other local speciality, the fruity Moscato d'Asti. *coppo.it; tel +39 0141 823 146; Via Alba 68, Canelli; daily by appointment* 💲

07 BRAIDA

Braida is forever associated with the name of the late Giacomo Bologna, a mythical figure of Piedmont wine. Planting the then humble grape of Barbera in the unsung region between Asti and Alessandria back in the 1960s, Bologna proved that Piedmont's great wines did not have to be restricted to the Nebbiolo-based Barolo and Barbaresco. Using 100% Barbera and ageing for long periods in small French oak barrels, he produced stunning vintages of what is now Braida's signature full-bodied Bricco dell'Uccelone. Today, this dynamic winery is run by Giacomo's children, Raffaella and Giuseppe, and after a visit to the state-of-the-art cantina, head to the village for lunch at the family Trattoria I Bologna. *braida.it; tel +39 0141 644 113; Via Roma 94, Rocchetta Tanaro; Dec-Aug Tue-Sat, Sep-Nov Thu-Mon* 💲

08 IL MONGETTO

North of the Langhe, the wilder, under-the-radar region of Monferrato is the place to discover rare indigenous grapes. The brothers Carlo and Roberto Santopietro have converted an 18th-century *palazzetto* (frescoed mansion) into an *agriturismo* where wines can be tasted, and at the weekend local specialities are served in a cosy dining room. They produce surprising reds, such as the fruity but tannic Grignolino, a *vivace* (lively) Cortese, the intense, oak-barrelled Barbera del Monferrato Superiore, and an easy-drinking Malvasia di Casorzo – sweet, fizzy and only 5% alcohol. *bit.ly/IlMongetto; tel +39 347 725 1306; Via Piave 2, Vignale Monferrato; Fri-Sun by appointment* * 🍴

WHERE TO STAY
CASA SCAPARONE
A wonderful working farm and vineyard with chic rooms and a raucous osteria serving organic vegan dishes, often accompanied by live music. Kids will love visiting the farm animals. *casascaparone.it; tel +39 0173 33946; Località Scaparone 45, Alba*

CASTELLO DI SINIO
This 800-year-old castle dominates the hamlet of Sinio, surrounded by vineyards producing the finest Barolo wine. You'll find sumptuous rooms and a great welcome by owner Denise Pardini. *hotelcastellodisinio. com; tel +39 0173 263 889; Vicolo del Castello 1, Sinio*

LE CASE DELLA SARACCA
A unique location where six medieval houses have been transformed into a labyrinth of grottoes, suspended glass walkways, swirling metallic staircases and bedrooms with features carved out of the rock.

saracca.com; tel +39 0173 789 222; Via Cavour 5, Monforte d'Alba

WHERE TO EAT
OSTERIA DA GEMMA
Visit Signora Gemma's osteria to taste her legendary Piemontese *cucina casalinga* (home cooking), where portions of razor-thin tajarin pasta are sprinkled with white-truffle shavings. *bit.ly/DiGemma; tel +39 0173 794 252; Via Marconi 6, Roddino; Wed-Sun*

PIAZZA DUOMO
Chef Enrico Crippa has won a coveted three Michelin stars in this futuristic temple of gastronomy in Alba. Simply sublime cuisine. *piazzaduomoalba.it; tel +39 0173 366 167; Piazza Risorgimento 4, Alba; daily*

WHAT TO DO
Turin was the first capital of modern Italy and is home to ornate baroque palaces, an amazing Egyptian Museum and the Museo Egizio di Torino, as well as a host of historical cafes that have made an art form of the evening aperitivo. *museoegizio.it*

CELEBRATIONS
Every weekend during October and November, Alba plays host to its renowned white-truffle festival. *fieradeltartufo.org*

[Italy]

LIGURIA

Wedged between the mountains and the sea, Liguria is one of Italy's most underrated wine regions, a place of 'heroic winemakers', cliffside vineyards and bold vintages.

Famed for its elegant beaches, pastel-tinted villages and decadent seafood, Liguria has long captivated visitors. Days here are spent gazing out from faded villas at turquoise waters, or walking rocky paths above ancient olive groves and vineyards first planted by the Romans. The wines have long played second fiddle to the region's more obvious charms: the grandeur of upscale seaside towns like San Remo, the candlelit dining rooms overlooking Portofino or the medieval lanes and sumptuous palazzi of Genoa.

In fact, until a few years ago, most Italians would shrug when asked about the attributes and virtues of a Ligurian wine. 'Red's a bit on the fizzy side,' a waiter might have advised – unkindly. 'How about something from Tuscany instead?' But things have changed dramatically in recent years in this crescent-shaped region anchoring

GET THERE
Genoa, on the coast near the centre of Liguria, has international flights, with more options from Milan (185km/115 miles north of Genoa).

Italy's northwest coast. A new generation of winemakers are introducing bold techniques while embracing a sustainable, back-to-the-land approach.

Italians often speak of *viticoltura eroica* (heroic winemaking) when describing the challenges of growing grapes in an extreme environment. No place seems to embody this more than Liguria. Working tiny plots on precipitously steep hillsides, protected by drystone terraces painstakingly built by hand – with heavy storms and landslides a perennial concern – discourages all but the most tenacious of winemakers. But after one taste of a Vermentino from Colli di Luni or a Rossese from Dolceaqua, you'll quickly realise why they go to all the trouble. Ligurian wines express a deep-rooted terroir: flavours can evoke Mediterranean herbs, forest berries, and the faint brininess of the salt-kissed air.

ITALY

CUNEO

GENOA

BORZONASCA

RAPALLO

PONTREMOLI

SAVONA

Gulf of Genoa

Riviera di Levante

SESTRI LEVANTE

FIVIZZANO

FINALE LIGURE

05

02

01

FRANCE

Riviera di Ponente

03

LA SPEZIA

MASSA

ALASSIO

Ligurian Sea

IMPERIA   04

06   SAN REMO

MONACO

MEDITERRANEAN SEA

🄌 BURANCO

A short stroll from Monterosso al Mare village, Buranco produces some fine DOC Cinque Terre white wines as well as grappa, *limoncino* (Liguria's answer to the Amalfi Coast's lemon-flavoured limoncello) and one tricky-to-pronounce dessert wine: Sciacchetrà (shah-keh-trah). Amber-yellow and aromatic, it has an intense nose and is richly complex with notes of dried fig, candied orange and hazelnut. It's quite labour-intensive to make: meticulously selected grapes are hand-picked then dried naturally indoors on trellises for two months before fermenting, followed by 16 months ageing in steel barrels. Before or after a tasting on the veranda, wander the vineyards to get a sense of the challenges of working the steeply terraced hillsides. Buranco rents out four apartments on the property, all with terraces (two overlooking the vineyards). It also runs a small restaurant above the vines and lemon groves, specialising in locavore cuisine. *burancocinqueterre.it; tel +39 349 434 8046; Via Buranco 72, Monterosso; by appointment* 💲✕

🄼 CANTINA CINQUE TERRE

High above the seaside village of Manarola, the Cinque Terre's largest wine producer has been cultivating vines since 1982. Over 200 grower-members make up this cooperative, which consists of dozens of lofty parcels of land, spread across the southern-facing hillsides above the crashing waves. Some of the best wines here hail from historic vineyards that date back centuries. Sipping the DOC Costa de Campu, you can almost taste the summer heat and Mediterranean wildflowers in this golden-hued wine with its notes of sage and citrus, while the Costa de Posa evokes the constant sea breezes with a delightfully briny mineral finish. This is also the place to find one of Liguria's best Sciacchetràs – an intense award-winning Riserva that is aged in small oak barrels for at least three years. Book ahead for a tasting or a tour of the cellars. *cantinacinqueterre.com; tel +39 0187 920 435; Località Groppo, Riomaggiore; Mon-Sat by appointment* 💲

01 Cinque Terre
coastline at Manarola

02 Liguria's
mountainous interior

03 Tasting Dolceacqua
at Terre Bianche

he produces on the 45 hectares (111 acres) of the Cantine Lunae estate. The Vermentino Riserva Etichetta Nera (or Black Label Reserve Vermentino) is a revelation: it exhibits outstanding structure, with aromas of wild herbs, spices and honey. The winery is set among restored 18th-century stone and terracotta-tiled buildings, with an atmospheric wine shop, tasting room and restaurant, as well as a small museum in the old manor house that pays homage to the people who worked the land in centuries past. *cantinelunae.com; tel +39 0187 693 483; Via Palvotrisia 2, Castelnuovo Magra; daily by appointment* 🟢✕

05 TERRE BIANCHE

This storied family-run winery dates back to 1870, when Tommaso Rondelli planted the first Rossese vines on the unusual white clay soil above the village of Dolceaqua in western Liguria. Successive generations of Rondelli have worked the land with passion, nurturing vines and continuing a centuries-old winegrowing tradition. Terre Bianche produces several top-notch white wines, including a golden Pigato and a luminous Vermentino. The star of the show, however, is the Rossese di Dolceacqua, a much-lauded ruby-red wine with a rich flavour

03 POGGIO DEI GORLERI

In a tiny settlement above the Riviera del Ponente (the western part of the Italian Riviera, from Genoa to the French border), the Merano family founded this winery back in 2003, determined to create a great Ligurian wine that marries a commitment to innovation with a respect for tradition. The south-facing slopes overlooking the sparkling Gulf of Diano Marino make a rugged setting for growing, though the iron-rich and limestone soils provide the foundation for excellent Vermentino and Liguria's native Pigato grapes. Their Albium, made of 100% Pigato, has a warm and bright character that's remarkably elegant and well-balanced on the palate, with notes of citrus fruits

and honeysuckle. Tastings are accompanied by locally sourced nibbles or a four-course wine-paired lunch; Poggio dei Gorleri is also a 'wine resort', with an inviting swimming pool and beautifully furnished rooms with vineyard views. *poggiodeigorleri.com; tel +39 0183 495 207; Via San Leonardo, Frazione Gorleri, Diano Marino; by appointment* 🟢✕

04 CANTINE LUNAE

Framed by the Apuan Alps to the north and the rolling hills of Tuscany to the east, the Colli di Luna proves to be a remarkable terrain for producing Vermentino and other varieties. In this easternmost corner of Liguria, Paolo Bosoni has become a legend for the brilliant wines

04 Francesca Bruna of Bruna winery

05 Pastel hues on the Ligurian coast

06 Antique vintages at Terre Bianche

profile and notes of cherry, wild berries and spices. It's aged in steel tanks, ensuring that every drop you taste is an unadulterated expression of the terroir. Terre Bianche also rents out holiday apartments nestled among the sloping vineyards set between mountains and sea (which you can explore using the mountain bikes available for guests). *terrebianche.com; tel +39 0184 31426; Località Arcagna, Dolceacqua; by appointment* ⑤

⑥ BRUNA

Winemaker Riccardo Bruna bucked the trend with his ambition to make a high-quality Pigato when he began producing wine back in 1970. Until then, this spotted white-wine grape (a relative of the better-known Vermentino) was largely made into an easy-drinking quaff for local consumption. Bruna, however, saw incredible potential in the forest-fringed heights around Ortovero in western Liguria, and within a decade he had won acclaim for his savoury, well-made wines. Today, Riccardo's daughter Francesca carries on the tradition, crafting not only brilliantly balanced Pigatos, but also juicy reds made from Granaccia, a grape variety native to Liguria and similar to the Grenache of France's Rhône Valley. *brunapigato.it; tel +39 0183 318 082; Via Umberto I 81, Ranzo; by appointment* ⑤

WHERE TO STAY
HOTEL GIANNI FRANZI
In picture-perfect Vernazza, Hotel Gianni Franzi has simple, atmospheric rooms with a retro feel; some have balconies. Breakfast on the deck delivers sublime sea-drenched views, and there's also a small garden under the Doria castle for guests to enjoy.
giannifranzi.it; tel +39 0187 812 228; Via San Giovanni Battista 41, Vernazza

VALLEPONCI
Only 5km (3 miles) from the pretty beach of Finale Ligure, Valleponci feels deliciously wild, tucked away in a rugged Ligurian valley. Horses graze, grapevines bud and the restaurant turns out fresh Ligurian dishes made with vegetables and herbs from a kitchen garden. Rooms are simple but show the keen eye of the Milanese escapee owners.
valleponci.it; tel +39 329 315 4169; Località Verse, Val Ponci 22, Finale Ligure

WHERE TO EAT
TRATTORIA DA BILLY
Hidden off a narrow lane in the upper reaches of Manarola, Trattoria da Billy fires up some of the best seafood anywhere in Cinque Terre. Start with a mixed platter – 12 different hot and cold dishes (octopus salad, lemon-drizzled anchovies, tuna with sweet onion) – then feast on lobster pasta or swordfish laced with black truffle.
trattoriabilly.com; tel +39 0187 920 628; Via Rollandi 122, Manarola; Fri-Wed

CASA E BOTTEGA
Join the daytrippers from France at this stylishly bucolic restaurant, cafe, homewares shop and general village epicentre in Dolceacqua. Lunch and dinner offerings are fresh, bold reworkings of local classics: perfect fare for alfresco dining with a bottle of Rossese.
ristocasaebottega.it; tel +39 320 333 9444; Piazza Garibaldi 2, Dolceacqua; Fri-Wed

WHAT TO DO
Liguria has hundreds of kilometres of well-signed trails, and some of its most famous lie near the Cinque Terre. One memorable 2.5hr walk heads from seaside Manarola up to the lofty settlement of Volastra (elevation 335m/1099ft), passing through terraced vineyards and olive groves before descending to the clifftop village of Corniglia. Manarola-based Arbaspàa can arrange guided walks and vineyard visits.
www.parconazionale 5terre.it; arbaspaa.com

CELEBRATIONS
Held in early April, Sciacchetrail is a challenging 47km-long (29-mile) endurance event that takes to the hills of Cinque Terre. Some 300 runners from around 20 different countries race along dirt paths that skirt past cliff edges and through terraced vineyards, ascending more than 2600 vertical metres (8530ft) over the 10-plus-hour race (though winners run it in less than six hours). True to its name, the race pays homage to the famed wine of Cinque Terre, and Sciacchetrà wine tastings, cooking demonstrations and discussions by winemakers are all essential parts of the weekend events.
sciacchetrail.com

[Italy]
TUSCANY

With its swaying cypresses, hilltop villages and exceptional red wines, Tuscany exudes an old-fashioned romance that's hard to resist.

W ine and Tuscany are so closely associated that, for many, the vintages produced in the storied Tuscan hills symbolise all the glamour and style of Italy in the same way that Champagne evokes France.

It was the Etruscans who first made wine here, using huge terracotta amphorae that some natural-wine makers are rediscovering today. As early as the 5th century BCE, Tuscan wines were exported to France and Greece; and Florence founded its own Wine Merchants Guild in 1282. So Tuscany has always been the ambassador of Italian wine, from ancient times through to the days when a straw-covered flask of Chianti featured as house wine across the globe. And today, the region's wine has moved onto the wine lists of the world's finest restaurants, with the top Tuscan producers appearing alongside those of Bordeaux and Burgundy.

Tuscany is the perfect location for producing outstanding red wine with the native Sangiovese grape, but centuries of tradition came under threat as winemakers started blending it with 'international' varietals like Cabernet Sauvignon and Merlot. These are the so-called Super Tuscans, wines produced outside the ancient regulations that offer immediate, accessible quality that is easier to sell internationally. While some Super Tuscans, primarily in the Maremma, have made

their mark and are here to stay, the mood is now returning to traditional winemaking based purely on the potential of Sangiovese. That is definitely the case in the historic Chianti Classico region, where the story of Tuscan winemaking began.

With vineyards nestling in undulating hillsides and valleys from the outskirts of Florence all the way to the Mediterranean, it is difficult to know quite where to start when planning a Tuscan wine journey. Exclusive wines such as Sassicaia and Ornellaia are produced in the relatively new maritime vineyards of windswept Maremma; the medieval cities of Montalcino and Montepulciano continue to impose strict rules on the making and ageing of their venerable Brunello and Vino Nobile vintages. But the Chianti Classico region remains the beating heart of Tuscany.

GET THERE
Pisa is the nearest major airport, 120km (75 miles) from Gaiole di Chianti. Car hire is available.

GREVE IN CHIANTI
07 06 05

VOLPAIA
04
RADDA IN CHIANTI

CASTELLINA IN CHIANTI

03 01

02

TUSCANY **SIENA**

🄰 CASTELLO DI BROLIO

The story of Chianti begins at the enchanting Castello di Brolio. It may have become something of a Disneyland castle, but it remains a must-see stop-off.

While wine in Tuscany dates back to Etruscan times, it was Barone Bettino Ricasoli, one-time prime minister of Italy and enthusiastic winemaker, who is credited with creating the blend of grapes that produce the distinctive personality of Chianti Classico, back in 1872. This perfect expression and interpretation of the Sangiovese grape has survived until today.

The Ricasoli dynasty owned Brolio from 1141, along with half the countryside between Florence and Siena, and the present descendant

Francesco, the 32nd Barone, has restored Brolio's reputation as a respected winemaker.
ricasoli.it; tel +39 0577 730 280; Località Madonna a Brolio, Gaiole in Chianti; daily 🅂✕

🄱 LE BONCIE

Giovanna Morganti, along with cult French winemaker Nicolas Joly, was one of the founders of Vini Veri, which today has grown into the influential 'natural wine' movement. She is an uncompromising *viticoltrice* (winegrower), planting her vineyard from scratch in 1990; today the freestanding *alberelli* (bush vines) of her tiny vineyard resemble immaculate bonsai trees surrounded by a jungle of wild plants and weeds. Her work in the

cantina is exceptional, fermenting in open-topped tanks with regular *batonnage* (stirring of the lees).

Giovanna makes just two wines, Il Cinque and the headline Le Trame, a *vino da tavola* that she has taken deliberately outside the official DOCG (Denominazione di Origine Controllata e Garantita) appellation, and is unlike any other Chianti Classico you will taste: incredibly intense, complex and concentrated. While 90% of the grapes are Sangiovese, she adds little-known local varietals such as Mammolo, Colorino and Fogliatondo, and is fiercely critical of fellow winemakers who have been influenced to add in so-called 'international grapes' Merlot and Cabernet Sauvignon.

01 Villa Pomona
wine tasting

02 Siena skyline

03 Chianti country

04 Vineyards in Chianti

05 Monica Raspi in the
cantina at Villa Pomona

bit.ly/LeBoncie; tel +39 0577
359 383; Località San Felice,
Castelnuovo Berardenga; daily
by appointment

03 FATTORIA POMONA

Traditions die hard in Chianti
country, as visitors will quickly
understand when they meet
the passionate, down-to-earth
winemaker Monica Raspi in the
charming *fattoria* where she makes
wine and olive oil. Guests can stay
in an ancient olive mill converted
into holiday apartments.

Monica explains, 'I was born here,
but went off to Florence to study
as a veterinarian. But as soon as my
mamma said she was going to sell
the villa and our vineyards I couldn't
bear to lose our family heritage.'

She abandoned her career, did a
crash course in oenology, started
making her own wines in 2007,
'and mamma looks after the bed
and breakfast.' Her tiny cantina is
a cluttered mix of giant wooden
botte (barrels) and steel and
cement vats, and the vineyard has
official organic certification.
*fattoriapomona.it; tel +39 0577 740
473; Località Pomona 39, Castellina
in Chianti; daily by appointment* $

04 VAL DELLE CORTI

A wine tasting with Roberto Bianchi
often ends up with an impassioned
discussion over several bottles of
his outstanding wines accompanied
by a plate of delicious Tuscan
sausage and cheeses. This feisty
artisan *vignaiolo* (winemaker) makes

a supple *vino da tavola*, perfect for
drinking young; a tannic but elegant
Chianti Classico bursting with fruity
flavour; and a Riserva only when
he feels the harvest merits it. His
organic vineyard is only 6 hectares
(15 acres), and he uses only aged
barrels in his cantina because
'there is already enough tannin in
the Sangiovese grape.'
*valdellecorti.it; tel +39 0577 738 215;
Val delle Corti, Località La Croce
141, Radda in Chianti; Mon-Sat
by appointment* $

05 FATTORIA DI LAMOLE

The road to Lamole weaves through
thick forest before emerging at
Greve in Chianti, one of the most
beautiful villages in the region, some
600m (2000ft) above sea level.

Paolo Socci is a fiercely traditionalist winemaker, favouring giant old wooden barrels in his cantina: 'I want my wine tasting of Sangiovese tannin, not oak.' His 2013 Gran Selezione Vigna Grospoli is sensational, made solely with grapes grown in the microvineyard within the 7km (4 miles) of centuries-old *terrazzi* that Paolo has painstakingly rebuilt.

He has also renovated a small medieval hamlet of cottages at the edge of Lamole into a comfy B&B for visitors.

fattoriadilamole.it; tel +39 0558 547 065; Lamole, Greve in Chianti; daily by appointment 💲

06 FONTODI

Down below Panzano lies a showpiece vineyard planted in a sunny amphitheatre known as La Conca d'Oro. It is the heart of the Fontodi estate, which covers some 70 hectares (173 acres) of vines and 30 hectares (75 acres) of olive groves. A 50-strong herd of Tuscany's iconic Chianina cows completes this far-sighted and sustainably run organic farm.

Unlike many of Chianti's big wineries, a visit here is a casual affair. The Manetti family bought Fontodi over 50 years ago and are experimenting with ageing a wine in an *orcio* (terracotta amphora) jar, a technique used by the Greeks and Romans. Their modern flagship wine, Flaccianello della Pieve, is 100% Sangiovese, while the luscious Vin Santo is made using grapes that have been straw-dried for five months and then barrel-aged for six years.

fontodi.com; tel +39 0558 52005; Panzano in Chianti; Mon-Sat by appointment

07 RIGNANA

Head off into the unknown along the *strada bianca*, the white-gravel dirt tracks crisscrossing the Tuscan countryside, and you'll discover romantic villas, vineyards, farms and restaurants. One of these hidden jewels is Rignana, the magical winery of the dashing Cosimo Gericke. His 18th-century frescoed villa has sumptuous guest rooms, an olive mill converted into a trattoria, a pool by an olive grove and even a medieval chapel used for weddings. Cosimo produces an absorbing mix of organic Chianti Classico; a tannic Merlot aged in small oak barrels; a rare white wine using Sangiovese; and a fruity, light Rosato, most of which is quaffed as sunset aperitifs at the villa itself.

rignana.it; tel +39 0558 52065; Via di Rignana 15, Greve in Chianti; daily by appointment 💲🍴

WHERE TO STAY

FATTORIA LA LOGGIA

This sprawling medieval wine and olive-oil *fattoria* has been transformed into an idyllic bolthole with spacious rooms, a heavenly pool and sculptures and paintings everywhere thanks to an artists-in-residence programme. *fattorialaloggia.com; tel +39 0558 244 288; Via Collina 24, San Casciano in Val di Pesa*

LE MICCINE

Canadian *vigneronne* Paula Papine Cook settled in Chianti a few years back, and her wines are now winning top awards. The guest villa and apartment next to her cantina features an inviting infinity pool. *lemiccine.com; tel +39 057 774 9526; Località Le Miccine 44, Gaiole in Chianti*

WHERE TO EAT

ANTICA MACELLERIA CECCHINI

Dario Cecchini is the 'King of Chianti', a dramatic master butcher famed for his *bistecca* *alla fiorentina* (T-bone steak). There is sit-down dining out back, from simple daily specials to more elaborate meals. *dariocecchini.com; tel +39 0558 52020; Via XX Luglio 11, Panzano in Chianti; daily*

A CASA MIA

This village osteria serves huge portions of *cucina casalinga* (home cooking) such as tagliatelle with porcini, presented by the rock'n'roll hosts, Cosimo and Maurizio. *acasamia.eu; tel +39 0558 244 392; Via Santa Maria a Macerata 4, Montefiridolfi; Wed-Sun*

BAR UCCI

Volpaia is a dreamy medieval village high up in the hills of Chianti. Tuck into Tuscan specialities on Ucci's sunny terrace. *bar-ucci.it; tel +39 0577 738 042; Piazza della Torre 9, Volpaia; Tue-Sun*

WHAT TO DO

Spend a relaxed day exploring Siena's Renaissance palaces, churches and museums. *visittuscany.com/en/ destinations/siena*

CELEBRATIONS

In September, head to Panzano or Greve in Chianti, which both host week-long wine festivals. *panzano.com/ vino-al-vino; bit.ly/ GreveChiantiWin*

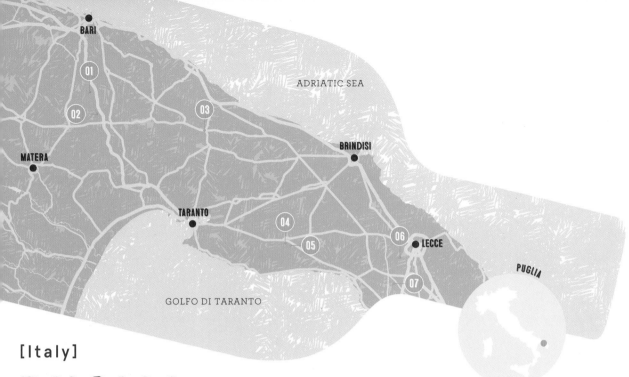

[Italy]

PUGLIA

Follow the sun down through the heel of Italy to olive groves and trulli – and a range of rustic, resurgent wines that perfectly accompany the local cuisine.

Puglia is the largest wine producer in Italy, a quintessentially rural region where cultivating grapes and olives is ingrained in the daily life of the *contadino* (farm worker). But for a long time it has been known for all the wrong reasons, historically supplying wine in bulk to Italy and much of Europe.

Things have changed, though, and today the world has woken up to the wine revolution taking place here. Forget so-called international grapes like Chardonnay, Cabernet and Merlot, and discover unique indigenous varieties – elegant Negroamaro; full-bodied Primitivo, cousin of California's Zinfandel; and fruity Minutolo and Malvasia Nera.

The prime vineyards begin just north of Bari and stretch down Italy's heel to Brindisi, Taranto, Lecce, Manduria and the Salice Salentino. The climate here is hot but tempered by breezes from the Adriatic

and Ionian seas, meaning the wines are intense and strong in alcohol but by no means overpowering. And today the region's small independent estates produce wines of exceptional quality, making use of modern cellar techniques and taking care in the vineyard to limit yield and to cultivate old *albarelli* (bush vines).

Don't expect too much picturesque scenery of hills covered with vines, of the type you'd find in Tuscany or Piedmont. In Puglia, running down through to the southeastern tip of the Italian mainland, landscapes are dominated by miles and miles of flat plains planted with hundreds of thousands of giant, gnarled olive trees, some more than three millennia old. Olive groves and vineyards alike are marked by the unique conical white-stone huts called *trulli* – some are still home to agricultural workers, while others are being converted into seductive B&Bs.

GET THERE
Bari is the nearest major airport, 40km (25 miles) from Acquaviva delle Fonti. Car hire is available.

01 TENUTE CHIAROMONTE

Located just south of Bari, Acquaviva is a medieval town with a long history of winemaking. 'We like to say that this is a mini-Reims,' explains owner and winemaker Nicola Chiaromonte, 'as more than 500 houses have their own cellar where wine has always been made.'

Nicola's intense Primitivo Riserva is made from 80-year-old *albarelli*. He is firmly against the trend to lower the alcohol volume of Primitivo to sell to a wider market. 'If you drink a Primitivo that is 13% you will never understand what the wine is about – the grape needs to develop, to mature, and for the Riserva I even favour a partial *appassimento* (desiccating the grape on the vine).'

tenutechiaromonte.com;
tel +39 080 768 156; Via Suriani 27,
Acquaviva delle Fonti; Mon-Sat
by appointment $

02 POLVANERA

Polvanera refers to the distinctive deep-red soil that surrounds the ancient manor house of innovative *vignaiolo* (winegrower) Filippo Cassano. 'I come from a family of winemakers who for generations produced bulk wine, without the financial means to bottle their own vintages,' Filippo recounts. 'So I am determined to prove that this part of Val d'Itria can make the finest Primitivo as well as great wines from other native Puglia grapes.' He has excavated a quite incredible cellar hewn out of limestone 8m

(26ft) underground. This is where he ages his wine for long periods – but there is not a barrel in sight. Filippo bucks the usual trend, refusing to use any wood and preferring to leave the wine in the bottle. The results are spectacular, especially the Polvanera 17, Primitivo in purezza, a dizzy 16.5% alcohol but still fresh and fruity. *cantinepolvanera.it; tel +39 080 758 900; Strada Vic.le Lamie Marchesana 601, Gioia del Colle; Mon-Sat by appointment* $

03 I PASTINI

While Puglia is making its name right now with Primitivo and Negroamaro red wines, there are also some highly original native white grapes grown in the region.

01 Old town, Bari

02 Tending the vines
at I Pastini

03 Harvesting by hand

04 Fermenting grapes
at Morella Vini

No estate quite compares to that of the Carparelli family, whose vineyards stretch around the historic city of Locorotondo through Val d'Itria, also known as the Trulli Valley. A tasting here includes a visit to the family's 17th-century *masseria* (traditional Puglian farmhouse) and ancient *trulli* still used during the *vendemmia* (harvest).

White wine is their speciality, and the Carparellis are credited with rediscovering the unique indigenous Minutolo grape from the Muscat family, wrongly named for decades as a Fiano from Campania. They vinify and age their wines only in steel vats, also producing Verdeca and the little-known Bianco d'Alessano.

ipastini.it; tel +39 080 431 3309; Strada Cupa Rampone, Martina Franca; Mon-Fri by appointment 💲

04 MORELLA VINI

For the moment, Gaetano Morella and Lisa Gilbee are making genuine garage wines in an industrial warehouse on the drab outskirts of Manduria. But these garage vintages are also winning Italy's top wine awards.

Finding the cantina is a problem, as there is not even a sign, but a tasting is fascinating, as Melbourne-native Lisa explains the experiments she is undertaking: old and new barrels, Nomblot cement eggs and strangely shaped cement vats called hippos. 'We came to Manduria specifically for

the ancient *albarelli* vines,' says Lisa. 'So many have already been dug up or abandoned, and we are just trying to save as many as possible because, quite simply, they produce incredible wines.'
morellavini.com; tel +39 099 979 1482; Via per Uggiano 147, Manduria; Mon-Sat by appointment

05 CONSORZIO PRODUTTORI VINI

The role of the cooperative cantina in Puglia's wine history has not exactly been glorious, and many still today prefer the economic security of supplying cheap wine in bulk. A notable exception is the venerable Consorzio Produttori Vini of Manduria, the oldest cooperative

*apolloniovini.it; tel +39 083 232
7182; Via San Pietro in Lama 7,
Monteroni di Lecce; Mon-Fri by
appointment* Ⓢ

07 CANTINA SEVERINO GAROFANO

If any master winemaker was
responsible for raising Negroamaro
to the heights it has reached
today, it was Severino Garofano.
For 50 years he held the reins
at the respected Cupertinum
cooperative – still very much worth
a visit – moving the conservative
soci (members) from bulk to quality
bottled wine. He also found the
time to set up his own winery, a
50-hectare (125-acre) vineyard,
which today is in the safe hands
of his son, Stefano. This stellar
azienda (company) is housed
in a wonderfully retro 1950s
cantina, and the vinification is
similarly traditional, still using giant
underground cement cisterns. But
the wines are absolutely modern,
especially the mellow Negroamaro
Le Braci, aged for at least seven
years, where a short *appassimento*
on the vine means alcohol levels
rise to almost 15% without affecting
the elegance of the vintage.
*vinigarofano.it; tel +39 083
294 7512; Località Tenuta
Monaci, Copertino; Mon-Sat by
appointment*

in Puglia, formed in 1932. Visiting
the immense cantina is the perfect
introduction to the region's wines.
A tasting (with locally sourced
bites) encompasses not just the
iconic Primitivo di Manduria, the
historic 'home' of Primitivo, but
Negroamaro, white and rosé
varietals, and a Fiano Spumante.
Beneath the cantina is a labyrinth
of cement cisterns, brilliantly
transformed into a museum
documenting the history of wine
and rural life here.
*cpvini.com; tel +39 099 973 5332;
Via Fabio Massimo 19, Manduria;
Mon-Sat by appointment* Ⓢ

06 APOLLONIO 1870

Marcello and Massimiliano Apollonio
run a huge modern winery, the
vineyards of which span the
prime Negroamaro and Primitivo
regions of Salento and Copertino.
The family comes from four
generations of winemakers who
are renowned for ageing Pugliese
wines in barrels; the oenologist of
the family, Massimiliano, could well
be described as the 'Wood King'
(though some young wines are
these days aged in steel vats).

The cantina is dominated by
wood – even the cement cisterns
are lined with oak. Massimiliano
experiments with different woods
for different cuvées – French,
American, Slavic, Hungarian and
Austrian. He even visits the coopers
to order the wood three years
before a barrel is made, when it is
still a tree. His philosophy? 'Wood is
fundamental for me, not just for the
profumo [scent], but for the colour
and stability of the wine, to age to
immortality if possible.'

WHERE TO STAY
CANNE BIANCHE
Right at the edge of the beach, this fashionably chic resort has a spa, cooking courses and even offers boat trips to catch octopus.
cannebianche.com; tel +39 080 482 9839; Via Appia 32, Torre Canne di Fasano

MASSERIA LE FABRICHE
Five minutes from the sandy beaches of the Ionian Sea, this perfectly restored 18th-century *masseria* is surrounded by vineyards. Guests stay down below amid a secluded olive grove in modern, minimalist junior suites.
lefabriche.it; tel +39 099 987 1852; C.da Le Fabbriche, SP130, Maruggio

WHERE TO EAT
L'ORECCHIETTA
Favourite haunt of local *vignaioli*, this creative pasta laboratory serves handmade orecchiette with *polpette* (meatballs) in rich tomato sauce, plus authentic Pugliese specialities such as

ciceri e tria (chickpeas and fried pasta).
lorecchietta.com; tel +39 083 270 5796; Via Vittorio Veneto 49, Guagnano; Tue-Sun

OSTERIA DEL POETA
Alberobella is replete with Puglia's unique *trulli* stone cottages, a must-see. Chef Leonardo Marco's gourmet osteria here is a perfect place for lunch.
osteriadelpoeta.it; tel +39 080 432 1917; Via Indipendenza 25, Alberobella; Jul-Sep daily, Oct-Jun Fri-Wed

RISTORANTE CIELO
Ostuni looks out over a sea of olive trees, some a thousand or more years old. This elegant restaurant features a gourmet reinterpretation of local cuisine by Michelin-starred chef Andrea Cannalire.
lasommita.it; tel +39 083 130 5925; Via Scipione Petrarolo 7, Ostuni; daily

WHAT TO DO
Don't miss exploring the brilliant baroque architecture of Lecce;

its labyrinth of lanes forming a maze of ornate churches and grand palazzi.
visitlecce.eu

CELEBRATIONS
Stretching over two months before and after the Lenten carnival period (February/March), the Carnevale di Putignano is both a sacred and profane celebration, combining religious rites with biting political satire.
carnevalediputignano.it

[Italy]
SICILY

Ancient grape varieties, adventurous winemakers and a myth-shrouded mountain combine to create one of Europe's most exciting wine scenes: Etna.

So, what does a volcano taste like? And who would make wine on the slopes of Europe's tallest active volcano? Those are the kind of questions you'll find yourself asking on this tour around Sicily's Mt Etna.

Shipwrecks show that Sicily has been exporting wine since at least 2 BCE, first in clay amphorae and then in wooden casks; the Greeks and then the Romans made wine on this crossroads of the Mediterranean. Today, a new generation of winemakers has revitalised the vineyards around Mt Etna. They've been attracted by a unique combination of factors: interesting indigenous grape varieties, a well-drained soil rich in minerals coupled with a high-altitude climate, and a wine-making culture based around *contrada* (parcels of land) and *palmenti* (old stone cellars) found only on Sicily.

This trail follows an ancient Roman road (now the SS120) as it curves around the north side of Mt Etna, passing (west to east) through the wine towns of Randazzo, Passopisciaro, Solicchiata and Linguaglossa, then bearing south to finish in the region around Milo that specialises in an unforgettable white wine. The major town in this corner of the island is Taormina, famed for its Greek amphitheatre. But it too is upstaged by the view of Etna: red earth, black rock and a smouldering white peak.

The 3357m-high (11,014ft) volcano is an ever-present companion on this trail. Lava flows from past eruptions leave walls of blackened rock and pumice in many of the vineyards. High above the searing heat of the Sicilian summer, the altitude of Etna's Denominazione di Origine Controllata means that the grapes ripen slowly as they grow. They share the land with olive trees and orchards of almond, hazelnut, walnut, fig, peach and citrus trees. Fresh seafood is landed on the coast. And the food and wines combine to create a local cuisine that tastes out of this world.

GET THERE
The most convenient international airport is Catania, a 1hr drive south. Trains from mainland Italy reach Palermo to the west.

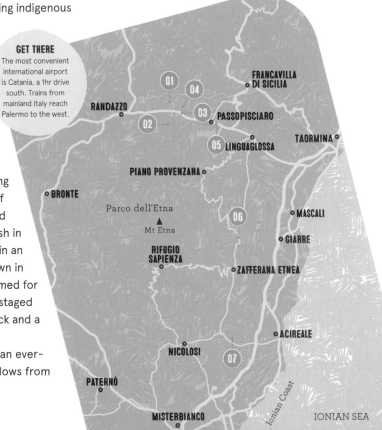

02

01 FATTORIE ROMEO DEL CASTELLO

For a first impression of how close the relationship between the volcano and the vineyards can be on this north slope of Etna, start at Chiara Vigo's organic farm on the outskirts of Randazzo. The vineyard is part of her family's centuries-old Romeo del Castello estate and in 1981, a lava flow destroyed 21 hectares (52 acres) before changing course away from the historic house, leaving a hinterland of blackened rock. After studying at the University of Bologna – she was tutored by Umberto Eco and published a thesis on wine labels – Chiara returned home in 2007 to take responsibility for the family's heritage: 'Wine was always made

here and we now produce three red wines, all from old-growth Nerello Mascalese vines.' Chiara's parcel of land is named Contrada Allegracore (meaning 'happy heart') and she believes in letting the grapes speak for themselves with minimal intervention. 'The soils around Etna come from different eruptions so each parcel produces different wine – that's why Etna wine producers specify the parcel on the bottle.'
romeodelcastello.it; tel +39 095 339 990; Contrada Allegracore, Randazzo; by appointment

02 PLANETA

If Fattorie Romeo del Castello epitomises small-scale Sicilian production, Planeta is an example

of big investment done well. The Italian wine group purchased plots of land in 2008 near Passopisciaro, the epicentre of Etna's wine country. Under the guidance of long-standing head winemaker Patricia Tóth, Planeta has restored old buildings, planted Nerello Mascalese and Carricante vines, nurtured long-lost varieties – the *reliquie* or relics – and developed vineyards such as Sciaranuova. Some terraces were turned into an open-air theatre that is the venue for the annual Sciaranuova arts festival. The new winery and tasting space, sympathetically constructed from lava rock, opened in 2012 in the *contrada* of Feudo di Mezzo. Visitor experiences include a vertical tasting of three wines at

the Sciaranuova *palmento*, plus a visit to the lava flows. *planeta.it; +39 092 5195 5460; Contrada Sciaranuova, Passopisciaro; Mon-Sat by appointment* Ⓢ

03 FRANK CORNELISSEN

'There are many reasons to be attracted to a place,' says Frank Cornelissen. 'The northern valley of Etna has something mystical: the obvious natural beauty but also its energy and contradictions, snowed under in the winter, hot and dry during the summer. We're living in the southern Mediterranean but on the side of a mountain. The result is the incredible elegance and structure of the wines.' Sometimes it takes an outsider

to appreciate a place fully: Frank Cornelissen is regarded as a radical but the Belgian winemaker, who is dedicated to creating the most natural wines possible, is responsible for many of Etna's most interesting wines. He bottles nine of his wines according to the vineyards or *contrada* in which the grapes grew. The Munjebel red from Monte Colla, for example, comes from Nerello Mascelese vines planted in 1946 on a steeply terraced site right before Mt Etna. All Frank's wines are produced without chemical preservatives and using indigenous yeasts. He's very happy to explain his processes and philosophy at his Passopisciaro cellar, after a tour of a vineyard (bookable only by email).

frankcornelissen.it; Via Canonico Zumbo 1, Passpisciaro; by appointment (email ahead: info@frankcornelissen.it) Ⓢ

04 VINI FRANCHETTI

Adventure ran deep in the veins of Vini Franchetti founder Andrea Franchetti, who died in 2021. Ernest Hemingway was a friend of the famed Tuscan Italian family; and after leaving school Andrea cycled and hitched his way to Afghanistan before returning to Italy by way of Manhattan. In 2000, having married his Sicilian girlfriend, and drawn by the drama of Etna's setting, he began to restore an old farm and cellars on its slopes just above the wine town of Passopisciaro. Here he worked

05 Pietradolce's
modern winery

06 Harvest in the
Pietradolce vineyards

mainly with the local Nerello Mascalese variety, which grows at up to 1000m (3280ft) above sea level so the grapes are late to ripen – temperatures here are up to 15°C (59°F) cooler than on the coast and downright chilly at night during September and October before harvest. The estate is now run by his children, and tours usually include a vineyard visit. *vinifranchetti.com; +39 094 239 5449; Contrada Guardiola, Castiglione di Sicilia; by appointment*

05 PIETRADOLCE

Look around the smart winery and tasting room at Pietradolce and you get the sense that the Faro family have long been Etna pioneers. 'My grandfather was a small-scale winemaker,' says owner Michele Faro. 'But we were convinced the territory had enormous potential –

although it was not certain that you were making the right choice!' Pietradolce's ambition is to produce elegant wines representative of the land – look for gentle tannins in the Contrada San Spirito, a Nerello Mascalese with red cherry and raspberry fruit, quite like a Pinot Noir from Burgundy. Old, pre-phylloxera vines are cultivated in wild, terraced vineyards in the local 'bush' or *alberello* method, surrounded by butterflies and flowers. 'The grapes are fermented, for the most part, in raw cement vats that recall the old traditional fermentation vats but with modern methods of temperature control. So tradition and innovation come together. We are really happy with the result.' *pietradolce.it; +39 344 064 0839; Contrada Rampante, Solicchiata; by appointment*

06 BARONE DI VILLAGRANDE

As you travel around Etna clockwise, Sicily's signature white wine, made from the local Carricante grape, comes to the fore. Etna's east side, notably cooler and cloudier, is where Carricante flourishes. For 10 generations the Nicolosi family – Sicilian nobility since the King of Naples made Don Carmelo a baron – has grown grapes in the vineyards of the Bosco Etnea region among their oak and chestnut forests. The

winery is well established for visits (there's a wine resort and hotel), and a guided tasting gives the lowdown on this unique wine: it's a savoury, almost saline experience, with aromas of white fruits, almonds and a fresh minerality that makes it a perfect match for seafood and cheese; low alcohol levels also make it an especially sociable wine – a good comparison would be the Albariño wines from Rias Baixas in Spain (p.233). *villagrande.it; +39 095 708 2175; Via del Bosco 25, Milo; by appointment Mon-Sun* 💲✕

07 BENANTI

Finish your tour of Etna at Benanti, one of the original new-wave wineries that inspired local gurus like Salvo Foti and Alberto Graci. The estate was revitalised in 1988 when Guiseppe Benanti decided to take winemaking seriously again, after the vineyards had languished for decades. It's based in Milo, the heart of Carricante country, and is now run by twin sons Salvino and Antonio. Benanti's benchmark white wine is the zesty Pietra Marina, made from Carricante and aged for three years (and will age well). Look for mineral lemon fruit in this Sicilian classic. Tastings are paired with locally sourced bites. *benanti.it; +39 095 789 0928; Via Guiseppe Garibaldi, 361, Viagrande; by appointment* 💲

WHERE TO STAY

HOTEL FEUDO VAGLIASINDI

Converted from a large *palmento* just outside Randazzo, this art nouveau manor house is drenched in wine history, with original barrels from the 19th century still lined up in the cool cellars. Olive trees and Nerello Mascalese vines are cultivated around the manor and fresh, local produce, including the hotel's own olive oil, is used in the kitchen. Lots of volcano-oriented activities, including bike and horseback rides, canyoning and 4WD tours are available.
feudovagliasindi.it; tel +39 095 799 1823; Contrada Feudo Sant'Anastasia, Strada Provinciale 89, Randazzo

SHALAI

After a day trekking round the wineries, retreat to this luxe boutique hotel, with 13 minimalist and contemporary rooms, all crisp white linen, flowing drapes and designer lighting, as well as a stucco-adorned 19th-century lounge, candlelit spa and a Michelin-starred fine-dining restaurant.
shalai.it; +39 095 643 128; Via Marconi 25, Linguaglossa

WHERE TO EAT

CAVE OX

Entering Cave Ox in Solicchiata is like finding a back door to Etna's wine scene, particularly the natural wine movement. Owner Sandro Dibella is a friend of Frank Cornelissen and they share an interest in traditional Etna winemaking methods. Lots of other local winemakers are also regular visitors, bringing along their latest releases to share. Pizza is served indoors or outside in a garden and is accompanied by an epic wine list.
caveox.it; tel +39 094 298 6171; Via Nazionale, 159, Solicchiata; Wed-Mon

WHAT TO DO

FERROVIA CIRCUMETNEA

This narrow-gauge railway, dating from 1888, runs around the perimeter of Etna, with a section forming part of Catania's Metro. If you depart Randazzo and head clockwise towards Riposto you'll pass through Etna's prime vineyards, lava fields and lemon groves. You can hop on and off at wine villages (six departures daily, Mon-Sat).
circumetnea.it

ETNA WINE LAB

Freestyle Sicilian driving can be rather challenging: a guided tour can allow you to focus on the wine and let someone else deal with the driving. Etna Wine Lab offers a range of experiences taking in the region's food and wine, meeting producers along the way.
etnawinelab.it

CELEBRATIONS

Part-tasting, part-party, the Contrade dell'Etna was first held in 2008 at the instigation of the late Andrea Franchetti and a few dozen local producers and friends; now the guest list spans a couple of thousand people and includes sommeliers and wine fans from around the world, drawn by the opportunity to taste wine from 100-odd Etna producers – and to have a good time.
lecontradedelletna.com

[Lebanon]
BATROUN VALLEY

Terraced vineyards and olive groves are scattered across the hills in this emerging wine region overlooking Lebanon's Mediterranean coast.

Most wine lovers have heard of the Bekaa Valley, but few outside Lebanon are familiar with that country's other major wine-growing area, the hilly hinterland behind the ancient port city of Batroun on the Mediterranean coast. Here, the terrain is scattered with stones, gnarled olive trees and drifts of wildflowers. Maronite monasteries are hidden among stands of oak trees, and village houses cluster around simple whitewashed churches.

It's an ancient and spectacularly beautiful landscape where the copious sunlight, cooling sea breezes and well-drained soil (a mixture of clay, sand and limestone) provide perfect conditions for growing premium grapes. Over the past two decades, a number of boutique producers have established vineyards, built wineries and produced vintages that are becoming more complex and impressive by the year. Cabernet Sauvignon and Syrah grapes do particularly

GET THERE
Beirut-Rafic Hariri is the nearest major airport, 63km (39 miles) from Batroun. Car hire is available.

well, and most vineyards focus on red varietals, with secondary plantings of Chardonnay, Riesling and other white grapes. Almost all the wineries have embraced organic growing methods and hand-harvest grapes. Only 56km (35 miles) from central Beirut, Batroun is easily accessed via the main coastal highway. Heading inland, it's possible to follow an itinerary known as La Route des Vins du Nord (Northern Wine Route), which wends its way uphill from Batroun through this picture-postcard landscape, passing terraced vineyards and hidden hamlets aplenty. As well as the wineries mentioned, the Monastery of Kfifane, part of the Adyar cooperative (adyar.org.lb), welcomes visitors by appointment. The first all-organic winery in Lebanon, Adyar grows grapes at eight Maronite monasteries across the country. Its best-regarded wines include the Monastère De Mar Moussa and Monastère De Annaya.

Courtesy of Ixsir

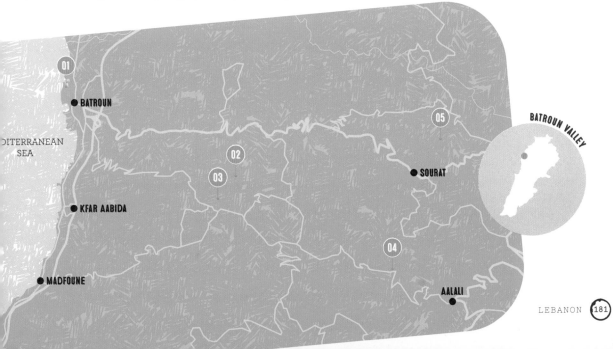

01 BATROUN MOUNTAINS

'I believe that a quality bottle
of wine is made in the vineyard
and not in the winery,' says Assaad
Hark, the winemaker and driving
force behind this family-run
business in Batroun. California-
trained, Assaad sources his
organically certified grapes from
narrow terraced vineyards in
six local villages overlooking the
Mediterranean Sea. These vineyards
were designed to maximise sun
exposure and this, along with
the dry, well-drained and stony
local soil, contributes to fruit of
intense colour and flavour, across
the 12 styles of wine that Batroun
Mountains produces.
batrounmountains.wine;
tel +961 34-84863; Rawabi Ave,
Batroun; by reservation 10am-
5pm daily 💲

02 IXSIR

There's been a buzz around this
company since its establishment
in 2008, and a visit to its winery
in Basbina helps to explain why.
Spanish-born, French-trained
winemaker Gabriel Rivero is
producing impressive wines here
using grapes sourced from vineyards
in six mountainous Lebanese regions,
and the guided tour and tasting is
a great introduction to his art. (You
can also take a free self-guided tour.)

The focal point of the estate is
a handsome 17th-century stone
house that now hosts a restaurant.
But most of the action occurs in
the state-of-the-art underground
winery, which was designed by
Raëd Abillama Architects and has
been recognised internationally for
its sustainable design. Over lunch at
the restaurant, consider sampling
the estate's highly regarded EL
IXSIR Red – a blend of Cabernet
Sauvignon, Syrah and Merlot. The
grapes for this are sourced from a
vineyard at an elevation of 1800m
(5900ft), one of the highest in the
northern hemisphere.
ixsir.com; tel +961 71-631613;
Basbina; by reservation 10am-4pm
Tue-Sun, to 6pm summer 💲 🍴

03 COTEAUX DE BOTRYS

Though the Lebanese have been
making wine for millennia, most of
the major producers are relatively
new to the business. Not so Neila
al-Bitar, whose family first settled
in the wildflower-carpeted hills
above Batroun in 1760 and started
to distil arak. This tradition turned
into a business in 1992, when Neila's
father, retired general Joseph al-
Bitar, decided to produce the fiery

aniseed spirit commercially. Wine production followed, with 5000 vines planted in 1998 and the first vintages appearing in 2002; the estate produces six styles of wine. *coteauxdebotrys.com; tel +961 32-38937; Main Rd, Eddé; by reservation Sat & Sun*

04 DOMAINE S.NAJM

Owned and operated by husband-and-wife team Salim and Hiba Najm, this small estate in the mountain village of Chabtine produces one wine (a blend of Cabernet Sauvignon, Grenache and Mourvèdre), an arak and a cold-pressed extra-virgin olive oil produced from the fruit of 200-year-old trees. Salim's training as an agricultural engineer and Hiba's as an oenologist (she studied in Bordeaux) make them a great team. *bit.ly/SNajm; tel +961 70-623023; Chabtine; by reservation*

05 AURORA VIN DE MONTAGNE

Spectacularly sited among a forest of oak and olive trees overlooking the Mediterranean, this family-run vineyard is one of two recognisable landmarks in the village of Rachkidde – the other is the 19th-century Maronite Church of Saints Sergius and Bacchus. Owner and self-taught winemaker Dr Fady Geara produces the Chateau, a blend of Merlot and Cabernet Sauvignon, as well as a Pinot Noir, a Chardonnay, a Sauvignon Blanc and red and rosé Cabernet Francs. All can be tasted during the weekend openings. *aurorawinery.com; tel +961 71-632620; Rachkidde; by reservation 12.30-4.30 Sat & Sun*

01 The stone house at Ixsir

02 Winemaking at Batroun Mountains is a family affair

WHERE TO STAY

L'AUBERGE DE LA MER
Tucked between two historic churches, this swish boutique hotel in a 19th-century stone building offers elegantly presented rooms, a rooftop jacuzzi and wonderful sea views. *laubergedelamer.com; tel +961 67-40824; Harbour, Batroun*

BYBLOS SUR MER
Overlooking the harbour of ancient Byblos, 17km (10 miles) south of Batroun, this classy hotel is a popular weekend getaway for Beirutis. Rooms are spacious, there's a seafront pool and the in-house restaurant features a glass floor floating above excavated ancient ruins. *byblossurmer.com; tel +961 95-48000; Rue du Port, Byblos*

WHERE TO EAT

CHEZ MAGUY
Head to this ramshackle fishers' shack near Batroun's Phoenician sea wall to enjoy fish so fresh it's almost writhing. The sea-facing terrace is an idyllic setting on warm evenings. *Tel +961 34-39147; Batroun; daily*

COLONEL BREWERY & DISTILLERY
Excellent craft brewery with tasty ales on tap, plus an attractive indoor space, outdoor deck and garden for drinking them. Identify your favourite beer via tasting flights; good bar food, too. *bit.ly/ColBD; tel +961 37-43543; Sea Side Rd, Batroun; daily*

WHAT TO DO

Once important trading ports, the ancient towns of Byblos and Batroun have retained significant traces of their Phoenician, Greek, Roman, Crusader and Ottoman heritage, and are well worth a visit to see their many sights.

CELEBRATIONS

Events are staged throughout the year celebrating Lebanese wine, such as June's three-day Blanc et Rosé in Byblos, and Batroun's two-day Beer, Wine & Seafood Festival. For more on what's on, check the Lebtivity listings pages. *lebtivity.com*

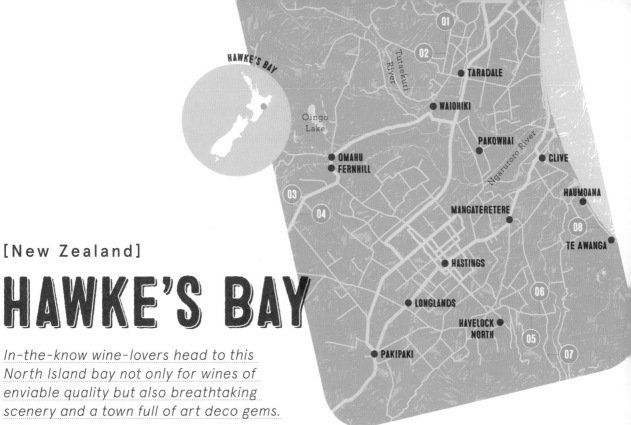

[New Zealand]

HAWKE'S BAY

In-the-know wine-lovers head to this North Island bay not only for wines of enviable quality but also breathtaking scenery and a town full of art deco gems.

Known as the 'fruit bowl of New Zealand', Hawke's Bay is a patchwork of orchards, vegetable gardens and vineyards, with pastures in between. Alongside such delectable largesse is a raft of attractions ranging from art-deco architecture, farmers markets and a sophisticated dining scene to surf beaches and cycle trails. And as well as being the country's second-largest wine region it's also the oldest, dating back to 1851 when Marist missionaries planted the first vines between Napier and Hastings.

While Hawke's Bay lacks a signature varietal such as Marlborough's Sauvignon Blanc or Central Otago's Pinot Noir, it grows a whole bunch of grapes very well. Warm, sunny conditions swiftly ripen fruit from highly varied soils throughout diverse sub-regions such as the Bridge Pa Triangle on the Heretaunga Plains and the cooler Esk Valley or coastal Te Awanga.

The most famous sub-region is the Gimblett Gravels, laid down by Ngaruroro River as it changed course over the ages. Once considered a barren wasteland, the first vines were planted here in 1981, but it

wasn't until the early '90s – when plans for a quarry were quashed – that winemaking in the Gravels really gathered momentum.

Full-bodied reds rule the roost across the bay, particularly the vast plantings of Merlot and Cabernet Sauvignon that lend the region its 'Bordeaux of New Zealand' moniker. Syrah is also produced in significant volume. The dense, peppery profile of this cooler-climate, Rhône-style red accounts for the locals' tactical move to eschew the name 'Shiraz', thus distinguishing it from the vibrant, jammy Aussie versions. Chardonnay is another leader, nosing its way through a respectable field of contenders – Pinot Gris, Gewürztraminer and Pinot Noir to name but a few. Like most other New Zealand wine-growing areas, however, experimentation is rife.

The abundance, quality and diversity of Hawke's Bay wines makes for enjoyable touring, amplified by the volume of restaurants, cafes and artisanal food producers all sandwiched together, with splendid scenery and the option of cruising around by bicycle.

GET THERE
Hawke's Bay has flights from Auckland, Wellington and Christchurch. By car it's about 3.5hr from Wellington; 1.5hr from Taupo and 2hr from Gisborne.

01 MISSION ESTATE

At the end of a tree-lined avenue, Mission Estate's centrepiece is the beautifully preserved seminary – La Grande Maison – built in 1880. Daily tours illuminate Mission's story and key chapters in the region's history (including a devastating 1931 earthquake), and foreground the wines available for tasting. Visitors can also sit down to a refined lunch in the seminary's formal front rooms, or out on the sunny terrace.

Made to 'gladden the human heart', originally by French Marist missionaries, Mission's wines have been tended by Paul Mooney for the last 30-odd years. The range features six tiers from the great-value Mission Estate wines through to the classy Jewelstone and Huchet drops made from Mission's most blessed grapes.

Hallmark Hawke's Bay exemplars include toasty Chardonnays from vines grown on-site, and Bordeaux-style reds and Syrah borne from the coveted Gimblett Gravels. A tasting at Mission, however, may also include aromatic Riesling, Pinot Gris and Gewürztraminer, an intense Marlborough Sauvignon Blanc or savoury Martinborough Pinot Noir. *missionestate.co.nz; tel +64 6-845 9353; 198 Church Rd, Taradale; 9am-5pm Mon-Sat, 10am-4.30pm Sun* 🛇 ✗

02 CHURCH ROAD

Red wines flowed from this site on Church Rd for most of the 20th century, but it took a new winemaking team to revive the winery in the '90s, setting its sights on creating reds in the Bordeaux style using fruit from Hawke's Bay.

Today, Chardonnay is the signature wine of talented winemaker Chris Scott, who has also won awards for his Syrah and blended reds. Locally sourced meals paired with estate wines are on offer in the restaurant, and the cellar door features a trio of tutored tastings and a range of wines for sale including old vintages and experimental labels only available here. Hot tip: try Church Road's big, juicy red made from the Italian grape Marzemino. *church-road.co.nz; tel +64 6-882 3098; 150 Church Rd, Taradale, Napier; 11.30am-4.30pm, tastings by reservation* 🛇 ✗

From top left: courtesy of Craggy Range (2); Elephant Hill | Brian Culy; Te Mata | Foto Grau

Iberian influences surface in a sturdy fruit-driven Tempranillo, and Touriga Nacional port-style wine.

Located in the thick of cellar door territory in the countryside west of Hastings, Trinity Hill is not to be missed. Their high-ceilinged, concrete-slab tasting room is spacious, with local-produce platters available.
trinityhill.com; tel +64 6-879 7778; 2396 State Hwy 50, Hastings; daily 🏷️✖️

varieties to shine include a fruity Pinot Gris, something winemaker Grant Edmonds thinks 'Hawke's Bay does a bloody good job of', and distinct Pinot Noirs from their cooler Plateau and Parkhill vineyards. Keep an eye out for the EV wines that flow from the best vintages. Visitors can join a winery tour, run twice daily in summer months.
sileni.co.nz; tel +64 6 879 4830; 2016 Maraekakaho Rd, Hastings; 10am-5pm Wed-Sun✖️

03 TRINITY HILL

John Hancock, former winemaker and co-owner of Trinity Hill, was an early pioneer and co-founder of the Gimblett Gravels Winegrowers Association. His impressive output helped elevate the Gravels' reputation as the Bay's premier winegrowing district, particularly well-suited to full-bodied reds.

Trinity Hill's current winemaker Warren Gibson produces a Rhône-rivalling Syrah, the Homage, made only in superlative years and ranked among New Zealand's greatest reds. Other varietals include exemplary Chardonnay and Merlot, as well as unusual and experimental varieties including a delicate Arneis and richly textured Marsanne/Viognier blend, both excellent with food.

04 SILENI

When a winery is named after Silenus, the most debauched, drunken and yet wisest of the Greek wine god Dionysus' followers, you get an inkling that there's fun to be had, here at one of the Bay's largest wineries. Sileni lives up to the name by offering one of the region's most enjoyable wine tastings, often hosted by ebullient cellar-door manager, Anne Boustead. The pomp-free flight through their wines is injected with fascinating facts and a measure of good humour. There's plenty to talk about. From its dramatic (and somewhat sci-fi) HQ secreted in the foothills of the Bridge Pa Triangle, Sileni produces consummate examples of Syrah and Chardonnay. Other

05 BLACK BARN

Black Barn has all sorts of ways to lure in the passing visitor: a stylish cellar door, a growers' market held beneath the trees on summertime Saturday mornings, a kitchen store crammed full of only-local produce, an outdoor concert venue and – for those who really want to make the most of all this bounty – luxurious cottages and retreats to rent.

The vineyard accompanying this mini-empire is decidedly boutique, with all wines estate-grown and many sold only through the cellar door. There's a good cross section of well-made varietal wines available to taste: barrel-fermented Chardonnay 'sur lie' (kept in contact with the residual yeast) is a favourite. Pick a nice day and enjoy

06 The oceanside
Elephant Hill

07 The cellar door
at Trinity Hill

savoured with something gamey in the excellent Terrôir restaurant. A treasure trove of other hen's teeth Craggy Range vintages can be found in its formidable wine list.
craggyrange.com; tel +64 6-873 0141; 253 Waimarama Rd, Havelock North; 10am-6pm daily Nov-Mar, 11am-5pm Wed-Sun Apr-Oct ⑤ ✕

a heavenly lunch under the vines at the Black Barn Bistro.
blackbarn.com; tel +64 6-877 7985; Black Barn Rd, Havelock North; 9am-5pm Mon-Fri, 10am-4pm Sat-Sun & by appointment ⑤ ✕

06 TE MATA

Te Mata is the country's oldest winery, with wines still being made in the original 1896 buildings and the vineyards recognised as important national heritage sites.

Best known for Coleraine, the country's most iconic and internationally respected red wine, Te Mata also makes a string of other stylish wines. No visit is complete without trying the peppery, Rhône-like Bullnose Syrah; rich, complex Zara Viognier; suave and sophisticated Elston Chardonnay; or the deliciously fruity Gamay Noir.
temata.co.nz; tel +64 6-877 4399; 349 Te Mata Rd, Havelock North; Oct-Apr 10am-5pm Mon-Sat, 11am-4pm Sun; May-Sep 10am-5pm Wed-Sat ⑤

07 CRAGGY RANGE

In a sublime setting alongside the Tukituki River, at the foot of Te Mata Peak – the Bay's chief landmark – Craggy Range is worth visiting for the journey alone. Add in a modernistic collection of buildings housing the cellar door, restaurant and upscale accommodation, and pour in some of New Zealand's finest drops, and you've got yourself a wine-tour stop that's hard to beat.

After a serendipitous meeting between Craggy Range founder Terry Peabody and Master of Wine Steve Smith in 1997, the pair set out to create 'single-vineyard New World classics' from various New Zealand wine regions including Martinborough, Marlborough and Central Otago, where they own their own vines.

Quality is certainly high across the board, but it's Craggy's top-flight range where memories are made. Well-heeled wine-lovers may wish to indulge in a bottle of Le Sol Syrah, a dense and luscious drop from the Gimblett Gravels best

08 ELEPHANT HILL

Contrasting starkly with the rustic charm of other wineries, Elephant Hill is a striking, monolithic form clad in patinated copper and fronted with epic windows offering unobstructed views of Cape Kidnappers and the Pacific Ocean.

Elephant Hill's German owners fell for Te Awanga while on holiday. With the goal of creating a state-of-the-art winery marrying traditional and contemporary styles and techniques, they planted their first grapes in 2003 and set to it. The results are impressive: their Reserve Chardonnay displays a lovely fruit purity and depth typical of Te Awanga terroir, and their reds blend local and Gimblett Gravels' characters.

The circular tasting bar is an enticing introduction to the restaurant, a classy affair complete with a white-leather sunken lounge, sundeck and infinity pool.
elephanthill.co.nz; tel +64 6-872 6060; 86 Clifton Rd, Te Awanga; Thu-Sun 11am-5pm ⑤ ✕

WHERE TO STAY
CLIVE COLONIAL COTTAGES
These courtyard cottages sit prettily amid gardens in a serene spot near the beach. Pick up the cycle trail alongside to ride around the vines. *clivecolonial cottages. co.nz; tel +64 6-870 1018; 198 School Rd, Clive*

MILLAR ROAD
Set in the Tuki Tuki Hills with vineyards and bay views, Millar Road is architecturally heaven-sent. Two plush villas (each sleep four) and a super-stylish house (sleeps eight) are filled with NZ-made furniture and local art. Explore the vast grounds or look cool by the pool. *millarroad.co.nz; tel +64 6-875 1977; 83 Millar Rd, Hastings*

WHERE TO EAT
HAWKE'S BAY FARMERS MARKET
If you're around on a Sunday morning (8.30am-12.30pm), don't miss one of New Zealand's best markets, a lively affair set in bucolic showgrounds and bursting with produce, coffee and gourmet picnic supplies. *hawkesbay farmersmarket.co.nz; Tomoiana Showgrounds, Kenilworth Rd, Hastings*

MISTER D
With something for everyone morning, noon and night, Napier's hottest dining ticket sets a hip and stylish standard with food from cinnamon doughnuts to bone-marrow ravioli. *misterd.co.nz; tel +64 6-835 5022; 47 Tennyson St, Napier; Wed-Sun*

WHAT TO DO
ART DECO NAPIER
Don your walking

shoes or hop on a bike to admire Napier's internationally acclaimed collection of art deco buildings, which emerged in the aftermath of the devastating 1931 Hawke's Bay earthquake. This fascinating chapter in the Bay's history is well told at the Art Deco Trust visitor centre, a good place to start your tour. *artdeconapier.com; tel +64 6-835 0022; 7 Tennyson St, Napier*

TE MATA TRUST PARK
Te Mata Peak (399m), part of the Te Mata Trust Park, rises dramatically from the Heretaunga Plains 16km (10 miles) south of Havelock North. The summit road passes sheep trails, rickety fences and vertigo-inducing stone escarpments, veiled in a bleak, lunar-meets-Scottish-Highlands atmosphere. On a clear day, views from the lookout fall away to Hawke Bay, Mahia Peninsula and distant Mt Ruapehu. The park's 30km (19 miles) of trails offer walks ranging from 30 minutes to two hours: pick up the Te Mata Park's Top 5 Walking Tracks brochure from local i-SITEs. *tematapark.co.nz; tel +64 6-873 0080; off Te Mata Rd, Havelock North*

CELEBRATIONS
The bay's major festival is the annual Art Deco Weekend in February, a 200-event extravaganza of art deco architecture, art, music and Gatsby-esque costumes. Epicures might like to coincide their visit with the Hawke's Bay's Food and Wine Classic (FAWC), a series of appetising events held in June and November. *artdeconapier.com; fawc.co.nz*

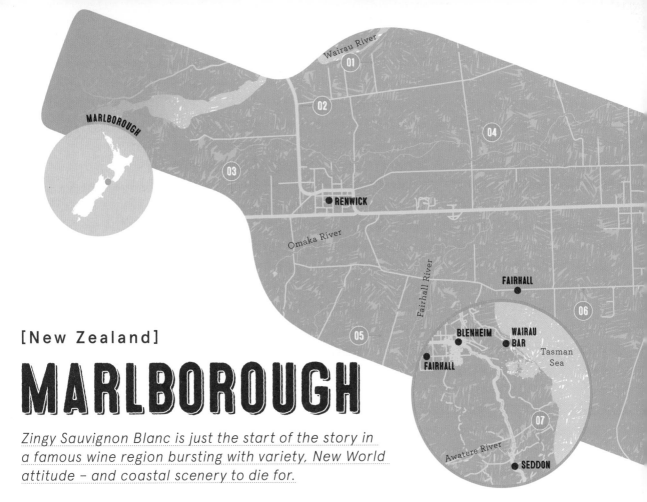

[New Zealand]

MARLBOROUGH

Zingy Sauvignon Blanc is just the start of the story in a famous wine region bursting with variety, New World attitude – and coastal scenery to die for.

Marlborough is a *vinous colossus*, accounting for around three-quarters of New Zealand's wine. At last count there were nearly 600 growers tending 23,000 hectares of grapes, working their way into the wines of 158 producers. Remarkably, it has taken just 40-odd years for the Marlborough region to grow from first vines into the billion-dollar industry it is today.

So that's why you've probably heard of Marlborough Sauvignon Blanc: this New World classic is pungently aromatic, fruity and herbaceous, a dominant varietal that has stormed the global wine scene. Indeed, the ubiquity of big brands flooding supermarkets worldwide has led to accusations that Marlborough 'sav' has become predictable – even one-dimensional – but the region produces plenty that is exciting and distinct.

The majority of vineyards line up around Renwick in the Wairau Valley, although side-valleys and coastal fringes have been colonised in response to the demand for land. While growing conditions throughout are generally sunny and dry, the soil is a veritable kaleidoscope of glacial stone, shingle, sand and silt, shifted and settled by river flows. The result is a highly varied terroir.

To home in on memorable Sauvignon Blanc, set your sights on smaller, independent wineries. They are more likely to offer tastings of single-estate wines, not just of Sauvignon Blanc but also of Marlborough's other notable varietals such as Pinot Noir and Riesling.

With lots of accommodation in its rural surrounds, just 10km (6 miles) from Blenheim, Renwick makes a good base for wine touring. More than 20 of the region's 35 or so cellar doors can be found around here, along with bicycle hire, guided tours and shuttle services.

GET THERE
Auckland is the nearest major airport, with connecting flights to Marlborough, 7km (4 miles) from Rapaura. Or cruise up the Marlborough Sounds.

(02)

01 HANS HERZOG ESTATE

Hans and Therese Herzog left behind, respectively, their winery in Switzerland and Michelin-starred restaurant to start anew in Marlborough. The result? Seriously good Kiwi wines with a distinctly European flavour from 29 different grape varieties, some in achingly small quantities, all estate-grown and made. The limited edition Nebbiolo and seriously concentrated Montepulciano wouldn't look out of place alongside the best Italian examples of both varieties. And while the cuvée Therese rosé sparkling might not fool you into thinking it's Champagne, it is still delicious.

They offer a choice of wine tastings and a 30-minute winery tour; platters of charcuterie or cheese are available, but the renowned bistro and restaurant have sadly closed post-pandemic. *herzog.co.nz; +64 3-572 8770; 81 Jeffries Rd, Marlborough; 9am-5pm Mon-Fri, Sat & Sun by reservation* 💲

02 NAUTILUS ESTATE

Nautilus wines are typically pure and ethereal, showing a clear expression of place but also packing a punch. So determined was the team to make great Pinot Noir that they built a separate, dedicated gravity-flow winery – the results speak for themselves. Elegant Chardonnay; seductively fruity Pinot Noir; taut, restrained Sauvignon Blanc; and a complex, yeasty bottle-fermented sparkling wine which has won many well-deserved accolades – Nautilus sweeps the board.

Taste the wines at the cellar door or book in advance to tour the winery with a Nautilus winemaker. *nautilusestate.com; tel +64 3-572 6008; 12 Rapaura Rd, Renwick; 10am-4.30pm daily* 💲✖

03 SERESIN ESTATE

Founded in 1992 by successful cinematographer Michael Seresin, who describes the estate as 'a New World winery with an Old World philosophy', Seresin is farmed biodynamically and organically and encompasses olive groves, orchards and vegetable plots as well as vineyards.

To home in on memorable Sauvignon Blanc, set your sights on smaller, independent wineries more likely to offer tastings of single-estate wines

The flagship Sun & Moon heads a list of six Pinot Noir labels, including the entry-level Leah Pinot Noir. A highlight of the two Sauvignon Blanc labels is the wild-fermented Marama; a sleek Chardonnay, spicy Pinot Gris and dry Riesling are also excellent. *seresin.co.nz; tel +64 3-572 9408; 85 Bedford Rd, Blenheim; 10am-4.30pm daily* Ⓢ

04 CLOUDY BAY
Visiting Marlborough without stopping at Cloudy Bay is like going to Agra without taking in the Taj Mahal. One of the region's pioneering winemakers, Cloudy Bay helped put New Zealand wine on the world map, particularly with its Sauvignon Blanc, which remains something of an international icon. Less well-known but even more delicious is its elegant and complex Chardonnay and plump, fruity Te Wahi Pinot Noir, the latter from Central Otago where Cloudy Bay has now purchased vineyards and a winery.

In summer, Jack's Raw Bar offers an exciting menu of fresh, local (mostly raw) produce that demands to be enjoyed alfresco. *cloudybay.co.nz; tel +64 3-520 9147; 230 Jacksons Rd, Blenheim; 10am-4pm daily* Ⓢ ✗

05 FRAMINGHAM
Marlborough may be best known for its Sauvignon Blanc, but Framingham is doing a stellar job of producing world-class Riesling

Ø5 Looking towards
Wither Hills

Ø6 Marlborough
Vintners Hotel

Ø7 YEALANDS FAMILY WINES

Yealands lies on the edge of the wine region, 31km (19 miles) southeast of Blenheim, but it's an easy trip for those driving to or from Kaikoura. Blanketing 1000 hilly hectares (2471 acres) in the Awatere Valley, it's the country's largest privately owned vineyard.

Yet despite its size, Yealands keeps its eyes on the prize – environmentally sustainable winemaking, a carbon-zero footprint and total self-sufficiency. These efforts are evident on the enjoyable self-drive tour that loops through Seaview vineyard, passing picnic spots, windmills, wetlands and compost piles along the way. There's also the odd peacock, sheep, chicken or duck. (The kunekune pigs have been banished from the vine terraces after they piggybacked one another to chomp the grapes.)

The corporate but casual cellar door experience is best started with the short film relaying the colourful Yealands backstory. As for tasting, while the winery is known for an abundance of super-value drops, there are plenty of delightful single-vineyard wines and Reserves. Its S1 Block Sauvignon Blanc is a winner, while relative newcomers Grüner Veltliner and aromatic blend PGR are making waves.

yealands.co.nz; tel +64 3-575 7618; cnr Seaview and Reserve Rds, Seddon, Blenheim; 10am-4.30pm daily 🟢 ✕

wines, described by Wine Trails writer Bob Campbell as 'ravishing'. The winery was founded in 1981 by engineer Rex Brooke-Taylor, from Framingham in Norfolk, England, and adheres to sustainable principles. Its cellar door is reached via a courtyard fragrant with flowers and the intoxicating scents continue inside once a bottle of Riesling is opened: lime, apricot, orange blossom. The winemaking team is led by Andrew Brown and viticulturist James Bowskill, who can also be seen playing bass in the winery's Underground creative arts venue, which hosts gigs and art exhibitions.

framingham.co.nz; tel +64 3 572 8884; 19 Conders Bend Rd, Renwick; 10.30am-4pm daily

Ø6 WITHER HILLS

This modern, midsized winery, nestled in among vineyards bordering the Wither Hills, incorporates a stylish restaurant and a full menu of wine-tasting experiences, from a straightforward guided session to the chance to experiment with your own blends.

Wither Hills own vineyards across Marlborough and produce benchmark examples of the region's high-performing grape varieties. The single-estate Sauvignon Blanc from the coastal Rarangi vineyard is one of Marlborough's more concentrated examples, while the sophisticated Pinot Noir from the Taylor River vineyard offers outstanding value for money.

Wither Hills takes sustainability seriously, having established the Rarangi Wetlands Conservation Project in their Rarangi vineyard to create biological diversity and help protect rare flora.

witherhills.co.nz; tel +64 3-520 8284; 211 New Renwick Rd, Blenheim; 10am-4.30pm daily 🟢 ✕

WHERE TO STAY

OLDE MILL HOUSE

On an elevated section in otherwise flat Renwick, this charming old house is a treat. Dyed-in-the-wool local hosts run a welcoming B&B, with stately decor, and home-grown fruit and homemade goodies for breakfast. Lovely gardens, hot tub and free bikes make this a tip-top base for exploring wine country. *oldemillhouse.co.nz; tel +64 3-572 8458; 9 Wilson St, Renwick*

MARLBOROUGH VINTNERS HOTEL

These smart suites make the most of panoramic, vine-lined Wairau Valley views. Opt for the Outdoor Bath suite to survey Marlborough's night skies while having a soak. The stylish reception building has a bar and restaurant opening out to a cherry orchard and organic veggie garden. *mvh.co.nz; tel +64 3-572 5094; 190 Rapaura Rd, Renwick*

VINTNERS RETREAT

These smart apartments make the most of the Wairau Valley setting. Each is self-contained, with kitchen and living room, and some have vine views from the patio; there's a pool and tennis courts on site. *vintnersretreat.co.nz; tel +64 3-572 7420; 55 Rapaura Rd, Renwick*

WHERE TO EAT

ROCK FERRY

This stylish cafe is a popular lunchtime spot for seasonal fare and stupendous sweet treats matched with Rock Ferry's own organic wines. *rockferry.co.nz; tel +64 3-579 6421; 130 Hammerichs Rd, Blenheim; Wed-Sun*

GRAMADO'S

Injecting a little Latin American flair into the Blenheim dining scene, Gramado's is a fun place to tuck into hearty meals such as lamb *assado*, *feijoada* (smoky pork and bean stew) and Brazilian-spiced fish. Kick things off with a caipirinha. *gramadosrestaurant. com; tel +64 3-579 1192; 74 Main St, Blenheim; Tue-Sat*

WHAT TO DO

OMAKA AVIATION HERITAGE CENTRE

Original and replica WWI aircraft are brought to life at this brilliant museum abetted by Peter Jackson's Wingnut Films and Weta Workshop. A new wing houses

Dangerous Skies, a WW2 collection. Survey the Wairau Valley from a vintage biplane flight. A cafe and shop are on site and next door is Omaka Classic Cars, with more than 100 vehicles from the '50s to the '80s. *omaka.org.nz; 79 Aerodrome Rd, Blenheim; 9am-5pm Dec-Mar, 10am-4pm Apr-Nov*

MARLBOROUGH FARMERS MARKET

Come rain, hail or shine, this market is open every Sunday (9am-12pm), and Thursday 2pm to 5pm at the A&P Showgrounds at the corner of Blenheim's Alabama and Maxwell Rd. *marlborough farmersmarket.org.nz*

CELEBRATIONS

New Zealand's largest and longest-running wine and food festival is held in Renwick each February. Watch a band, take in a cooking demo or just chill out on the grass enjoying the sun. *marlborough winefestival.co.nz*

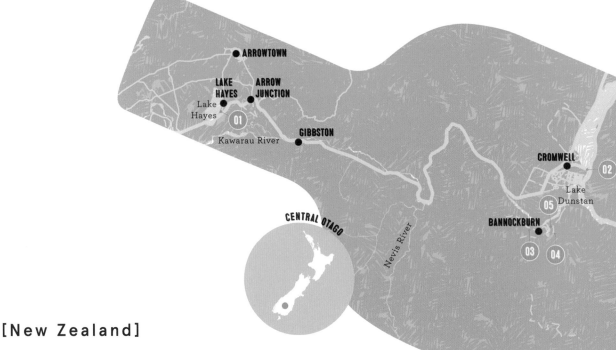

On the map: ARROWTOWN, LAKE HAYES, ARROW JUNCTION, Lake Hayes, 01, Kawarau River, GIBBSTON, CENTRAL OTAGO, Nevis River, CROMWELL, 02, Lake Dunstan, 05, BANNOCKBURN, 03, 04

[New Zealand]

CENTRAL OTAGO

New Zealand's most beautiful wine region has the country's only continental climate, with hot summer days and cool nights that ripen Pinot Noir to perfection.

Central Otago is the pin-up of New Zealand tourism, famed for sublime alpine scenery and the resort town of Queenstown. Vaunted for adrenalised pursuits such as skiing, hiking and biking, it's also the setting for some world-class winemaking.

The region's wild landscapes make up the world's southernmost wine region and New Zealand's highest, ranging between 200m and 450m (650ft and 1500ft) above sea level. Vineyards are spread through the deep valleys and basins of six subregions – Gibbston, Bannockburn, Cromwell Basin, Wanaka, Bendigo and Alexandra. In all, Central Otago boasts some 6% of the country's grape-growing area (although its wine output is less than 3%).

The few vines planted back in 1864 were an early forerunner of an industry that has burgeoned since the mid-1990s. The scene remains largely in the hands of friendly boutique enterprises, with winemakers experimenting with a terroir not yet fully understood. Soils are predominantly glacial, with a high mineral content, while various microclimates share a common theme of hot days, cold nights and low rainfall. These conditions have proven excellent for aromatics, particularly Riesling and Pinot Gris, but the hero is Pinot Noir, which accounts for more than 75% of the region's plantings. Indeed, Central Otago is lauded as one of the best places outside of Burgundy for cultivating this notoriously fickle grape.

With some 30 wineries regularly open to visitors, and many more by appointment only, it would take a good two days' touring to get a comprehensive taste of the terroir. One focus could be on the Gibbston Valley (with cycle touring a possibility), but a much broader picture is revealed beyond the gates of the dramatic Kawarau Gorge at Cromwell Basin, where two-thirds of Central Otago's grapes are grown.

GET THERE
Auckland is the nearest major airport, with flights to Queenstown airport, 9km (5.5 miles) out of town. Car hire is available.

Courtesy of Amisfield / Shantanu Starick

01 AMISFIELD

Since it opened in 2005, Amisfield's cellar door restaurant has been an essential stop for gourmands and vinophiles visiting Central Otago. And given the winning blend of fine wine, exciting cuisine, enviable architecture and stupendous views, it is arguably the region's ultimate winery experience.

Capitalising on its proximity to the tourist hubs of Queenstown and Arrowtown, the winery and its renowned bistro lie within the mountain-lined Wakatipu Basin, overlooking Lake Hayes. The muscular building – fashioned from local schist and recycled timbers – is a fabulous setting for an alfresco lunch. Chef Vaughan

Mabee's tasting menu is the way to go, with wines matched to local ingredients. In season, Bluff oysters may arrive with a glass of bright, zesty Amisfield Brut, or Catlins *paua* (abalone) alongside a flinty, dry Riesling. Local venison is a heavenly pairing with Amisfield's plummy Pinot Noir.

The bistro and tasting room are the public face of the winery, located at Lowburn, north of Cromwell. On a former merino sheep station, it's one of Central Otago's largest single-vineyard estates, though still relatively modest at 80 hectares (200 acres). *amisfield.co.nz; tel +64 3-442 0556; 10 Lake Hayes Rd, Queenstown; 10am–6pm daily* 💲✕

02 WILD EARTH WINES

Test your nerves as you cross the cascading Kawarau River and imagine stepping back 150 years to gold-mining days: crude huts, harsh winters and the slim chance of making a fortune. Nestled right at the river's edge, Wild Earth's cellar door and restaurant will return you to modern-day comforts with gold-standard wine and fantastic food. Owner Quintin Quider has come up with a novel way of reusing old French oak wine barrels, transforming them into outdoor 'stoakers', or cookers, to create tasty mains and platters to accompany his excellent wines in the Stoaker Room Bistro & Bar.

There is treasure here with old vintages of Wild Earth Pinot Noir

01 Amisfield's Lowburn vineyard, one of Central Otago's largest single-vineyard estates

02 Dining in the Amisfield Bistro

03 Wine and food at Wild Earth

04 Cromwell, on Lake Dunstan, is a great base

Central Otago is lauded as one of the best places outside Burgundy for cultivating the notoriously fickle Pinot Noir grape

dating back more than a decade – delicious, award-winning wines that demonstrate just how well good Pinot Noir can improve with bottle age.
wildearthwines.co.nz; tel +64 3-445 4841; 180 State Hwy 8B, Cromwell; noon-9pm daily ✖

03 MT DIFFICULTY

The Gibbston Valley Hwy funnels through the rocky narrows of Kawarau Gorge before emerging into the Cromwell Basin, where the undulating brow of the Carrick Range casts a rain-shadow across Bannockburn's famous vines. One of the forerunners here is Mt Difficulty, established in the early 1990s when five growers collaborated to produce wine from

the promising but then-unproven Central Otago region.

Having taken over from Matt Dicey in 2021, winemaker Greg Lane is producing excellent Pinot Noir and continuing to develop a range of wines of enviable breadth and quality. We love their luscious lemon-and-lime Target Riesling, although some of the most captivating drops come from the Grower's Range, bursting with concentrated, nuanced flavours expressive of the local terroir.

But wait, there's more. Perched on a hill with vast views over Cromwell Basin, Mt Difficulty's alluring restaurant encourages lingering over lunch. Sharp and modern with scrumptious fare and spectacular alfresco tables on the

05 Dessert at Amisfield

06 Working in the Amisfield vineyards in Lowburn, north of Cromwell

terrace, it will pay to book a table and sort out well in advance who's responsible for driving home. *mtdifficulty.co.nz; tel +64 3-445 3445; 73 Felton Rd, Bannockburn; 10.30am-4pm Wed-Sun* 💲✕

04 AKARUA

Like most great Central Otago wineries, Akarua is the architect of delectable Pinot Noir, but it's the rosé and crisp bubbles – particularly the complex, citrussy Vintage Brut – that really pop our corks. A victory lap, however, should be reserved for Akarua's 100% Pinot Noir rosé: a bouquet of strawberries and cream and pretty hard to top on a classic Central Otago summer's day.

The wines speak for themselves, so there's no need for bells and whistles at the cellar door. Accordingly, Akarua keeps it simple but smart, focusing on the warm welcomes and informative tastings that have been a hallmark of our repeated visits; you can now add to your visit in nearby Arrowtown, where Akarua's new restaurant and cellar door offers tastings and wine-paired meals. *akarua.com; tel +64 3-445 0897; 210 Cairnmuir Rd, Bannockburn; 10.30am-4pm Mon-Fri*

05 CARRICK

The beauty of Central Otago's cellar doors is that they offer a classy wine experience low on snoot-factor, with Carrick a case in point. This slick outfit may host plenty of jetsetting types, but it treats visitors with equal fervour regardless of the taster's knowledge. Like Mt Difficulty, Carrick is a spectacular spot for an indulgent lunch. The airy, art-filled atrium dining room opens on to a shady terrace and lush lawn. Framed by willows and vines is a view over Lake Dunstan's Bannockburn inlet to the Carrick Range, its foothills sculpted by old gold-mining sluices.

Starring its own olive oil and other local ingredients, Carrick's platters are a great complement to its wine range, which includes an intense, spicy Pinot Noir – its flagship drop – as well as a rich, toasty Chardonnay and citrusy aromatic varietals.

Between the wine, food and wonderful setting, Carrick rises to the occasion. To take things totally over the top, take a helicopter trip from the winery around the super-scenic Cromwell Basin with a landing atop the Pisa Range. *carrick.co.nz; tel +64 3-4453480; 247 Cairnmuir Rd, Bannockburn; 11am-5pm daily* 💲✕

WHERE TO STAY

VILLA DEL LAGO

With unobstructed lake views and a scenic 25-minute walk to downtown, these fully self-contained suites and villas make an ideal Queenstown base. *villadellago.co.nz; tel +64 3-442 5727; 249 Frankton Rd, Queenstown*

MILLBROOK RESORT

Set in 200 hectares (500 acres) of parkland with epic mountain views, this luxurious but unstuffy golf resort piles up the plaudits for its recreational facilities, day spa, 175 rooms and popular restaurants. *millbrook.co.nz; tel +64 3-441 7000; Malaghans Rd, Arrowtown*

WHERE TO EAT

CROMWELL FARMERS & CRAFT MARKET

Held in the Old Town heritage precinct on the lake edge, this sweet little summertime market (Sunday 9am-1pm Oct-Feb) has everything from hot pies to produce, with

the bonus of live music and the chance to have a yarn with the locals. *cromwellfarmerscraft market.co.nz; Cromwell Town Heritage Precinct, Erris St, Cromwell*

PROVISIONS

Just one of many cafes housed in Central Otago's charming historic buildings, Provisions serves excellent espresso alongside irresistible home baking. Make a beeline for the sticky bun. *provisionsofarrowtown. co.nz; tel +64 3-442*

0714; 65 Buckingham St, Arrowtown; daily

WHAT TO DO

The extensive, mostly easy tramps of the Queenstown Trail network offer a memorable way to reach wine-tour highlights while soaking up the scenery and working up an appetite. Bike hire and regular shuttles make for enjoyable loops or tours around Lake Hayes and Gibbston Valley wineries, taking in AJ Hackett's bungy jump base at

historic Kawarau Bridge. *queenstowntrail.co.nz*

CELEBRATIONS

With its endearing old schist-stone buildings and interesting hydro-dam location, Clyde is an ambient setting for the annual Clyde Wine and Food Harvest Festival, held on Easter Sunday. Central Otago's largest culinary festival, it features 20-odd wine stalls and a raft of food producers, alongside live music and local art. *promotedunstan.org.nz*

[Portugal]

DOURO

Take a slow boat (or train) along the beautiful Douro Valley in northern Portugal to experience historic estates, riverside vineyards and some of the world's best reds.

Still enough to reflect the slowly shifting clouds overhead, the Douro flows westwards for more than 850km (530 miles) from central Spain (where it's called the Duero) to Porto, on the Atlantic coast. Gorge-like in parts, the rugged 100km (62-mile) valley which bears its name is the world's largest mountainside vineyard. Rising up on either side of the river, its steep schist slopes have been carved into neat dry-stone terraces, ribbed with vines, whose leaves shimmer in the heat haze.

The whitewashed manor houses dotted among the riverbank terraces are the wine estates known as *quintas*, ranging from the grandly traditional 18th-century farmhouse of Quinta de la Pacheca to the sleek architecture of the Quinta do Seixo. On these estates, world-famous port wines, boosted by a touch of *aguardente* (distilled grape spirits similar to brandy)

have been produced since the 17th century. They also make superb dry red and white wines, and rosés – the perfect showcase for the beguilingly floral perfume of grapes Touriga Nacional and Touriga Franca.

Douro winegrowing harks back to Roman times, when the arduous process of hand-carving the stone terraces began. The valiant efforts of generations past, who pruned and harvested vines and maintained terraces by hand, continue today. And although robotic 'treading machines' can emulate the process, old habits die hard. During harvest in September, when golden light bathes the valley and dust clouds billow after truckloads of grapes en route to the wineries, workers still crush grapes with their bare feet in *lagares* (shallow stone fermentation vats), accompanied by accordion music and, of course, wine. It's a beautiful time to tour the Douro.

GET THERE
The nearest airport is Porto, 127km (79 miles) from the Douro. Reachable by boat, train or car, Pinhão is the best base.

① QUINTA DO CRASTO

The Roquette family run this 400-year-old estate, perched on an outcrop overlooking the Douro River. The astounding view from the infinity pool has become almost as famous as the family's pioneering red wines. Among the region's best old field-blend vines – a mix of native varieties (49, at the last count, in top parcel Vinha Maria Teresa) – produce terrific complexity, structure and rich fruitiness (look for raspberry, cherry and blackberry) tempered by a mineral edge. They make an interesting contrast with Crasto's single varietal range (a Touriga Nacional, Touriga Franca and Tinta Roriz) and wines from a younger vineyard, Quinta da Cabreira, in the drier, warmer Douro Superior subregion. Do try the ports; unfiltered (unlike most big-volume examples), the Late Bottle Vintage Port punches above its weight. *quintadocrasto.pt; tel +351 254 920 020; Gouvinhas, Sabrosa; daily by appointment* 💲🍴

② QUINTA NOVA DE NOSSA SENHORA DO CARMO

Acquired in 1999 by the Amorim family, the world's largest cork producers, this estate's name (meaning 'new') is apt. Sprawled along a bend in the river, its south- and west-facing, sun-soaked vineyards originally produced Burmester Port. Today, they're mostly used for wine. Diverse and well executed, from easy-going Pomares to refined flagships Mirabilis white and red, the range includes a sophisticated rosé. Enjoy a glass and the view of the Douro River from the tasting room's terrace or stay longer at the 18th-century manor house's boutique hotel or highly regarded restaurant, Terraçu's. Three scenic vineyard walks of varying distances take in the chapel, orchards, olive-oil mill and Marquis de Pombal milestone, one of 335 demarcating the region's original boundary. History fans will also enjoy the small wine museum. *quintanova.com; tel +351 969 860 056; Covas do Douro; Tue-Sat by appointment* 💲🍴

During harvest in September, when golden light bathes the valley and dust clouds billow after truckloads of grapes en route to the wineries, workers still crush grapes with their bare feet

03 QUINTA DE LA ROSA

This small, pretty Douro riverside estate was given to owner Sophia's Bergqvist's grandmother, Clara, as a christening present. Rows of vines plunge from 400m (1312ft)

right down to the river, where the high, heat-reflective walls of the Vale do Inferno vineyard help explain the high-quality white and red wines and ports that are made here. Handily located within walking distance of Pinhão, the property has 23 rooms (21 with river views). Facing the river, the glass-fronted restaurant, Cozinha da Clara, also has a sizeable terrace. *quintadelarosa.com; tel +351 254 732 254; Pinhão; tours daily Apr-Oct, private visits by appointment* 🟢✖

04 WINE & SOUL

The careers of Douro's younger generation often start by making garage wines. Sandra Tavares da

Silva and Jorge Borges Serôdio had larger ambitions and bought a warehouse in the sought-after Pinhão Valley. The warehouse came with granite *lagares* in which their first batch of grapes, from a tiny plot of 70-year-old vines, was crushed by foot. This wine became the muscular, award-winning Pintas. The *terroirists* have since acquired more old field-blend vineyards and artfully tease out the differences. Quinta da Manoella is slightly higher and breezier, with humid, forest influences; it produces an elegant, spicy red. The Pintas vineyard is the basis of a brooding Vintage Port, while Manoella has traditionally produced Tawny Ports, including 5G, a limited-edition Very Old

05 Quinta da Gricha's
Patio das Laranjeiras

07 Stylish sleeping
at Churchill's

06 Churchill's Quinta
da Gricha grounds

Tawny Port first made by Serôdio Borges' great-great-grandfather at the end of the 19th century. Guru, a stunning, flinty white, is from even higher vineyards in Porrais. *wineandsoul.com; tel +351 254 738 076; Avenida Júlio de Freitas, Vale de Mendiz, Pinhão; Mon-Fri by appointment* 💲

05 DOW'S

Five generations of the Symingtons have made port at Quinta do Bomfim, just a short walk from Pinhão station. Rising to almost 400m (1312ft), the estate's position is key to Dow's relatively austere style. Guided visits explore its history, supported by photographs and port wine paraphernalia from the family archive. During harvest, you can see port wine in the making from a viewing area over the robotic *lagares*. Year-round, the visit includes the 19th-century lodge, with its imposing *balseiros* (huge, upright wooden casks) and port pipes. Tastings extend to the family's other port brands, including Graham's and Warre's. Order a traditional picnic basket and enjoy it (and fine views) from the visitor centre or vineyard terraces. You can also book a self-guided vineyard walk to wander among the vines. *symington.com; tel +351 254 730 370; Pinhão; daily by appointment, closed Mon Nov-Mar* 💲✖️

06 CHURCHILL'S QUINTA DA GRICHA

In contrast to the other stops on this trail, Quinta da Gricha is located on the north-facing bank of the Douro, near Ervedosa do Douro. The company was established in 1981 by Johnny Graham, whose great-great-grandfather founded Graham's Port in 1820 – port clearly runs in the blood. Churchill's acquired Quinta da Gricha in 1999, and has since embarked on making Douro wines as well as ports – all foot-trodden in traditional granite *lagares*. The single-estate red wine is particularly mineral, with resinous notes of esteva (a local wild plant) – a thumbprint which you will also find in wines from Quinta de S. José, with whom Churchill's share a jetty (boat transfers from Pinhão can be arranged). Lunch is served alfresco on the Patio das Laranjeiras (meaning 'orange trees') or in the beamed *caseiros'* (caretakers') kitchen, with its traditional bare stone walls. *churchills-port.com/quinta-da-gricha; tel +351 254 422 136; Ervedosa do Douro, S. João da Pesqueira; daily by appointment* 💲✖️

WHERE TO STAY

CASA DO VISCONDE DE CHANCELEIROS

Despite the grand facade, this 18th-century manor house hotel has an unpretentious, homely feel to it. Extensive views over the valley, and the hotel's spectacular terraced garden (with patios, pool and tennis court), make breakfast a leisurely affair. It's a ten-minute drive from Pinhão. *chanceleiros.com; tel +351 254 730 190; Pinhão*

QUINTA NOVA DE NOSSA SENHORA DO CARMO

Located on the Quinta Nova winery estate, this 19th-century manor house offers luxurious rooms with a mix of

traditional furniture and modern fittings. The restaurant is exceptional, serving contemporary takes on classic Douro dishes, which are expertly paired with wines from the estate. *quintanova.com; tel +351 254 730 430; Quinta Nova, Covas do Douro*

WHERE TO EAT

DOC

Famous for its superb wine list and waterfront setting (with outdoor deck), this is acclaimed local chef Rui Paula's first restaurant. DOP in Porto city centre followed in 2010, and then Casa de Chá on the beach in Leça da Palmeira, which earned Paula a Michelin

star in 2016. *ruipaula.pt; tel +351 254 858 123, Estrada Nacional 222, Folgosa, Armamar; daily*

O PAPARICO

It's worth the short taxi ride north of Porto to O Paparico. Portuguese authenticity is the name of the game here, from the romantically rustic interior of stone walls, beams and white linen to the menu that sings of the seasons. Dishes such as veal with wild mushrooms and monkfish are cooked with passion, served with precision and expertly paired with wines. *opaparico.com; tel +351 225 400 548; Rua de Costa Cabral, Porto; Tue-Sat*

WHAT TO DO

DOURO CRUISING

Cruise all the way from Porto and pick up a hire car in Régua or Pinhão. *cp.pt*

MUSEU DO DOURO

Get the lowdown on the Douro Valley's history, landscape and cultural traditions, and check out

the permanent exhibition centred on Douro and Porto wines. *museudodouro.pt*

WALKING

A short distance north of the Douro Valley is the Parque Nacional da Peneda-Gerês, a spectacular region of mountains and forests where wild horses, boar and wolves still roam. The park is created by the folds of four mountain ranges and is the perfect place for a couple of days of hiking, punctuated by cooling dips in the clear rivers and pools. *natural.pt*

CELEBRATIONS

Midsummer is when one of Europe's most enthusiastic street festivals takes over Porto: Festa de São João do Porto, celebrating St John the Baptist. The party starts on the afternoon of 23 June and features live music and dancing, barbecues, fireworks and a lot of wine. *wow.pt/sao-joao*

[Romania]
DRĂGĂŞANI

At the heart of Eastern Europe, Romania is steeped in myth and tradition, but the wine-producing region of Drăgăşani pulsates with new methods and rare local grapes.

Wolves, deer and bears roam brooding Carpathian Mountain forests, and impressive castles – including Bran, supposed lair of Bram Stoker's fictional count – loom on rocky hilltops. But there's more to Romania than spurious Dracula connections, from ancient monasteries, cathedral-like salt mines and a hospitable culture to its fabulous and fascinating wines.

Romania is a wine country through and through, with grapevines grown just about everywhere. Wine may have been made here for at least 4000 years and certainly before the region became Roman Dacia; and it's said that ancient Thrace (part of today's Romania) was the birthplace of Dionysius, the god of wine. Nowadays the country is Europe's fifth-biggest winegrower and produces more wine than New Zealand (though is nowhere near as famous). Travellers will find familiar grapes such as Merlot, Pinot Noir and Pinot Grigio, but more intriguing are Romania's local varieties, including the widespread Fetească group: Fetească Albă (the white maiden grape), Fetească Regală (royal maiden) and Fetească Neagra (black maiden), as well as the rare white grape Crâmpoşie Selecţionată, and reds such as Novac and Negru de Drăgăşani, many of which are grown nowhere else in the world.

Recent years have seen a revolution in winemaking here, with exciting wines being crafted

GET THERE
The nearest airport is 70km (43 miles) from Drăgăşani at Craiova. Bucharest has more flights but is a 2.5-3hr drive away (200km/ 124 miles).

by passionate people. This is epitomised in the southwestern Drăgăşani region, likened to Romania's Tuscany for its sunny climate and gentle hills overlooking the River Olt. Wine has been renowned here since the 16th century, and today, Drăgăşani is home to some of Romania's most innovative small family wineries, offering a warm and very personal welcome, and situated conveniently close together to form an easy wine trail.

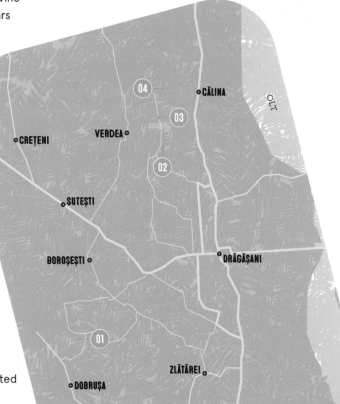

01 AVINCIS

Sitting on a plateau, surrounded by vines in every direction, this winery must be a contender for the most beautiful in Romania. The family connection dates back to 1927 when Iancu Râmniceanu (a Romanian army officer) and his wife Maria bought the neo-Romanian mansion with vineyards. It was confiscated by the state in the communist era, but in 2007, their great-granddaughter Cristiana (together with her husband Valeriu) returned to the family estate. They restored the ruined mansion and built a dramatic modern winery in local stone, with an eco-friendly grass roof to fit into the landscape.

A gently sloping 40 hectares (99 acres) of vines are managed with low yields and fanatical attention to detail. The year 2011 marked the first vintage of the new era, made by a young Alsace winemaker Ghislain Moritz. Today, the winery's consulant is Federico Giotto, and Avincis' local varieties are a real strength, from the refreshingly elegant Crâmpoșie Selecționată and the fine Fetească Regală to the wonderfully juicy red, Negru de Drăgășani. Tastings of three or five wines include a tour of the winery and the vineyards. *avincis.ro; tel +40 751 199 416; Vila Dobrușa, Valea Caselor Strada 1A; Mon–Sun by appointment* 💲✕

02 PRINCE ȘTIRBEY

It's not often that you set foot in the home of actual blue-blooded royalty, but extending a warm welcome to visitors has always been important at Prince Știrbey. The effortlessly gracious Ileana Kripp comes from a long line of Romanian nobles – her grandmother was Princess Maria Știrbey – though the family's vineyards were seized by the communists in 1949. Ileana escaped to France aged 15 and somehow 'lost' her return ticket. She later met her husband, Jakob Kripp, in a German vineyard and, perhaps inevitably, the idea of recovering Ileana's inheritance began to play on the couple's minds. In 2001, the

estate eventually returned to their hands. Luckily it had been well looked after by the state, under Dumitru Nedelut – Ileana and Jackob have kept on Dumitru as their vineyard manager today.

Their German-born winemaker Oliver Bauer has also been a key influence. He originally came to Romania for a couple of months but found the chance to rebuild a historic winery from scratch too hard to resist. From the start, the concept was unusual for Romania – with special focus on local grape varieties, such as the first Crâmpoșie varietal wine, the first dry Tămâioasă Românească, and the first Novac. Some two decades on, Prince Ştirbey is

German-born Oliver Bauer found the chance to rebuild a historic Romanian winery from scratch too hard to resist

firmly established as one of the country's most consistent and exciting wineries.
stirbey.com; tel +40 751 252 272; Dealul Olt Strada; daily by appointment Ⓢ

⓸ CRAMA BAUER

Oliver and Raluca Bauer, who both work at Prince Ştirbey, which is just 2km (1.2 miles) up the

road, met at a wine tasting. They started planning their own family winery in 2010. Oliver was keen to explore Romania's winemaking potential further – his approach is to seek out rare varieties and parcels from old vineyards, creating what is effectively a single-vineyard wine from each batch. He is also conducting various winemaking experiments, such as producing orange, skin-fermented Sauvignonasse, semi-sweet Crâmpoșie Selecționată in a Mosel style, and using Negru de Drăgășani for rosé. His Fetească Neagră is excellent, too. The Bauers take a very personal approach to guiding visitors around their winery and can offer guided tastings accompanied

01 Aerial view
of Avincis estate

02 Harvesting by hand

03 The modern winery
at Avincis

04 Avincis tasting

05 Domeniul Drăgăși's
Pelerin guest rooms

06 Pelerin's vintage
decor

07 Terrace views at
Domeniul Drăgăși

by local foods, or special horizontal
or vertical tastings.
*cramabauer.com; tel +40 757 098
940; Dealul Olt Strada; Mon-Sat by
appointment* 🟢 ✕

04 DOMENIUL DRĂGAȘI

Former lawyer Magdalena Enescu
visited Drăgășani to work on a
legal case and fell in love. She
subsequently took a 180-degree
turn in her life and devoted herself
to establishing this small wine estate.
It has just 7 hectares (17 acres) of
vineyards, planted in 2012, with
breathtaking views over the River
Olt. The vineyards' international
varieties offer the chance to explore
how the grapes suit the Drăgășani
landscape, with good Cabernet
Franc and an unusual pink Pinot Gris
called Ramato under the Pelerin
(Pilgrim) label.

Close to both Știrbey and Bauer,
Domeniul Drăgăși also offers
five well-appointed rooms in the
historic Pelerin house and makes an
ideal place to stay. Leisurely days
can be filled with wine tastings,
wine-matched dinners based on
delicious local ingredients and
cooked by a professional chef, plus
guided tours of the winery itself
and the vineyards on request.
*domeniul-dragasi.ro; tel +40 766
995 929 or 0740 222 270; Dealul
Viilor din Pruddeni; Mar-Oct daily
by appointment* 🟢 ✕

06

© Vitalie Brega | 2020. Domeniul Dragasi

WHERE TO STAY & EAT

AVINCIS

Enjoy panoramic views from one of three apartments built on the grass-covered roof of this stunning winery. There are also nine comfortable modern double rooms overlooking the vines. In addition to wine tasting and meals, you can make use of the sauna and tennis courts and walk through the vines and down to the village of Dobruşa, with its small orthodox monastery. *avincis.ro; tel +40 751 199 416; Vila Dobruşa, Valea Caselor Strada 1A*

HOTEL KMZ

In the centre of Drăgăşani, this edgy, young-at-heart boutique hotel, where the 'boutique' label feels tongue-in-cheek, offers clean and cosy rooms with period design touches, such as striped bedding and gold headboards. There's a handy street-level cafe that does great sandwiches and gyros. *kmz.ro; tel +40 250 814 093; Regele Carol Strada 16*

WHAT TO DO

LOCAL TRIPS

In addition to wine tastings and walks in the area, the Drăgăşani winegrowers' association can help organise trips to nearby sights, such as the impressive Horezu monastery, with its Unesco World Heritage-listed pottery, as well as other significant monasteries Ike Dintr-un Lemn and Arnota. It's also well worth asking about a visit to the dramatic salt mines of Ocnele Mari. *info@cramabauer.com; tel +40 751 252 272*

WALKING

Horezu is also a good starting point for hiking and wildlife-spotting in the lovely and very wild Carpathian Mountains. The Crame Romania website is a helpful resource, and also provides plenty of winery information and useful maps. *crameromania.ro*

[Slovenia]

BRDA

Taste thrilling experimental and historic wines in this multicultural frontier zone, defined by gentle hills and unforgettable hospitality.

In western Slovenia, home to the beautifully contoured wine region of Brda, the Italian border is fluid; it's possible to cross between the two countries several times a day without noticing. Understanding this frontier status through an encounter with the wines on both sides of the border is critical to an appreciation of the Brda's wines. Brda literally means hills, and defines the Slovene extension of the wider Gorizia Hills, once an ancient seabed, which continue into Italy under the name Collio. Although deeply influenced by both countries, there is a special culture here that one could call 'Gorizian', and which predates the European nation-state. Extraordinary wines are made on both sides of the border from the same grape varietals, mostly white, and with very similar techniques. Often, the fermentation vessel is clay, and the wine rests on its skins to become honey-coloured, layered and captivating.

Some of the most violent and drawn out battles of both world wars happened here, resulting in massive depopulations in the early part of the 20th century. Conflict has left deep scars, some of which are still visible, yet Gorizians remain warm and generous, and fiercely loyal to their land, which in many cases they fought and paid dearly to keep. That pride of place is illustrated by one of the local realities of winegrowing: above solid rock there is a lack of topsoil; often, in order to plant a viable vineyard, earth must be brought from elsewhere and layered directly on the stone.

Take a walk with a family grower – the meaning of 'family' here carries special weight – and they'll make sure to explain the historical significance of their surrounding landmarks, before taking a moment to admire the many vistas the landscape affords.

GET THERE
Trieste–Friuli Venezia Giulia is the nearest major airport, 30km (19 miles) from Dobrovo. Car hire is available.

01 MOVIA

There's no denying that Movia's restless, charismatic winemaker Ales Kristančič has almost single-handedly brought Slovenian wine to the world stage. Movia currently stands as a true 'border wine': half of the vineyards lie in the Italian Collio, and some 80% of production is exported. When he's not in the vines or cellar, Ales travels the world promoting his region and his wines. And what wines! There's little that hasn't been tried here, from biodynamic viticulture or deeply extended skin macerations to undisgorged sparkling wines. These techniques were all put in place to achieve, as Ales would put it in his inimitable language, an ultimate goal of purity and soul, a transparent connection to the earth.

Don't miss his entirely additive-free Lunar bottling, from Ribolla, and the Puro sparkling rosé, served with local cheese and charcuterie on a view-heavy balcony.
movia.si; tel +386 51 30 45 80; Ceglo 18, Dobrovo, Slovenia; by appointment Mon-Sat $

02 MARJAN SIMČIČ

From Movia, you can walk across the street to visit fifth-generation winemaker Marjan Simčič at his impressive modern winery. As with Movia, Marjan's vines straddle the Italo-Slovene border, yet the wines are less idiosyncratic and enjoy a wider appeal. Marjan bottles his wines in three distinct tiers: entry-level Brda Classic; specially selected Complex Wines; and the Opoka Cru, released in exceptional years and matured in oak. Together, they provide an easy-to-understand portrait of the varietals the region is best known for, including Ribolla, Sauvignon and Merlot.
simcic.si; tel +386 53 95 92 00; Ceglo 3b, Dobrovo, Slovenia; by appointment

03 RADIKON

Stanko Radikon's estate is home to some of the most radically appealing, complex wines in the world. His terraced vines form an amphitheatre around his family's home and winemaking facility, where he and son Sasa craft wines with as little intervention as possible. The tasting experience here is one of the region's warmest and most intimate. Their white wines, largely based on Tokaj and Ribolla, are perhaps better understood as 'amber', or 'orange'; they see several months of extended skin contact in Slavonian oak (and sometimes several years of bottle age), before release, and convey richly layered, honeyed textures alongside powerful acidity.
radikon.it; tel +39 48 13 28 04; Località Tre Buchi 4, Oslavia, Gorizia, Italy; by appointment $

04 ČOTAR

Branko Čotar (pronounced 'Chó-tar') began making wine for his restaurant in 1974, and eventually became drawn into winemaking full-time, bottling his first commercial vintage in 1990. Today, he's joined by his son Vasja. Ancestral methods are the rule here, from vineyard to winery. The Čotars are amazing hosts, offering intimate, detailed views of their cellar and vineyards; if there's time, pair their selection of dried hams with their wines.

They primarily work with local varietals to produce a small range of still and sparkling wines. Each of their bottlings are delicious, but pay special mind to the dry, sparkling red Teran, labelled Crna Penina, and the still, cidery, white Vitovska.
cotar.si; tel +386 41 87 02 74; Gorjansko 4a, Komen, Slovenia; by appointment

05 EDI KANTE

Edi Kante is regularly referenced as a pioneer of Carso winemaking. Carving a three-storey cellar and winemaking facility into the karst rock beneath his home has enabled him to give his wines the controlled temperature needed for elaboration and maturation. The resulting wines are taut and lean, clearly reflecting the ruggedness of their source. The unique KK spumante stands as one of the region's finest sparkling wines.
kante.it; tel +39 40 20 02 55; Prepotto 1/A, Trieste, Italy; by appointment

06 VODOPIVEC

The famous estate of Paolo Vodopivec lies 35 minutes southeast of the Gorizia/Oslavje zone, yet it's very much worth the trip. Paolo works with one varietal, the Vitovska grape, which is currently elaborated in three separate bottlings, aged in Georgian clay amphora and Slavonian oak. Dark-hued and fragrant, often recalling qualities of rooibos tea and fine sake, they stand as a benchmark for the region and varietal.
vodopivec.it; tel +39 40 22 91 81; Località Colludrozza 4, Sgonico, Italy; by appointment

01 The hilly landscape of Brda

02 Marjan Simčič winery in Dobrovo

WHERE TO STAY
HOMESTEAD BELICA
Perched high atop the village of Medana, this eight-room homestead offers lovely views and an outdoor pool.
belica.si; tel +386 53 04 21 04; Medana 32, Dobrovo, Slovenia

PALAZZO LANTIERI
Historic Gorizia is a gorgeous city, and this palazzo-stay offers light, spacious, art- and antique-filled rooms overlooking a glorious Persian-styled garden.
palazzo-lantieri. com; tel +394 81 53 32 84; Piazza San Antonio 6, Gorizia, Italy

WHERE TO EAT
ARKADE CIGOJ
The friendly Cigoj family make their own Vipava wines, grow veg and raise livestock, all of which end up at their farm-to-table restaurant. Sample barley and wild mushroom risotto, gnocchi with radicchio and sausage or tempting strudel.
arkade-cigoj.com; +386 53 66 60 09; Črniče 91, Črniče, Slovenia; daily

ČEBRON FAMILY ESTATE
Featuring tables set on a shady terrace overlooking the Vipava hills, this farm and vineyard uses seasonal ingredients in its food, from minestrone to pasta with wild boar ragu or olive-oil ice cream.
cebron.eu; tel +386 41 58 20 51; Preserje 59, Branik, Slovenia; daily

WHAT TO DO
In the Slovenian capital of Ljubljana, take a lazy river cruise or board the funicular up to the 15th-century castle. For a break from the grape, sample the craft ales at buzzing Union Brewery.
union-pivnica.si

CELEBRATIONS
In late April, the Brda & Vino festival is held in the tiny Slovenian border town of Smartno; a few weeks later, the nearby village of Višnjevik hosts a Rebula (wine grape) and Olive Oil festival. On the second Sunday in September, the Italian town of Cormons celebrates the new grape harvest.
brda.si

WELLINGTON, SWARTLAND & TULBAGH

MALMESBURY

WOLSELEY

Bergrivier

WELLINGTON

01 02 08 05 03 06 07 04

[South Africa]

WELLINGTON, SWARTLAND & TULBAGH

Small vineyards with enthusiastic, independent owners offer the visitor
a special insight into the future of winemaking in this fertile region.

Cape winemaking has long been symbolised by the grand old estates in Stellenbosch, Franschhoek and Constantia, where the first vines were planted on the African continent as far back as 1659. But today there are a host of regions further afield in the Cape that are developing their own terroir characteristics, and are not limiting themselves to the classic Chenin Blanc and Pinotage for which South Africa is famous. With its maritime climate, Walker's Bay is well known for Chardonnay, a flinty Sauvignon and Pinot Noir, while Elgin's higher-altitude vineyards favour Sauvignon Blanc and Bordeaux blends. For sheer variety, and for smaller family-run wineries who offer a friendly, genuine welcome, the adjoining regions of Wellington, Swartland and Tulbagh offer a refreshing alternative. Instead of hearing a tour guide reciting a set speech, winery tastings here can still mean a face-to-face

encounter with the winemaker. It quickly becomes clear that in these emerging regions, estate owners are happier to take risks, experiment and plant new grape varieties.

Swartland is known as the 'bread basket of the Cape', farming wheat and breeding cattle and horses. But the immense vineyards, owned by anonymous cooperatives producing bulk wine and brandy, have all but been replaced by a band of cutting-edge vintners with small, manageable estates; many are experimenting with biodynamic production. And vineyard owners here are some of the most progressive in the Cape, with the Black workforce genuinely having a voice in the running of an estate. In the remote valley of Tulbagh, visitors discover farms producing certified organic wines and taking important steps to preserve the fragile ecosystem surrounding the vineyards.

GET THERE
Cape Town is the nearest major airport, 70km (43 miles) from Wellington. Car hire is available.

01 RIJK'S WINE ESTATE

Tulbagh is one of the under-the-radar wine regions of the Cape, a fertile valley ringed by a bowl of three tall mountain ranges. Between 2012 and 2021, the cellar at Rijk's was run by one of South Africa's most renowned winemakers, Pierre Wahl, who modestly declared, 'With the top-quality grapes that are harvested here, I am simply entrusted with gently guiding the wine into the bottle with the least interference possible.' Now under the helm of winemaker Adriaan Jacobs, Rijk's is something of an experimental winery. The vineyard was planted from scratch with many different cultivars in this largely schist soil, and three years later, after the first harvest,

plants producing Merlot, Cabernet Sauvignon and Franc were dug up, with production now concentrated on Chenin Blanc and Pinotage. While Rijk's presents a range of younger wines, with slight oak influences, what's really interesting is the Private Cellar selection, kept in oak barrels for two years, then bottle-aged for three years. Attached to the winery is a traditional whitewashed country house, transformed into an elegant hotel. The perfect place to sample Rijk's intriguing wines is the sunny terrace of the restaurant, which offers idyllic views over a lake, with the vineyard and the imposing mountains in the background. *rijks.co.za; tel +27 23 230 1622; Van der Stel St, Tulbagh; 10am-4pm Mon-Fri, 10am-2pm Sat* 💲✕

02 WAVERLEY HILLS

While Rijk's is just at the edge of bustling Tulbagh, Waverley Hills sits alone in the middle of a wild landscape in the foothills of Witzenberg Mountains, right at the other end the valley. The vineyard was founded in 2000 and has very different objectives to most other wineries. To begin with, this is one of the few Cape vineyards to produce genuine organic wines, with a biodiversity programme that ranges from a flock of ducks to combat snails to a huge parcel of virgin land set aside to conserve endangered veld and keep out alien vegetation.

Johan Delport is Waverley's vintner, supervising not only the vineyard and olive groves, but also a plant nursery. Generally, the wines

are light, mineral and not strong in tannin, as much ageing is done in steel vats rather than wooden barrels, while screw tops have replaced cork. The real surprise comes when Johan opens his Cabernet Sauvignon, a 'natural' wine made without sulphites.

After a tour of the modern cellar, with its huge steel vats, visitors arrive in the minimalist tasting room, which doubles as a deli for the farm's organic olive-oil production. And for the whole healthy, sustainable experience, indulge in a meal at the restaurant, which serves great food with suggested wine pairings for each dish.
waverleyhills.co.za; tel +27 23 231 0002; R46, Tulbagh; 10am-4pm Mon-Sat, 11am-3pm Sun 💲✕

03 DOOLHOF

You have to drive well out of Wellington to the remote end of the snaking Bovlei valley to get to the splendid Doolhof estate. The farm is enormous, with 40 hectares (98 acres) planted in the 1990s with vines, although grapes for wine and brandy have been grown here since the early 1700s. It is a complex vineyard made up of a labyrinth of vines parcels planted on different terroirs with different microclimates, meaning a lot of careful blending is required in the cellar. Only three whites are produced – Sauvignon, Chardonnay and Chenin Blanc – while the red blends are dominated by Merlot, Pinotage, Shiraz and Petit Verdot. Sample the wines in the tasting room or, even better,

forego the indoors entirely, order a picnic with chilled wine and follow a leisurely river trail through the estate. Those who want to splash out can stay in the luxurious Grand Dédale Country House, where guests are pampered by a private chef.
doolhof.com; tel +27 21 864 2805; Bovlei, Wellington; tastings by reservation 10am-4pm Sat, 10am-3pm Sun 💲✕

04 NABYGELEGEN PRIVATE CELLAR

James McKenzie bought this idyllic property in the shadow of the looming Snow Mountains some two decades ago, but the estate dates back to 1748. He lives in the original manor house, while the vines run down to a lake, the perfect spot for a chilled glass of his distinctive, mineral Chenin Blanc. James works the small farm and 17-hectare (42-acre) vineyard on his own, saying: 'It is a lot of hard work, but for me this is like living in paradise. This used to be a farm supplying the local wine cooperative, so I inherited fabulous 40- to 70-year-old bush vines. Most winemakers around here would just dig them up and replant, but I couldn't be happier, as the quality they yield is exceptional.'

After a tasting in the old forge, visitors are given a vineyard tour by this gentle giant of a man. His latest project is planting blocks of Malbec and Cabernet for bottlings in 2022 and beyond.
nabygelegen.co.za; tel +27 21 873 7534; Bovlei Division Rd, Wellington; by reservation Mon-Fri 💲

baby vines of over 50 different varietals to winemakers all over South Africa.
bosmanwines.com; tel +27 21 873 3170; Hexberg Rd, Wellington; by reservation 9am-4pm Mon-Sat ⓢ✕

ⓞ⁵ VAL DU CHARRON

Arriving at the entrance to this 1920s estate is more Sunset Boulevard than South Africa, with palm trees lining the monumental driveway against a backdrop of neatly spaced vines and the gaunt rocky cliffs of Groenberg Mountain. When Catherine and Stuart Entwistle decided to change lifestyle and become *vignerons*, they embarked on a huge project. This was a fruit farm with no vines, and in 2002 they planted 22 hectares (54 acres) from scratch with quite a startling variety of 18 different grapes 'because we didn't want to say 20 years later, "Oh, why didn't we plant this?"' says the spirited Catherine with a smile. Fortunately, they are advised by one of the Cape's top cellar masters, Bertus Fourie, and use the varietals in blends, waiting till the vines are older to concentrate on a reserve selection with single grapes such as Chardonnay, Cabernet Sauvignon and Shiraz.

The 'Theatre of Wine' tasting, led by a costumed actor, is a dramatic experience; guided tours and regular tastings are also available.
vdcwines.com; tel +27 21 873 1256; Bovlei, Wellington; tastings by reservation ⓢ✕

ⓞ⁶ BOSMAN FAMILY VINEYARDS

Eight generations of the Bosmans have been producing handcrafted wine in Wellington. Jannie Bosman, his children and their families still live together in the estate's grand mansions, and though the flagship domaine covers 150 hectares (25 acres), there are two other sizeable vineyards in nearby Swartland and the emerging Walker's Bay. After tasting the Chenin and Pinotage in the historic 260-year-old cellar, visitors gain a sense of the family's winemaking heritage. But the Bosmans look to the future too, setting up a vine nursery supplying

ⓞ⁷ DIEMERSFONTEIN

Diemersfontein is another South African winery brimming with new ideas. It offers travellers plush accommodation in a lavish Cape Dutch mansion, a deli stocking local specialities, and a performing-arts centre that promotes local musicians and actors. The latter is run by the workers association, who also control one third of the estate and produce their own line of wines, Thokozani. The wines are a surprise too, from the Malbec Reserve to the Coffee Pinotage, invented by Diemersfontein's cellar master and a huge commercial success. Toasted barrel staves are dropped into steel vats to give the rich red Pinotage wine a Mocha aroma and flavour. Experts consider it heresy, but people love it. The owner, David Sonnenberg, is often to be found reminiscing during tastings: 'During

apartheid I was disillusioned and left to live in London for 20 years working as clinical psychologist, but it was Nelson Mandela and the changes here that inspired me to come back to the winery, and I have never regretted it'.
diemersfontein.co.za; tel +27 21 864 5050; Jan van Riebeck Dr, Wellington; 10am-5pm daily ⓢ✗

08 ADI BADENHORST

Swartland is all about rock-and-roll winemaking. Just finding the windswept farm of Adi Badenhorst is challenging, though the welcome of this friendly bear of a man quickly makes up for it. He works in his cellar like an anarchic alchemist, using everything from huge old oak casks to 500L French barrels, cement and steel vats, and a couple of Noblot cement eggs. The tastings, which are followed by lunch, might feature stellar bottles as Secateur Chenin Blanc; Secateur Red, an explosive blend of Grenache, Carignan and Cinsault; and Funky White, which one year might be a Vin Jaune, the next a Muscat de Frontignan. This whole area was historically dominated by the Swartland Cooperative, but when farmers couldn't afford to replant their old vines in favour of high-yield young ones, many were forced to sell. This allowed maverick vintners like Adi to inherit low-yield bush vines that can date back over 100 years.
aabadenhorst.com; tel +27 82 373 5038; Kalmoesfontein, Jakkalsfontein Rd, Malmesbury; by reservation 11.30am Wed & Fri ⓢ✗

01 Adi Badenhorst

02 A festival at the Bosman family estate

03 Val du Charron's old cellar

04 Adi Badenhorst inspects the vines

05 Val du Charron's Wellington estate

06 An angel in Val du Charron's vineyard

WHERE TO STAY

TULBAGH HOTEL

Smack in the middle of Tulbagh's high street, this imposing 1850s hotel mixes contemporary design with nostalgic antique touches. Cosy restaurant, pool and sunny terrace bar.
tulbaghhotel.co.za; tel +27 23 230 0071; 22 Van der Stel St, Tulbagh

OUDE WELLINGTON WINE ESTATE

This wine and brandy estate welcomes guests in enchantingly rustic 18th-century Cape Dutch thatched cottages. Try the *braai* barbecue in the poolside garden.
kapwein.com; tel +27 21 873 2262; Bainskloof Rd, Wellington

WHERE TO EAT

READERS RESTAURANT

The oldest house in Tulbagh dates back to 1754 and hosts this cosy restaurant, where Carol Collins creates inventive recipes that reinterpret traditional dishes. Great homemade ice-cream, rib-sticking malva pudding and an outstanding list of local wines, many available by the glass.
readersrestaurant.co.za; tel +27 23 230 0087; 12 Church St, Tulbagh; Wed-Mon

STONE KITCHEN

On a gravel road just outside Wellington, Stone Kitchen is part of the unpretentious Dunstone Estate winery. The play areas are child-friendly, the menu features classics like quiche, burgers, pies and ribs, and you can enjoy a wine tasting at your table.
dunstone.co.za; tel +27 21 873 6770; Bovlei Rd, Wellington; daily

WHAT TO DO

The Cape is a nature paradise, so take a day off to explore a wildlife reserve or head to the coast for whale-watching.

CELEBRATIONS

Swartland Independent Producers organise special events throughout the year, like November's Swartland Street Party in Riebeek Kasteel.
swartlandindependent. co.za

[South Africa]

FRANSCHHOEK & STELLENBOSCH

Wine lovers are spoiled for choice in buzzy Stellenbosch and French-flavoured Franschhoek, with excellent wines and gourmet restaurants.

Tasting the exceptional wines produced in South Africa's Cape region while in the actual vineyards themselves is a unique experience. Just half an hour's drive from Cape Town and the iconic Table Mountain are the immense open landscapes of South Africa, where vast estates with hundreds of hectares of vines blend in with towering mountain ranges, lakes and wild vegetation.

The heart of the Cape winelands is the buzzing town of Stellenbosch, a wine lover's paradise of bars and bistros, and the perfect place to be based for a few days of serious vineyard visiting. Grapes have been cultivated around Stellenbosch for more than 350 years, and wine tourism is a highly developed business here: every winery seems to offer everything from guesthouses and restaurants to wine-paired picnics, and kids' playgrounds so parents can enjoy a serious tasting.

GET THERE
Cape Town is the nearest major airport, 35km (22 miles) from Stellenbosch. Car hire is available.

For many years, Stellenbosch has dominated wine awards, especially for South Africa's signature Pinotage, a hybrid of the Pinot Noir and Cinsaut grapes that was bred in the local university back in 1925.

But recently, attention is turning to nearby Franschhoek, which draws on the French heritage of its original Huguenot settlers, who brought vine seedlings with them from France. With restaurants and hotels named Le Bon Vivant or Quartier Francais, you could almost be in a Provencal village (though no one speaks French any more). The Franschhoek restaurant scene is gourmet, the resort hotels luxurious and young *vignerons* are making sensational wines – classic Chenin Blanc and Pinotage as well as intense Syrah, complex Pinot Noir and Sauvignon. And here, too, estates are finally, if slowly, implementing inclusive ownership programmes for their Black workforces.

© Walter Bibikow | Getty Images

FRANSCHHOEK & STELLENBOSCH

01

04

03

● PNIEL

02

● BANHOEK

06

07

FRANSCHHOEK ●

05

● STELLENBOSCH

● ROBERTSVLEI

❶ KANONKOP

The historic estate of Kanonkop is a 30-minute drive outside Cape Town, at the outskirts of Stellenbosch, South Africa's unofficial capital of wine tourism. The entrance is marked by a black cannon, and the surprise as you drive towards the huge cellars through the vineyards that line the slopes of the Simonsberg Mountain is that there are as many traditional free-standing bush vines here as the more modern Guyot. In fact, Kanonkop oozes tradition. The estate tour takes you into a hall of shallow open concrete vats used for hand-punching and fermenting after harvest, which the winemaker, Abrie Beeslaar, claims is the secret of the high quality of Kanonkop's wine. The Pinotage range is intense and tannic, taken from minimum 50-year-old bush vines and aged in French oak – certainly not to be drunk young.
kanonkop.co.za; tel +27 21 884 4656; R44, Stellenbosch; 9am-5pm Mon-Fri, 9am-3pm Sat Ⓢ

❷ TOKARA

Under the guidance of oenologist Miles Mossop and now with Stuart Botha at the reins, Tokara is the modern face of Stellenbosch winemaking. It's a stunning example of futuristic architecture, filled with daring contemporary art and sculpture. Botha creates distinctive wines from three different vineyards, reflecting personality and characteristics of Stellenbosch and the emerging regions of Elgin and Hermanus. Tokara's signature, berry-rich Pintotage is the big hitter – but don't miss the straw-coloured Director's Reserve White, a vibrant blend of Sauvignon and Semillon; or the award-winning Syrah, hand-picked on the slopes of the Simonsberg Mountain and incredibly intense in flavour and colour. Tastings are held in the Wine Lounge; be sure, also, to try the fruity olive oil made on their olive farm. There is also a casual deli, and a gourmet restaurant with spectacular panoramic views as far as Cape Town's mythic Table Mountain.
tokara.co.za; tel +27 21 808 5900; Helshoogte Rd, Stellenbosch; by reservation daily Ⓢ✕

❸ ALLÉE BLEUE

Like many large Cape wine estates, Allée Bleue is owned by foreign investors who have transformed a fruit farm by replacing some of the orchards with 25 hectares (61 acres) of vines. And their *vigneron*, Van Zyl du Toit, a beefy rugby enthusiast, could not look happier, as he has been given carte blanche to create a state-of-the-art cellar. Allée Bleue is the place to taste Pinotage, South Africa's most famous grape – a cross of Burgundy's Pinot Noir with Chateauneuf-du-Pape's Cinsault, or Hermitage – created in 1925 in Stellenbosch. The vines at Allée Bleue are young, aged in steel vats to produce what Van Zyl calls 'our quaffing wine'. But their flagship, full-bodied and tannic Pinotages are made from grapes that come by lorry from 50-year-old vines three hours away, a method Van Zyl mischievously describes as 'terroir by truck'. He pinpoints three key characteristics for Pinotage: 'colour – a very deep, ruby red; a very intense nose, plums and cherry; and then there is the tannin, which the old-school winemakers prefer supple, aged in large old wood barrels, while the newer generation like me prefer to emphasise by using small new *barriques*.'
alleebleue.co.za; tel +27 21 874 1021; Intersection R45 & R310, Groot Drakenstein; 9am-5pm Mon-Fri, 10am-5pm Sat & Sun Ⓢ✕

❹ SOLMS DELTA

Though it has been through some troubled times in recent years, having faced down liquidation in 2018 following the withdrawal of government funding, Solms Delta has endured. It's certainly a winery with a vision, making a concrete attempt to empower the cooperative Black workforce, which has been given 50% ownership. 'The owners are trying to address the post-apartheid heritage,' explains former winemaker Hagen Viljoen. The choice of wines to taste are daring blends of highly

02

03

04

concentrated Rhone varietals such as Syrah, Grenache, Carignan and Mourvèdre, made essentially from desiccated grapes. And the restaurant, Fyndraai, is perfect for a wine-pairing lunch, with dishes such as smoked ostrich and fynbos greens; chef Shaun Schoeman uses herbs from his native African heritage and Cape Malay spices. *solms-delta.co.za; tel +27 062 457 5647; Delta Rd, Groot Drakenstein; by reservation 9am-5pm daily* 💲✗

05 GLENWOOD

GlenWood is Franschhoek's hidden secret, tucked away in a remote valley at the end of a dusty 7km (4-mile) dirt track. The domaine resembles the Big Country ranch, with vines dramatically enclosed by steep mountain slopes. The genial cellar master, DB Burger, has been making award-winning wines here for over 30 years, and suggests that 'visitors give a call first, because our tasting is more personalised than most places, I hope. I try to be available, and there is not the feeling you are being told what to think by some student taster who is repeating comments learnt by heart.' He is most proud of his elegant Chardonnays, both the oaky Vigneron Selection and the crisper GlenWood Unoaked Chardonnay, but the spicy Syrah is also excellent. Burger explains, 'Franschhoek has metamorphosed into perhaps the leading Cape wine region. In my early days, grapes were just grown to be sold to the cooperative. Then winemakers started replanting

vines that are only now growing into maturity, explaining the recent radical improvement in quality.' *glenwoodvineyards.co.za; tel +27 21 876 2044; Robertsvlei Rd, Franschhoek; by reservation 11am-4pm Tue-Sun* 💲✗

06 CHAMONIX

Chamonix is a vast domaine encompassing vineyard, farmland and sprawling game reserve with guest lodges surrounded by wildebeest, zebra and springbok. But the wines stand out, masterminded by dynamic oenologist Gottfried Mocke and now in the hands of winemaker Niel Bruwer, who is experimenting in the cellar, ageing in a mix of concrete tanks, steel vats, *barriques*, large casks and the latest trend, high-tech concrete 'eggs'. The stars here are the Chardonnay and Sauvignon, Pinot Noir and a supple Pinotage, made *passito*-style similar to Amarone. Chamonix also restarted production of Chenin Blanc in 2020 and, according to Mocke: 'Chenin was planted here in vast amounts 50 to 60 years ago, primarily to make brandy, but I think over the years the vine has mutated to our climatic conditions to become virtually an autochthonous South African grape.' *chamonix.co.za; tel +27 21 876 8500; Uitkyk St, Franschhoek; by reservation 10am-5pm Mon-Sat* 💲✗

07 HAUTE CABRIÈRE

It is worth driving out from the edge of Franschhoek and up the

mountainside just for the views over the valley from the sunny wine-tasting terrace of Haute Cabrière. The estate was named in 1694 by one of the founding French Huguenot settlers, Pierre Jourdain, after his home town, when this area was still known as Olifantshoek – Elephant's (rather than French) Corner. The present owners, Achim von Arnim and his son Takuan, are on a mission to produce high-quality Champagne-standard sparkling wines, and have planted Chardonnay on the sandstone soil on one side of the vineyard, and Pinot Noir on the stony clay terroir of the west-facing slopes. Yes, these are officially South African Methode Cap Classique, but it is difficult to tell them apart from a French Champagne in a blind tasting – especially over a meal in their restaurant, which overlooks the cathedral-like cellar. *cabriere.co.za; tel +27 21 876 8500; Lambrechts Rd, Franschhoek; 10am-5pm daily* 💲✗

05

WHERE TO STAY

HOLDEN MANZ
Just outside Franschhoek, the modern boutique winery and restaurant contrasts with the irresistible old-world charm of this property, housed in a romantic 17th-century Cape Dutch thatched manor.
holdenmanz.com; tel +27 21 876 2738; Green Valley Rd, Franschhoek

RICKETY BRIDGE COUNTRY HOUSE
Dating back to 1792 when it was part of La Provence, one of Franschhoek's original Huguenot estates, Rickety Bridge is a boutique winery with three sumptuously furnished guest rooms.
ricketybridge.com; tel +27 21 876 2994; R45, Franschhoek

STELLENBOSCH HOTEL
A comfortable country-style hotel with a variety of rooms, some self-catering. A section dating from 1743 houses the Stellenbosch Kitchen, a good spot for a drink and some people-watching.
stellenboschhotel.co.za; tel +27 21 887 3644; 162 Dorp St, Stellenbosch

WHERE TO EAT

LA PETITE COLOMBE
This breezy Franschhoek sister branch of the award-winning Cape Town restaurant offers French-inspired 'Reduced' or Chef's Experience' menus of 10 or 13 courses (including entirely vegetarian menus); you can opt to pair each course with a different wine.
lapetitecolombe. com; Le Quarter Français, Huguenot Rd, Franschhoek; tel +27 21 202 3395; daily

REUBEN'S
Franschhoek's favourite son, celebrity chef Reuben Riffel, is behind this French-inspired restaurant in a fabulous, light-filled space off the main road. Seasonal two- or three-course set menus, a carefully curated wine list and beers from a nearby microbrewery.
reubens.co.za; tel +27 21 876 3772; 2 Daniel Hugo St, Franschhoek; Wed-Mon

RUST EN VREDE
Expect innovative dishes such as rabbit-leg wontons or beetroot chocolate fondant at this stylish winery restaurant. Book ahead.
rustenvrede.com; tel +27 21 881 3757; Annandale Rd, Stellenbosch; Tue-Sat

WHAT TO DO
A favourite Cape Town activity is learning to cook Cape Malay-style. Gamidah Jacobs of Lekka Kombuis will show you how to make perfect *dhaltjies* (chilli bites), *rootis* (flatbreads) and chicken curry at classes in her historic turquoise-painted Bo-Kaap home.
lekkakombuis.co.za

CELEBRATIONS
Franschhoek goes back to its French roots with a huge 14 July party to celebrate Bastille Day.
franschhoekbastille.co.za

Map labels: CORNAZO, 04, O LAGO, VILANOVA DE AROUSA, CARDALDA, Río Umia, 03, CASAL DO RÍO, PONTE ARNELAS, 05, RÍAS BAIXAS, 01, CAMBADOS, 02, RIBADUMIA

[Spain]
RÍAS BAIXAS

For sea, shellfish and a very special wine, make a pilgrimage to this rugged nugget of Galicia.

Perched just above Portugal, on the Iberian Peninsula's northwest coast, Galicia is a corner of Spain with a rich seafaring tradition and sought-after seafood. All year round its granite headlands are blasted by the Atlantic's wind and waves, but in between those rock bulwarks lie sheltered inlets – or *rías*. It is these that lend their name to Galicia's Rías Baixas wine region, the most interesting of the five Denominación de Origen (DO) regions in Galicia.

They do things differently in Galicia. Here, vines are suspended 2m (6.5ft) above the ground from granite pillars, all the better to gain extra ventilation in this humid region and prevent mould. And the grapes that hang from these canopies are also a little bit special. Stony yet fruity, the Albariño grape that grows in Rías Baixas produces a white wine that is a tangy alternative to Chablis (Chardonnay) and Sauvignon Blanc – and this is its heartland.

This grape is the key to how Rías Baixas' white wines manage to meld the savoury, saline flavours of their surroundings with a Viognier-like fruitiness, to mouthwatering effect. On a sunny afternoon, there is no better companion to a plate of seafood – oysters and octopus are the obvious options, but don't fear the local speciality of *percebes* (goose barnacles, harvested from cliffs in between crashing waves and tasting something like lobster). Outside Galicia, spicy Asian food is another great partner for Albariño.

Many visitors to Galicia arrive on foot, having made the pilgrimage to Santiago de Compostela on the Way of St James. Rías Baixas is a couple of hours' drive south of the Galician capital, and the revitalising coastal setting, with its wide and sheltered beaches, backed by aromatic pine and eucalypt forests in the interior, appeals to footsore pilgrims and wine-seeking sybarites alike.

GET THERE
The closest international airport is at Santiago de Compostela. It's a 1hr drive south to Cambados.

01 BODEGAS DEL PALACIO DE FEFIÑANES

Hidden in the granite cloisters of a vast, austere palace in the centre of Cambados, this winery was one of the earliest producers of wine in Rías Baixas, releasing its first bottles in 1928, and the first to be recognised as Denominación de Origen Rías Baixas. Today there are five Rías Baixas subregions and this tour focuses on the original source of the Albariño grape, here in the Val de Salnés.

The Palacio de Fefiñanes dates back to the 17th century and the stone with which its built is a clue to Albariño's savoury edge: the mineral-rich, granitic soil. As owner Juan Gil de Araújo puts it: 'a wine must be loyal to its origins'.

fefinanes.com; tel +34 986 542 204; Plaza de Fefiñanes, Cambados; daily by appointment

02 MARTÍN CÓDAX

From the tasting terrace at Martín Códax, high on a hilltop behind Cambados, visitors enjoy views over the mussel and oyster beds in the bay that produce the ideal accompaniment to its white wines.

It's all about Albariño at this cooperative, where 280 members pool harvests from their small plots every September and October; unlike most Spanish regions, co-ops are common here.

A great way to understand the grape is to book a tasting; there are four different tasting options available, during which you'll sample two or three wines. The 'Cantiga de Amigo' option features Organistrum (the label shows the cathedral in Santiago de Compostela), the only Albariño aged in French oak and bottled in small batches; you should detect fresh citrus and apples from this one. Lías, named for the yeasty lees on which the wine sits and which add flavours of brioche, is a rounded Albariño wine with a long finish. And the Martín Códax Albariño is a bright, intense wine with aromas of green apples, fresh herbs and citrus fruits. It's not aged – this is as honest a taste of the Val de Salnés as it gets. Three wines made from the same grape – but each deliciously different.

01 A break from
tending the vines at
Martín Códax winery

02 Pazo de Rubianes

03 Vineyard at Pazo de
Rubianes

*martincodax.com; tel +34 9986 526
040; Burgáns 91, Vilariño; Tue-Sat
by appt, plus Mon Jul-Sep* 💲

03 PAZO DE SEÑORANS

You can tell the importance of a
property by the size of the *horreo*
(the outdoor food store for a
house, raised above the ground
to stop vermin getting in), and the
horreo at Pazo de Señorans has
10 pillars per side, an indication
that this was a wealthy estate – yet
in the 1970s the building was a ruin.
It was restored by Marisol Bueno
and Javier Mareque and is now run
by their children Marisol, Vicky,
Javier and Santiago. Today, it's at
the heart of the Rías Baixas DO,
and celebrated its 30th anniversary
in 2020. Before you try the wine,
the *pazo* (country house) itself
is a fascinating place to explore:
pagan and Christian symbols
above the gate show typically
pragmatic loyalties: a small chapel
is decorated with palm trees, a
symbol of travelling the world. And
there's also a panic room where
Edward, the last king of Portugal, is
thought to have hidden.

In Galicia, explains Javier Izurieta
Romero, land was more important
than money. 'Family inheritances
split each parcel of land so
none could be sold without the
agreement of all. Each family had
its own vines, its own pig and a cow.
They optimised the land, growing
potatoes beneath the vines.' The
result is that Pazo de Señorans is
supplied with grapes by 110 growers
who work 400 parcels of land. The
sugar and acidity of the grapes
is measured at each. 'If you do a
good job in the vineyard you can
leave the wine alone,' says Javier.

The winemaking is similarly
simple, with no oak used. Just three
wines are made by winemaker
Ana Quintela, but the difference
between the years is striking.
'Albariño is not just a wine to drink
young and cold,' explains Javier. As
it ages, the flavours mellow from
citrus and green apple (and, some
years, rose petals) to nectarines
and apricots, becoming ever more
buttery. After pressing, the skins
of the grapes are used to make
aguardiente, a punchy digestif, in a
distillery on the property. Nothing
goes to waste in Galicia.
*pazodesenorans.com; tel +34 9986
715 373; Lugar Vilanoviña, Meis; by
appointment* 💲

04 PAZO DE RUBIANES

While there may be more than
20,000 small plots of vines and
some 6500 growers in Rías Baixas,
this 15th-century ducal palace
in the town of Rubianes is the
place to explore the region's
largest vineyards. The official
tour leads guests through the
palace's botanical gardens, which
were planted in the 17th and 18th

04 Chilled Albariño with seafood at Martín Códax

05 Pontevedra, the capital of Rías Baixas

06 *Pulpo a la gallega* (Galician octopus)

centuries and are now resplendent with giant eucalypt, camphor and oak trees, and more than 4000 varieties of camellia (the garden is a stop on the Ruta de la Camelia; see What To Do, opposite). Next, visit the vineyard, then the palace and chapel. The tour concludes with a well-earned tasting of Pazo de Rubianes' wines in the cellar, the result of agronomist Guillermo Hermo's hard work growing and selecting the best grapes. *pazoderubianes.com; tel +34 9986 510 534; Rúa do Pazo 7, Rubianes; by appointment* ⑤

⑤ BODEGA GRANBAZÁN

To complete a loop, head back to the coast and the town of Vilanova de Arousa, just north of Cambados. When the sun is shining, the small sandy beaches here lure daytrippers who then check out the tapas menus in the old town's bars. The grandest local winery is Granbazán, a short drive inland. Its Etiqueta range is the go-to Albariño, with the Etiqueta Verde being a dry, floral and decidedly salty example; and the minerality-meets-melon of the Etiqueta Ambar making it the pick of the bunch. *agrodebazan.com; tel +34 9986 555 562; Lugar de Tremoedo 46, Vilanova de Arousa; Tue-Sat by appointment (Sun & holidays on request)*

WHERE TO STAY

PARADOR DE CAMBADOS

The coastal town of Cambados is the best base for exploring the Salnés region. Set in an ancestral country house in the old quarter of Cambados, this parador has grand bedrooms (some with air-con), a restaurant serving Galician specialities, and good sea views from the promenade. *parador.es; tel +34 9986 542 250; Paseo Calzada, Cambados*

NOVAVILA

Novavila is a rural boutique hotel run by the same family as Spain's Vilanova Peña interior design brand (yes, all the furniture is available to buy). Wine is another sideline, so guests are also invited to taste the family's Albariño. *novavilariasbaixas.com; tel +34 9609 111 023; Santo Tomé de Nogueira, Meis*

WHERE TO EAT

There are several restaurants on Rua Albergue, Rua Real

and Rua Principe in Cambados. In Pontevedra, the Rías Baixas capital, the majority of the restaurants are concentrated in the streets of the old town.

EIRADO DA LEÑA

Enjoy a deliciously creative culinary experience in an intimate little stone-walled restaurant, set with white linen and fresh flowers. The Menú Curricán features nine beautifully presented courses of Galician produce for around €70. *oeirado.com; tel +34 9986 860 225; Praza da Leña 3, Pontevedra; daily*

BEIRAMAR

From Cambados, take a 30-minute drive to the town of O Grove on the peninsula that shelters Cambados from the full force of the Atlantic. Seafood, of course, is the town's speciality, and Beiramar is a reliable restaurant in which to enjoy scallops, oysters, fresh fish and more. *restaurantebeiramar. com; tel +34 9986 731 081; Avenida Beiramar 30, O Grove; daily*

WHAT TO DO

RUTA DE LA CAMELIA

If you're not ready for the Way of St James, the pilgrimage/hiking route across the Pyrenees that winds up in Santiago de

Compostela, the Ruta de la Camelia is a gentler, more floral alternative. It follows the southern coast of Galicia, taking in 12 ornamental gardens. Two close to Pontevedra are Pazo de Quinteiro da Cruz, with its 1500 varieties of camellia; and the grand estate of Pazo de Rubianes. *turismo.gal*

CELEBRATIONS

FIESTA DEL ALBARIÑO

On the first Sunday of August, Cambados' annual wine festival was born out of a contest between local winemakers, but is much more than that today: parades, live music by night and the naming of the year's winning wines. *fiestadelalbariño.com*

FIESTA DEL MARISCO

In October, the region's shellfish festival is hosted by the 'seafood paradise' of O Grove. Scoff local oysters while quaffing Albariño as the town's seafaring culture is celebrated with music, dance and sport. *turismogrove.es*

01

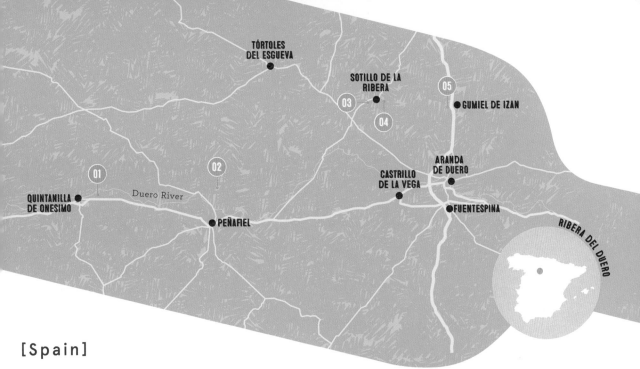

[Spain]

RIBERA DEL DUERO

Enjoy Tempranillo and slow-cooked lamb in the rustic, riverside region that
threatens to usurp Rioja as the source of Spain's most sophisticated red wines.

In a country where traditions are slow to change, some of the wineries in Ribera del Duero (as they are in Priorat too) are at the frontier of winemaking. Just two hours' drive north of Madrid, what Ribera del Duero lacks in scenic majesty – these are Spain's high plains, without the sea views of Rias Baixas, the mountains of Rioja and the rugged valleys of Priorat – it makes up for with its wonderful wines. Violet when young, the Tempranillo – the grape attraction here – is seemingly inkier than Rioja, with a flavour that is less dependent on oak, more open to the winemaker's influence. It was only in 1982 that Ribera del Duero gained a Denominación de Origen: 'This is a young DO,' says winemaker Rafael Cuerda. 'We can try new things, we're more flexible than Rioja.'

Thanks to its altitude – this is one of the highest winegrowing places in the world – the growing season in Ribera del Duero

is short, and it can be very hot during the day and very cold at night. But it's this variation, of up to 25°C (77°F), that creates the special conditions for producing incredible wines from vineyards along the Duero River (known as the Douro in Portugal; see p205). Those vineyards include Vega Sicilia, source of Spain's most famous wine, from plots developed by Eloy Lecanda y Chaves in 1864.

Younger Riberas taste fresh and are great with ham and fish. The Crianzas, aged for 12 months, are a perfect accompaniment to the local speciality of *lechal al horno* (slow-cooked lamb).

Make no mistake, however: aside from the wine, this is an undeveloped expanse of Castile and León. The landscape of bare plateaus, sometimes topped with a gimlet-eyed castle, is bleak; the towns and villages are functional. But the wines? The wines are just wonderful.

GET THERE
Madrid is the closest city to Aranda del Duero, which makes the best base for a weekend.

01 VIÑA MAYOR

Depending on where you're staying, it makes sense to start at the far end of Ribera's 'Golden Mile', a strip of wineries strung along the very fast and straight N-122 (be warned!) before venturing off the beaten path. Viña Mayor near Peñafiel offers an excellent introduction to the region, with a guided tour of the winery explaining such nuances as the difference between American and French oak barrels (it's all about the pores in the wood), before concluding in a glass-fronted tasting room overlooking the orange, iron-rich earth and vines stretching down to the road. Wines are produced in both a classic style and, under the Secreto label, a modern style;

a tour and tasting highlights the differences. Other tour options include learning how to blend a wine or pick and press grapes. *grupobodegaspalacio.es; tel +34 983 680 461; Carretera de Valladolid a Soria km325, Quintanilla de Onésimo; by appointment* ⑤

02 BODEGAS COMENGE

'This is nature, but controlled,' says Comenge's winemaker Rafael Cuerda. The organic-certified winery has earned its reputation as one of Ribera del Duero's best thanks to an approach that blends technology with ecology. An example: Comenge uses its own natural yeast – but that yeast was selected as the best for the wine

at the University of Madrid (where Rafael studied) from 300 samples taken from its vineyards.

Comenge is a small, young winery, with 32 hectares (79 acres) of Tempranillo vines, half of them surrounding the modern building, which was built by the Comenge family in 1999. At a lofty 800-900m (2600-3000ft), the tasting room and terrace overlook the valley of the River Duero, and in turn are overlooked by Curiel's hilltop castle. Pesticides and herbicides are not used; instead the grass is left to grow (the competition for water is good for the vines), then cut to insulate them later in summer. Comenge is looking for fewer clusters and smaller grapes. 'We don't try to make the same

wine every year,' says Rafael. 'It's important to express what happened in the vineyard that year and every year is different. The most important thing is the grape.'

Grapes are picked by hand in autumn; the local Tempranillo is quick to ripen in the warm, sunny days but the cold nights help the wine retain its distinctive colour. Rafael's skill and the winery's attention to detail ensures that the Don Miguel, made from grapes grown in the highest plots, strikes a great balance between fruit and toasty oak flavours – and it sells at around half the price of comparable wines.
comenge.com; tel +34 983 880 363; Camino del Castillo, Curiel de Duero; daily by appointment $

03 FÉLIX CALLEJO

It's a family affair at Félix Callejo: father Félix is from Sotillo and returned to the village in 1989 to start his winery, which now employs his children – Beatriz and Cristina are on the business side, while Noelia and José Félix, who studied winemaking at the University of Madrid with Rafael Cuerda from Comenge, are winemakers. Félix's mission was not only to make better wine (isn't that the goal of every winemaker?) but to revive an old-fashioned local white grape called Albillo. Previously in this part of Spain, families made their own wines and had their own cellar. They would plant a small plot with eight or nine vines of white, for eating, around a walnut tree.

But the white grapes they didn't eat were mixed with red wine to make Clarete – named for its clear colour – which they pressed with their feet. 'Our grandparents' generation,' explains Beatriz, 'drank a lot of wine so it had to be lighter.' Callejo has been making the El Lebrero wine from a 3-hectare (7-acre) plot of these white grapes since 2009 and, more recently, the Viña Pilar Clarete, with Albarillo and Tinto Fino, aka Tempranillo.

But the main focus is on Tempranillo, which is grown on limestone at a height of 860-930m (2820-3050ft). This elevation means that it's cold at night, so the local variety of Tempranillo has developed a thicker skin, allowing more flavour to be extracted at

pressing. And it's not the only advantage this part of Ribera del Duero enjoys over Rioja: the weather is warmer and drier. Callejo uses only its own grapes and some of the vines are almost 30 years old; these go into a Gran Reserva that is aged for five years. *bodegasfelixcallejo.com; tel +34 947 532 312; Avenida del Cid km16, Sotillo de la Ribera; Mon-Fri by appointment* $

04 BODEGAS ISMAEL ARROYO

To understand even more of Ribera del Duero's history, continue to Bodegas Ismael Arroyo on the other side of Sotillo (the village lends its name to Arroyo's award-winning ValSotillo wine). As was usual in many of the region's villages, every building in Sotillo had a *lagar*, a cave for storing wine, tunnelled into the hills in the village. Owner Miguel Arroyo explains: 'Villagers would

carry wine in goatskins which, when full, were just the right size to lift to the *lagares* after the grapes had been pressed.'

These cellars were built between the 16th century and the 1960s and Arroyo is one of very few wineries still using its family cellar, which is in the hill behind the winery and the location for tastings. 'You can understand how important wine was culturally,' says Miguel, 'because the stones inside were expensive and only otherwise used for palaces and churches.' Inside the narrow cellar it's cool – always 11°C (52°F), winter or summer – and, when lit by flickering wall lights, slightly eerie. The family started making their own wine in 1979, breaking away from the local cooperative. They still do things the old-fashioned way, using no pesticides and only the natural yeasts present in the grape skins.

valsotillo.com; tel +34 947 532 309; Los Lagares 71, Sotillo de la Ribera; Mon-Sat by appointment $

05 BODEGAS PORTIA

Wine meets architecture on the road into Aranda de Duero from the north. Here stands Portia, a vast, low-slung, high-tech winery designed in the shape of a three-pointed star by British architect Norman Foster. It's a stark contrast to wineries such as Arroyo, and is one of two star-architect-designed projects in Ribera del Duero; the other is Richard Rogers' Bodegas Protos in Peñafiel. But while Protos resembles a provincial airport, Portia has more of a spaceport look to it – which is why we prefer it; it's also home to the elegantly upscale Triennia Gastrobar restaurant. Portia's wines are good examples of the region: at the 2019 Concours Mondiale de Bruxelles, an annual international blind tasting, Portia scored a gold medal. At the same competition of 9000 wines from five continents, Spain and Ribera del Duero headed the medal table.

Portia is also rather creative when it comes to the events front: as well as tours and tastings, it offers stargazing evenings and 'VIP' events.

bodegasportia.com; tel +34 947 102 700; Antigua Carretera N-1, Gumiel de Izán; tastings & tours daily by appointment $ ✕

WHERE TO STAY

HOTEL TORREMILANOS

West of Aranda de Duero, this winery hotel promises spacious rooms and a great location, plus tastings and tours at the biodynamic bodega. *torremilanos.es; tel +34 947 512 852; Finca Torremilanos, Aranda de Duero*

HOTEL CASTILLO DE CURIEL

Just north of Peñafiel in Curiel de Duero, this is the hotel of choice for castle romantics. Occupying the oldest castle in the region (dating from the 9th century), the renovated hotel has lovely, antique-filled rooms, all offering sweeping views, and a well-regarded restaurant. *castillodecuriel.com; tel +34 983 880 401; Plaza Adolfo Muñoz Alonso, Peñafiel*

WHERE TO EAT

EL LAGAR DE ISILLA

In central Aranda de Duero, El Lagar de Isilla is the go-to place for traditional, ribsticking Ribera cooking – slow-cooked lamb, not many vegetables – which is the perfect companion to the region's wines. The restaurant is part of a winery business that also owns ancient cellars beneath Aranda de Duero, with tours and tastings available. *lagarisilla.es; tel +34 947 510 683; C/Isilla 18, Aranda de Duero; daily*

MOLINO DE PALACIOS

If visiting in autumn, fans of fungi should head for this converted watermill in the west of the region. Wild mushrooms are a seasonal obsession in northern Spain, and Molino de Palacios does them best. *molinodepalacios. com; tel +34 983 880 505; Avenida de la Constitucion 16, Peñafiel; Tue-Sun*

WHAT TO DO

As there's not much happening on the *meseta* (plateau), most locals head for Burgos, which might seem like a typically sombre northern-central Spanish city but has plenty of good restaurants and nightlife along C/de San Juan, C/de la Puebla and C/del Huerto del Rey, northeast of the city's standout Gothic cathedral.

CELEBRATIONS

Sonorama is an annual music festival hosted in Aranda de Duero each August – it must be one of the few pop, rock and dance music festivals in the world to also feature wine-tasting courses and events in the city's underground wine cellars. *sonorama-aranda.com*

[Spain]

RIOJA

Hemmed by mountains, sustained by adventurous Basque cuisine and home to spectacular wineries, Rioja is arguably the world's most rewarding wine region.

Rioja is Spain's rock-star region, the Jagger to Ribera's Richards. It's moneyed, flamboyant – and fantastic fun for a wild weekend away.

Firstly, it was blessed with natural good looks: the region sits at the foothills of the Cantabrian mountains, beyond which lie the Basque country and the city of San Sebastián. The mountains are a barrier to clouds from the north, creating a sunny microclimate. Next, it had perfect timing, hitting the heights as French wine faltered and attracting wealthy investors who splashed out on star architects (more on this later), state-of-the-art wineries and winemaking talent. The result is that there are now more than 550 wineries in Rioja. Not all are open for tastings, but those that do offer some of the most fascinating visitor experiences in the wine world.

GET THERE
Bilbao's international airport is 1hr 30min north of Logroño by car.

The River Ebro flows eastward through the region, on its way to the Mediterranean, passing through Logroño. This university city is the fulcrum for Rioja's three subregions. To the south is Rioja Baja; north of the river is Rioja Alavesa, which includes the fortified hilltop town of Laguardia; and to the west of Logroño is Rioja Alta. The focus of this wine trail falls on the latter two regions.

Laguardia, just north of Logroño, makes a good base for exploration. From here it's easy to reach Haro, where Rioja's original winemakers set up shop in the 1800s. Tradition is still at the heart of Rioja's wine, but the old-fashioned leathery Tempranillo is fading away in the face of fresh competition from Ribera del Duero. Its wineries range from fascinating time warps to engineering marvels and contemporary curios.

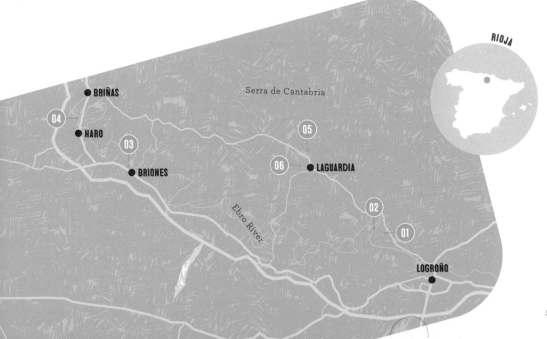

RIOJA

BRIÑAS

Serra de Cantabria

04

HARO

03

05

BRIONES

06

LAGUARDIA

02

Ebro River

01

LOGROÑO

01 VIÑA REAL

Seven years in the making, when Viña Real was completed in 2004 it was one of Rioja's first modern wineries. And it's an engineering marvel on a grand scale, courtesy of Bordeaux architect Philippe Mazières, whose father was a winemaker. First, a corner was cut out of a tabletop mountain between Laguardia and Logroño. Two tunnels were bored 120m (390ft) deep into the remaining mountain using the machines that excavated the tunnels of Bilbao's metro system. Then a 56m-wide (184ft) barrel-shaped building was sunk into the levelled-off corner. In the centre of this twin-storey circular room is a revolving crane arm that moves huge vats around, using gravity to pour grape juice from one to another. Head winemaker María Larrea monitors everything from a laboratory reached by a walkway. It's a little like winery-meets-Bond-villain-lair.

Beneath the production area is a raw concrete bunker where 2000 barrels of the Reserva are stored. In the cave there are 14,000 barrels of the Crianza, which is aged for at least two years, one of which must be in a barrel. Viña Real is part of the CVNE group, which started in 1879 when French winemakers relocated to Rioja, bringing with them barrel-ageing techniques. *visitascvne.com; tel +34 941 304 809; Carretera Logroño-Laguardia km4.8, Araba; Wed-Sun by appointment* 🟢 ✕

02 CONTINO

Cradled in a loop of the River Ebro, Contino is a château-style, single-estate vineyard, part of the CVNE (Compañia Vinícola Norte Espana – the Cune on the bottle is a misprint) empire. But it's a very different experience to Viña Real on the hill nearby. The stone property, just outside Laserna, is sheltered – ideal for sitting outside in the shade on old millstones, catching your breath while listening to the birdsong with a glass of the white Rioja in hand. Contino's vineyards reach all the way down to the river Ebro, past ancient olive trees (one is 800 years old).

Seven grape varieties are permitted in Rioja wine, three white and four red: Tempranillo,

04 LÓPEZ DE HEREDIA VIÑA TONDONIA

The story of López de Heredia Viña Tondonia is the story of Rioja wine. Founder Rafael López de Heredia was a Basque who lived in Chile but returned to fight for the Spanish king, lost, and was exiled to France, where worked for a Bayonne wine merchant, absorbing tips and techniques from French winemakers. The disaster of phylloxera, a vine disease that destroyed the French industry, was a blessing for Rioja. People like Raphael returned to Spain bringing new ideas and French winemakers. Recognising the region's similarities with Bordeaux, he settled in Haro in 1877, close to the train station, invested all his money in five vats and began making table wine, selling it fast and cheaply.

Fast-forward four generations and one thing has changed at López de Heredia, now managed by María José López de Heredia: the wine is outstanding (but not as cheap). Other things haven't changed: it still uses a bunch of dried Viura vine stalks as a filter, as was traditional; it doesn't use steel vats, only 100-year-old oak vats; and it still makes (some) of its own barrels.

A tour begins in a modern annexe designed by Zaha Hadid to resemble a wine decanter. But the real interest lies in the old winery next door. Here, the hand-excavated wine gallery dates from 1890 and extends all the way back to the river – workers were given

Garnacha (or Grenache, which adds a bit of weight), Carignane and Graciano. Contino is notable for having developed the rare and delicate Graciano grape and produces a 100% Graciano wine, which is worth comparing with a typical Tempranillo-driven Rioja. *visitascvne.com; tel +34 941 304 809; Finca San Rafael, Laserna; Tue-Sat by appointment* 🟦✕

03 VIVANCO

Not satisfied with just building a modern winery on the outskirts of Briones, in the west of Rioja Alta, the Vivanco family added a restaurant and a museum (full name: Vivanco Museum of the Culture of Wine). And it's by no means a half-hearted effort: with

4000 sq metres (43,055 sq ft) of space and items from the family's personal collection spanning 8000 years of winemaking, from amphorae to art by Joan Miró, you're guaranteed to learn something about human ingenuity (though you might want to skip a few of the 3000 corkscrews).

At weekend tasting courses, you can explore Vicanco's wine. The winery itself is next to the museum and underground. 'I've always felt that our wines had to tell a story,' says winemaker Rafael Vivanco Sáenz – but the museum also does a great job of telling it. *vivancowineculture.com; tel +34 941 322 323; Carretera Nacional N-232 km442, Briones; Wed-Sat by appointment* 🟦✕

05 Central Logroño

06 *Patatas a la Riojana*
(potatoes with chorizo
and onion)

4L (7 pints) of wine a day, two of which they could drink in the winery. In its darker corners the cave is coated with furry-white penicillium mould, which helps keep the temperature constant by absorbing humidity.

The last stop is in the tasting room to sample López de Heredia's Viña Bosconia, a five-year-old Burgundy-style wine; and the Viña Tondonia, a six-year-old Bordeaux style wine. After more than a century of practice, both are sublime.
lopezdeheredia.com; tel +34 941 310 244; Avenida de Vizcaya 3, Haro; Mon-Sat by appointment Ⓢ

05 BODEGAS RUIZ DE VIÑASPRE

This family-owned winery is set in the foothills between Laguardia and the Cantabrian mountains to the north. Its neighbour, Bodegas Ysios, is one of Rioja's most iconic wineries, thanks to its spectacular wave-like roof, designed by Spanish architect Santiago Calatrava to reflect the mountain backdrop. Sadly, the roof proved to be less waterproof than desired, which kept lawyers busy. Ruiz de Viñaspre is a smaller operation, with all the Tempranillo grapes coming from the winery's own vineyards. 'You can only make the best wines from the best grapes,' says Ainhoa Ruiz de Viñaspre, who now runs the winery with her sister Jaione. 'Our vineyards are in Laguardia and Elvillar, in the heart of Rioja Alavesa, sheltered below the Sierra Cantabria. The unique microclimate makes this one of the best vine-growing areas in the world.'

The Ruiz de Viñaspre family is at the heart of the winery: 'Being from Rioja means everything. That is why it is always someone from the family who receives visitors. We want them to feel that our house is theirs.'

bodegaruizdevinaspre.com; tel +34 945 600 626; Camino de la Hoya, Laguardia; Mon-Fri by appointment Ⓢ

06 CASA PRIMICIA

According to legend, King Sancho Abarca of Navarra once climbed a hill at the foot of the Cantabrian mountains, which overlooked the River Ebro and what is now Rioja. Recognising the hill's strategic importance, he founded La Guardia de Navarra at its top in 908 CE. More than a thousand years later and Laguardia offers a (very popular) glimpse into the past. The hill is riddled with unexplored tunnels and blessed with beautiful architecture. Casa Primicia, the 'first house', is the oldest property in the medieval hamlet, dating from the 15th century. It was here that grapes taxed from the local area were stored. From the 16th century, wine was made on the site and the restoration of the building, which owner Julián Madrid began in 2006, has revealed how it was done. And the tunnels that form a subterranean twin town are perfect cellars for storing Bodegas Casa Primicia's own wines.

Visits include tastings and tours of the building; you can also opt for a tasting with a meal.
casaprimicia.com; tel +34 945 600 256; C/Páganos 78, Laguardia; Tue-Sun by appointment Ⓢ ✕

WHERE TO STAY

If you're based in the walled hilltop town of Laguardia you'll be able to reach all of this trail's featured wineries easily. The town is popular with tourists, though hotels and restaurants can be pricey – but it's easy to escape to Logroño for better-value meals.

CASA RURAL ERLETXE

This guesthouse, in the thick walls of the town, is hosted by María Arrate Aguirre. She makes delicious homemade breakfasts that include honey from her bees, stationed up in the Cantabrian hills. *erletxe.com; tel +34 945 621 015; Rua Mayor de Peralta 24-26, Laguardia*

MARQUÉS DE RISCAL

For a less understated stay, try the upscale Marques de Riscal hotel. The Frank Gehry-designed property, a cascade of ribbons of steel, lies between Logroño and Haro. *hotel-marquesderiscal. com; tel +34 945 180 880; C/Torrea 1, Elciego*

06

WHERE TO EAT
LA TAVINA

This wine club in Logroño serves 60 wines by the glass (at shop prices) and modern tapas plates. In winter it hosts group tastings and courses. *latavina.com; tel +34 941 102 300; C/Laurel 2, Logroño; daily*

LA COCINA DE RAMON

Chef Ramón Piñeiro updates traditional Spanish recipes at his restaurant in central Logroño. There's a three-course set menu for €26 or his three-course 'Tempranillo' and 'Garnacha' menus for €55/€60, composed of creative dishes of market-fresh ingredients

paired with Rioja wines. And the impressive wine list features some 50 local labels. *lacocinaderamon.es; tel +34 941 289 808; C/ Portales 30, Logroño; Tue-Sun*

WHAT TO DO
SAN SEBASTIÁN

One of Europe's most delightful coastal cities, San Sebastián is Spain's epicentre of cutting-edge gastronomy. Well worth including on a food and wine pilgrimage, it has hundreds of bars serving pintxos, the Basque equivalent of tapas, as well as a constellation of garlanded restaurants, including Arzak.

PARQUE
NATURAL DE IZKI

Pack a pair of hiking boots (or cycling shoes) and head into the Parque Natural de Izki, north of Laguardia, on one of the many signposted hiking trails that weave through the Pyrenean oak forests. *izkiparkea.eus*

CELEBRATIONS

If you're in the area in October, the annual mushroom festival at Ezcaray is a treat for fungi fans, with autumn's bounty on display, expert talks, guided mushroom-picking walks in the Cantabrian mountains and lots of tastings in the village square. More famous is the annual Batalla del Vino (wine fight – really) in Haro at the end of June. The fiesta begins on the night of 28 June with a street party, then the battle commences the following morning. And in September the Rioja Wine Harvest Festival brings costumes, music and grape-crushing to the streets of Logroño. *wine-fight.com*

[Spain]

JEREZ

Sherry is stylish again. Head to the source of the ultimate tapas companion in this handsome Andalucían city for the lowdown on Fino.

Beware: you could get lost for days, maybe weeks in the Sherry Triangle. Formed by the three towns of Jerez de la Frontera (known as Sheris in medieval times), Sanlúcar de Barrameda to the west and El Puerto de Santa Mariá, this corner of Spain's southern region of Andalucía is the only source of sherry, the fortified wine that has regained well-deserved favour among food-lovers.

Every evening in bars right across Andalucía a pre-dinner ritual is repeated. Patrons take a seat and the bartender pours a small glass of pale gold liquid, the colour of an eagle's eye, then slides across the counter a plate of *jamón ibérico*, the air-dried local ham, or some cubes of cheese. The drink is Fino, the palest and driest of sherries, alive with a mouth-puckeringly savoury tang and, as legions of bar-hoppers are discovering, the perfect companion to sociable snacking.

The world of sherry is small but it can be bafflingly complex – it's not one drink but about five or six, and it's not immediately obvious how a refined Fino relates to the sickly, orange sherry from your great-aunt's drinks cabinet. This wine trail will set you straight.

Sherry's journey back to the bar-top began in the mid-1990s when inland Jerez, El Puerto de Santa María and Sanlúcar de Barrameda on the Spanish coast gained recognition and protection from the European Union as Protected Designation of Origin (PDO). Your journey starts in Jerez, where all the big producers have a bodega that's open to the public. It can be quite a commercial experience, but it's a good introduction.

Afterwards, take to Jerez's paved streets to get a flavour of Andalucían flamenco, then hit the bars to test your new-found know-how. The trail continues out of the city to the coast; make sure you find time to stop in fabulous, dissolute Cádiz along the way.

GET THERE
Sherry is stylish again. Head to the source of the ultimate tapas companion in this handsome Andalucían city for the lowdown on Fino.

01 GONZÁLEZ BYASS

Close to Jerez's cathedral, the bodega of González Byass is the city's most visitor-oriented. Fittingly, its Tio Pepe Fino is the world's biggest-selling sherry, and this is *the* place to come to get a grip on the basics of sherry production. There are several different types, from dry to sweet. At the driest end of the spectrum (and these have led sherry's revival) are Fino and Manzanilla. The tangy flavours of Fino are caused by a yeast known as *flor* that forms a film on the surface of sherries as they rest in the barrel for a minimum of three years (often much longer for the high-end vintages). This layer protects the sherry from the air, keeping it pale in the process.

After Fino, the next step for a sherry is the bone-dry Amontillado, a Fino that has continued ageing in contact with the air. As a result, it's darker and richer: expect woody and dry citrus flavours. The González Byass Amontillado is an attention-grabbing treat, and so are most of the bodega's older sherries.

Next on the sherry sweetness scale is Oloroso, which is fortified after fermentation to stop the *flor* forming. As it ages in the barrel, in contact with air, it grows darker, richer and fruitier. Pedro Ximénez is a dessert wine made from the grape of the same name; the more mature the better. Any extra-sweetened sherries beyond this point are for export only.

bodegastiopepe.com; tel +34 956 357 016; C/Manuel María González 12, Jerez; daily ⑤ ✕

02 SANDEMAN

Harvey, Osborne and Sandeman: the names that reveal sherry's genesis. Sherry's character might be Spanish but the business is British. Blame Sir Francis Drake for Britain's sherry obsession: the Elizabethan privateer sacked Cádiz in 1587 and made off with 3000 barrels of the local vino. Before long the Brits back home had developed a taste for Spain's fortified wine and a new industry was born. Entrepreneurs such as George Sandeman from Perth, Scotland set up businesses in Jerez and the rest, as they say, is history.

'When we start out, the wines are like little children. We have to teach them how to grow so that they can become adults we can be proud of'

–José 'Pepe' Blandino, cellar master at Bodegas Tradición

The Sandeman bodega was established in 1790, close to the Royal Andalusian School of Equestrian Art in the heart of the city. With guided tours in multiple languages and a museum, it's a good place to get the background of sherry's story (trivia: Sandeman's logo, the dashing, caped figure, was designed by the Scottish artist George Massiot Brown). Three tours are offered, each ending with a tasting of several sherries. *sandeman.com; tel +34 675 647 177; C/Pizarro 10, Jerez; Tue & Thu by appointment* ⑤

⑬ BODEGAS TRADICIÓN

In the cellar of Bodegas Tradición – boutique producer of rare aged sherries – amid the gloom of 625L

casks of American oak, the aroma of sherry is overwhelming. In the tasting room, among artworks by Goya and Velázquez and ceramic tiles painted by an eight-year-old Picasso, visitors seek out the unusual Palo Cortado, a nutty, smoky style somewhere between an Amontillado and Oloroso. The bodega's own full-bodied Oloroso combines vanilla, ginger, and the scent of Christmas cake.

Sherry, more than any other wine, requires human intervention at every step, and José Blandino, the cellar master (or *capataz*) at Bodegas Tradición, who has worked in the industry for some five decades, treats his sherries like his own offspring. 'When we start out, the wines are like little children. We

have to teach them how to grow, to help them through the varying stages of getting older. It takes a lot of time and hard work, so that they become adults we can be proud of.'

But even José admits that each person's response to the final product is as important, and as personal as his own role in the process. 'We can show people what to look for. But the only standard that really matters is whether or not you like it.'
bodegastradicion.es; tel +34 956 168 628; Plaza Cordobeses 3, Jerez; Mon-Fri & Sat mornings by appointment ⑤

④ OSBORNE MORA

You'll recognise the Osborne bull: that black silhouette that glowers from numerous Spanish roadsides, a stroke of advertising genius from a 1956 marketing campaign by the company (the original billboards had 'Veteran Brandy' emblazoned across them). The full story is revealed in a gallery at Osborne Mora's winery in El Puerto de Santa María.

This recently renovated bodega, sitting just 300m (985ft) from the sea of the Costa de la Luz, is the most southern point of the Sherry Triangle. The company was started by an Englishman, Thomas Osborne Mann, in 1772 but has since added Cinco Jotas *jamón ibérico* from acorn-fed black Iberian pigs and olive oil to its portfolio – meaning

that it's an ideal location for a ham-and-sherry tasting, one of the options offered.

Visitors can also learn about the *solera* system for blending sherries, in which wine of varying ages is decanted from one barrel to another, keeping barrels filled with younger wine that feeds the *flor* – this is what the stack of barrels in the cellar is all about. The company's collection of VORS (Very Old and Rare Sherries) is available for tasting (on the €35 tour). Its rare sherries include wines drawn from a single *solera*, such as the Antonio Osborne Solera, started in 1903 to mark the birth of the second Count of Osborne's son. Sherry ageing is only an average; a sherry from a solera started 10 years ago will have 10-year-old wine in it but also younger wine. Figure it out over some *jamón* and a glass of the classy Fino Quinta in the tapas tavern.
bodegas-osborne.com; tel +34 956 869 100; C/los Moros 7, El Puerto de Santa María; daily by appointment ⑤ ✕

⑤ DELGADO ZULETA

It's a tough gig being a sherry grape. The three varieties permitted in the production of sherry are Palomino, Moscatel and Pedro Ximénez; all have to cope with summer temperatures touching 40°C (104°F), their metres of roots driving deep down into the *albariza* soil – limestone – in the search for water. At Delgado Zuleta, those grapes have, since 1744, been turned into Manzanilla, a speciality of Sanlúcar de Barrameda, where the *flor* grows thickest and the saline tang is enhanced by the cool seaside climate. A basic tour of the bodega takes in the winery and the vineyard plus a tasting of four to five sherries (from €10). Delgado Zuleta's best-known Manzanilla is La Goya, first launched in 1918 and still a deliciously savoury sidekick to the local *langostinos* (prawns).
delgadozuleta.com; tel +34 956 360 543; Avendia Rocío Jurado, Sanlúcar de Barrameda; Mon-Sat by appointment ⑤

WHERE TO STAY

HOTEL YIT CASA GRANDE

This hotel occupies a carefully restored 1920s mansion, with rooms spread over three floors and set around a patio or beside the roof terrace, which has good views of Jerez's rooftops. *hotelcasagrandejerez. com; tel +34 956 345 070; Plaza de las Angustias 3, Jerez*

LA ALCOBA DEL AGUA

Modern, central and stylish, La Alcoba del Agua is the place to book for a night or two in Sanlúcar de Barrameda at the end of the trail. *laalcobadelagua.com; tel +34 956 383 109; C/ Alcoba 26, Sanlúcar de Barrameda*

WHERE TO EAT

LA CARBONÁ

Dishes at this family-run restaurant in Jerez are paired with different sherries. Inventive plates feature the best of Spanish ingredients, from spicy *chistorra* sausage from Navarra to langoustines from

Sanlúcar de Barrameda. It's a trick that works well for both partners; cooking-with-sherry classes with chef Javier Muñoz are sometimes available if you want to learn more. *lacarbona.com; tel +34 956 347 475; C/San Francisco de Paula 2, Jerez; Wed-Sun*

WHAT TO DO

DOÑANA NATIONAL PARK

One of Europe's great wildlife reserves covers the marshes, lagoons and scrub of the Guadalquivir River's estuary. Birdlife is the big draw, with half a million birds wintering here, but the Unesco-protected park is also home to the rare and threatened Iberian lynx (though you'll be lucky to see one). Wildlife-spotting visits must be booked in advance. *donanareservas.com*

CÁDIZ

Spend a day in shabby-chic Cádiz, one of Europe's oldest continuously inhabited settlements. Romantic,

mysterious and much-contested over the ages, Cádiz intoxicates with its edgy aura. *cadizturismo.com*

CELEBRATIONS

FIESTA DE LA VENDIMIA

Most winegrowing regions of Spain celebrate the annual grape harvest; in Jerez it kicks off at the end of August or in early September. The two-week festival opens with a ceremonial grape crush, or *pisá*, and a blessing in Jerez de la

Frontera's cathedral. There follows two weeks of exhibitions, fireworks and food and wine tastings, with extra wineries and vineyards throwing open their doors to visitors. *jerezdelafrontera.com*

CADIZ CARNAVAL

No other Spanish city celebrates Carnaval with as much fervour as Cádiz, which is overtaken by a ten-day singing, dancing and drinking fancy-dress party spanning two weeks in February.

07

Parc Natural de la Serra de Montsant

03 SIURANA

02 ESCALADEI

POBOLEDA

LA VILELLA BAIXA · LA VILELLA ALTA

GRATALLOPS

01

PORERRA

04

PRADELL DE LA TEIZETA

05

FALSET

PRIORAT

[Spain]

PRIORAT

Meet the pioneers of Spain's most adventurous viticultural region and experience some of the wildest wines – and landscapes – in the country.

Less than two hours' drive south of Barcelona lies the Wild West of Spanish winemaking. Bordered by the great escarpment of the Parc Natural de la Serra de Montsant to the north, compact and rugged Priorat was once the sort of place where undrinkable wine was sold by the litre. In this impoverished corner of Catalonia, the older generation eked out a living and the young yearned to escape to Barcelona.

But in the late 1970s, a band of five long-haired pioneers, including René Barbier and Alvaro Palacios, realised Priorat's potential. On dry, sun-drenched slopes grew Carignane and Garnacha vines of 70 or 80 years old, on gradients so steep – up to 60 degrees – that the vines delve deep into the rock to find water. The resulting yields are so low that seven to 10 plants make just one bottle of Priorat. These visionary winemakers knew that hardworking vines meant complex, potent wines were waiting to be unleashed. But first they had to tame the alcohol content, which could

GET THERE
The closest airport is in Barcelona; it's an easy 2hr drive south to Priorat via Tarragona.

hit 18% – and tame the land. They succeeded at the first challenge, but Priorat remains a wild and densely beautiful landscape dotted with old villages and tiny vineyards, most at an altitude of 375m (1230ft), but some at 900m (2952ft) and even 1000m (3280ft).

Today, Priorat boasts one of Spain's most expensive wines, Alvaro Palacios' L'Ermita, and is a fascinating place to tour. 'It was a wine region about to disappear,' says René Barbier, 'but now young people are coming back and they're proud to be part of it.'

01 Clos Mogador
vineyards

02 The Carthusian
monastery of Escaladei

03 Catalonian
porrones (wine
pitchers)

04 Priorat countryside

01 CLOS MOGADOR

Born in the port city of Tarragona, Clos Mogador's shaggy-bearded founder René Barbier would go hiking in Priorat as a youth: 'It was pure, untouched and wild.' Inspired by the hippie movement of the late 1960s and 1970s he returned, as he says, 'to plant the seeds of a better world'. The place he chose to settle, with his wife Isabelle, was just outside the hilltop village of Gratallops. More a wine safari than a wine tour, Clos Mogador will drive you to two vineyards before a wine tasting. An exploration of its steeply sloping vineyards is a geology lesson: the ground high up here consists of shards of schist, a rock known locally as *llicorella*.

Gnarled old Carignane and Garnacha vines emerge from this poor soil, which lends Priorat wines their unique mineral edge.

The next lesson is botany, for René Barbier is obsessed with biodiversity. He wants wine to be part of the natural environment, which is why 30 types of flowers and wild herbs such as fennel, rosemary and thyme flourish in his vineyards. Almond, olive, fig, cherry and walnut trees punctuate the vines. 'We want nature to be free', he says (up to a point: wild boar from the forest are kept away from the grapes by electric fences).

His self-professed hippie philosophy extends to his winemaking, now aided by his son

René Jnr and his brother Christian. They use only rainwater for irrigation and plant wheat around the wines which, when cut, reduces evaporation. Grapes are picked and sorted by hand in September, then pressed using a small cast-iron press, allowing the winemaker to keep tasting the must; just 50,000 bottles are produced in an average year. And although Barbier is one of the forefathers of Priorat, and has studied its vineyards and villages for dozens of years, he's still experimenting.

So, how best to enjoy Priorat's big personality? It's a wine that benefits from being decanted; these are not light wines and, once allowed to breathe, a classic Priorat blend

of Garnacha, Carignane with a dash of Shiraz and Cabernet Sauvignon, such as Clos Mogador's eponymous wine, will reveal a smoky swirl of cherries, cedar and herbs. 'Wine is all about passion and patience,' says René. 'What I want is for what you have in your glass to be what you see outside.'
closmogador.com; tel +34 977 839 171; Camí Manyetes, Gratallops; Mon, Fri & Sat by appointment $

02 CELLERS DE SCALA DEI

Continuing northeast from la Vilella Baixa to the quiet town of Escaladei, you'll reach one of the oldest wineries in Priorat. Monks introduced vines to the region in the 12th century and at this monastery, founded in 1194, you can tour the cellars in which wines are still aged. The monks seem to have taken the responsibility of winemaking very seriously and by 1629 they had produced a manual noting the varieties that grew best (Garnacha and Mataró, also known as Mourvèdre). Places to eat here include El Rebost de la Cartoixa.
cellersdescaladei.com; tel +34 977 827 173; Rambla Cartoixa, Escaladei; daily by reservation $

03 MARCO ABELLA

The drive to Porrera is spectacular, crossing a high plateau from where you can watch the weather rolling across the hills. The altitude of Priorat's vineyards is as important a factor as the soil and the sun, and few vineyards are loftier than those of Marco Abella, a winery owned by a family with roots in the region that go back to the 15th century.

The premium tour takes in La Mallola vineyard at 680m (2230ft) above sea level, where Carignane and Garnacha grapes grow, cooled by the Llevant wind from the Mediterranean. Bottles of Marco Abella's highly regarded wines bear artwork by Barcelona-born abstract artist Josep Guinovar.
marcoabella.com; tel +34 977 262 825; Carretera Porrera a Cornudella del Montsant, Porrera; tours Wed-Sun by appointment (other times by arrangement) $

subterranean winemaking levels the alchemy happens, with gravity doing a lot of the work.

Sergi and Raül remain ambitious: 'Despite the prestige of Priorat's wines and their international success, the region has to work harder on attracting wine-lovers, while preserving the beauty of this landscape and its quiet lifestyle.' *ferrerbobet.com; tel +34 609 945 532; Carretera Falset a Porrera km6.5; by appointment Mon-Fri plus first & third Sat* 💲

05 EL CELLER COOPERATIVA DE FALSET

Back in Falset, stop by the town's venerable wine cooperative, built in 1919 by architect Cèsar Martinell, a disciple of Gaudí, though eschewing his flourishes for a cathedral-inspired modernism.

A guided tour ushers visitors through a history of winemaking in the region. You can opt for an entertaining actor-led tour and tasting, or just book a tasting of the cooperative's wines, made by Marta Ferré Mallofré. Wines by the glass and platters of local morsels are also on offer in the wine bar, in front of the great wooden tanks used for vermouth (another of the cooperative's products). *etim.cat; tel +34 977 830 105; Carrer Miquel Barceló 31, Falset; Wed-Fri by appointment* 💲 🍴

04 FERRER BOBET

Best friends Sergi Ferrer-Salat and Raül Bobet began making wines together at the turn of the millennium, and with that auspicious date came a desire to do things a little differently. 'We wanted to emphasise freshness and elegance above all, we wanted to create a more "Burgundian" style of Priorat, more, let's say, drinkable,' explains Sergi, 'but without losing the incredible complexity and minerality of the century-old Carignane vines.' To achieve this, they found a base high up in Porrera, one of the coolest

corners of Priorat, and planted away from the sun's fierce glare. 'By avoiding over-ripeness, our wines better express both the terroir and the minerality of Priorat,' say Sergi. 'Also, the winery is gravity-fed, which makes for a much more gentle treatment of the grapes.'

Ferrer Bobet's contemporary winery – rare in these parts – follows the contours of the hilltop, like the vines below. Designed by Catalan architects Espinet-Ubach, it's highly energy-efficient, with glass walls providing mesmerising views of the surrounding hills from the visitor area, while down on the

WHERE TO STAY

CLOS FIGUERAS

One day in 1997, René Barbier introduced Christopher and Charlotte Cannan to an abandoned vineyard north of Gratallops – it is now the esteemed Clos Figueras winery. In addition to tours, tastings and meals, Christopher and Charlotte offer several B&B rooms. *closfigueras.info; tel +34 977 262 373; Carrer de la Font 38, Gratallops*

CAL COMPTE

Plumb in the centre of the region, in the village of Torroja, this guesthouse is allied to the Terroir Al Límit winery. With bedrooms in a baroque 16th- to 18th-century building and open-air dining, this is a romantic spot to stay in Priorat. *calcompte.com; tel +34 977 262 373; Carrer Major 4, Torroja del Priorat*

CAL LLOP

Cosy Cal Llop in the hilltop village of Gratallops has balconies overlooking Priorat's undulating vine terraces. *cal-llop.com; tel +34 977 839 502; Carrer de Dalt 21, Gratallops*

WHERE TO EAT

RESTAURANT LA COOPERATIVA

Seasonal, locally produced food (the olive oil is from Falset) and Priorat wines without a markup ensure that La Cooperativa is a popular place to eat in Porrera. This is rural Spain: expect rabbit, lamb or even boar. *bit.ly/lco-op; tel +34 977 828 378; Carrer Unió 7, Porrera; Tue-Sat*

EL CELLER DE L'ASPIC

Chef Toni Bru cooks updated Catalan classics at this Falset fixture. The wine list is notably good. *cellerdelaspic.com; tel +34 977 831 246; C/Miquel Barceló 31, Falset; daily*

WHAT TO DO

PARC NATURAL DE LA SERRA DE MONTSANT

Pack your hiking boots, because Priorat is laced with outstanding trails, especially to the north, along the edge of the Parc Natural de la Serra de Montsant. From an eyrie at the top of this wall of rock you look out over the whole of Priorat's amphitheatre; a network of via ferrata cables aids novice climbers. Book guides and get maps from the visitor centre in La Morrera de Montsant. It's not only climbers who head to the cliffs in the northeast of the region around the lost-in-time clifftop village of Siurana – a fabulous place in which to explore and enjoy a meal with a view.

CELEBRATIONS

In early May the annual wine fair takes over Falset for a week, with more than 60 producers showcasing their wines, including Clos Mogador and Alvaro Palacios. It's a hugely sociable event, with a programme of events plus organised activities for children. A Bus de Vi (wine bus) runs from Tarragona and Reus to Falset. *firadelvi.org*

[Spain]

EMPORDÀ

This up-and-coming region revolves around the fantastic city of Girona in the northeast of Spain, and makes for a rewarding wine-touring itinerary.

Once part of a Catalan kingdom that extended north past the Pyrenees and into what is now French Languedoc-Roussillon, Empordà is only recently emerging as wine region. Until now this arid area just north of Girona was best known for Figueres, the birthplace of Salvador Dalí. But the rapidly increasing appeal of Girona as a charming, regional city that has taken some of the tourist pressure off Barcelona, has meant that there are many more people interested in exploring this diverse and interesting wine region. In fact, a new trend is for visitors to base themselves in Girona, enjoying the quieter pace and beautiful historic architecture, and take day trips by high-speed train into Barcelona for sightseeing.

Adding a two- to three-day wine tour of the Empordà region means you can take in some of the interesting estates in the foothills of the Pyrenees to the north (Alt Empordà) and also visit the coast around the arty town of Cadaqués and the Costa Brava's beaches to the south, near Pals (Baix Empordà). You'll need a car to get around but the driving is straightforward on Spain's roads, with the first stop being around an hour's drive north. The itinerary is split between two areas, north and east of Girona. You can either base yourself in the city and try a few of the excellent restaurants and wine bars, or book accommodation in each area.

The wine itself doesn't receive the attention of Spain's superstar regions such as Priorat or Rioja, and because much of it is sold locally to restaurants in Girona and Barcelona, it's rare to find in other countries. But the region does have a fascinating history, traditions and a wide range of mostly family-owned wineries to discover, from boutique to blockbuster.

GET THERE
Both Barcelona and Girona have international airports and it's a fast 40min train ride between the cities.

01 MAS LLUNES

The Roig family offers a unique introduction to Empordà's wines: a sensory journey that takes place in the darkened barrel room of their winery, Mas Llunes. Host Miriam Compte guides guests to a round table and the show begins: music and slides illustrate the influence of ancient Greeks and Romans, who were the first to plant vines here.

Other influences on Empordà's wines include the tramunatana wind, which reduces humidity (good). But, says Miriam, 'it also drives people crazy, which is why there are lots of artists in the area.'

The Roigs have been making wine here since 2000, steadily increasing the number of vines planted. 'Our goal was to be distinctive and focus on the expression of the wine,' says Miriam. The work has paid off, with Finca Butaros, made with grapes from vines planted in 1900 and aged for five years, regularly rated as one of Spain's top wines.
masllunes.es; tel +34 972 552 684; Ctra de Vilajuïga, Garriguella; tours, tastings by appointment Ⓢ

02 LA VINYETA

A short drive west, La Vinyeta has a very different feel: it's rural and ringed with vines that are patrolled by sheep. But the winery itself is an airy, modern building with a large outdoor area for performances. It's a young business. The Serra family, Josep and Marta, bought a parcel of old Carignan and Grenache vines from a local grower, who helped them understand the soil and climate on the proviso that the family developed the winemaking. They've been true to their word. 'The region had a culture of quantity not quality,' says Josep Serra, 'but winemakers are changing that. In Spain, minds were closed for too long. Young people don't like oaky wines and young people are the future. So, we are adventurous: less oak and more acidity.'

La Vinyeta's experimental Micro Wines are short runs of five wines, each trying something new. For example, says Josep: 'We might keep one microwine in amphoras and we can compare it with the

04

01 Top, Perelada's winery; below, coastal Cadaqués

02 Music at La Vinyeta

03 Sol y serena wine aging at Martin Faixo

04 Tasting wines at La Vinyeta

05 The sound and light show at Mas llunes

06 Brugarol's winery

07 Girona's old town

05

same grape kept in barrels. After the oak, there's added hints of toast and vanilla. With the clay you taste the fruit without other influences.'

A visit to La Vinyeta can take in a walking tour of the vines followed by a sommelier-led tasting with food, including their own cheeses. ***lavinyeta.es; tel +34 647 748 809; Carretera de Mollet a Masarac; see website for times***

03 MASIA SERRA

You may not make it to Masia before lunch (especially if you have a picnic at La Vinyeta) but if you do, you could find a party in full swing. This is '*vermut*', a Catalan tradition that sees friends get together for a glass of vermouth and snacks such as olives and anchovies (this is Spain and lunch isn't until around 3pm). At Masia Serra, *vermut* also includes a DJ playing bouncy dance music on the winery's shaded terrace.

Hosts and owners Jaume Serra and Sílvia Vilà might encourage the lively vibe but they're serious about their wine. The winery, sitting on the border of a national park, was started in 1961. Jaume's grandfather was a wine dealer in Figueres who fell in love with the piece of land, which is now planted with three varieties of Empordà's only indigenous grape variety, Grenache. Jaume studied winemaking in Bordeaux and worked at Chateau Pétrus so he planted French vines too. In 1996 they made their first wine in their garage. You can still watch the winery at work but there are lots of other experiences available, including food pairings. ***masiaserra.com; tel +34 689 604 905; Carrer del Solés, 20, 17708 Cantallops; see website***

4 HOTEL PERELADA WINE SPA & GOLF

Perelada is another family-owned winery, but the family is Suqué Mateu, one of Spain's wealthiest industrialists. They bought Castle Perelada in 1923 and it came with a Carmelite monastery, underneath which was a wine cellar. Wine has been produced at Perelada at least from the 14th century. Today, it's made in an astonishing

fortified wines too. These are aged in bottles on the roof using a Catalan technique called *sol y serena*. martinfaixo.com; tel +34 972 159 401; C/ de Cadaqués; Wed-Fri by appointment 💲✗

06 CELLER BRUGAROL

Deep in a web of steep dirt tracks, Brugarol emerges like a little Eden. Gardens surround a boutique hotel, which also has its own small chapel. To one side is perhaps the most inventive winery in Empordà, designed again by RCR. It delves into the ground, an entrance panelled with steel from recycled ships. Inside, some dark corridors tilt as if you're at sea. A lab has a glass wall that opens into a forest. Then you emerge into the light to try wines and olive oils on the terrace. brugarol.com; tel +34 972 601 071; Camí de Bell Lloc s/n de Palamós

07 CELLER MAS GELI

Make a final, sunset stop at this family-owned winery a stone's throw from beaches such as Sa'Tuna, Sa Piera and Mas Pinell. Brother and sister team of Lluis and Anne planted the organically-grown vines and opened the winery in 2019. They farm as sustainably as possible, encouraging bats and wild hawks.

They make nine wines, served with cheese, sausage, bread and tomato, followed by a chocolate flavoured with the grape mousse. 'We try to do soft and elegant wines that are lighter,' says Anne. 'Wine is about sharing.' masgelipals.cat; tel +34 629 694 428; Pals; book tours online 💲✗

contemporary winery – Spain has a penchant for these – designed by the award-winning Catalan architects RCR. They integrated the buildings into the landscape and built the winery underground. You'll take a lift down to the labyrinth, a web of concrete corridors leading to a vault that is larger than that of Girona's cathedral. It's a stunning space, filled with barrels, bottles and egg-like amphoras. The wine is also good, such as Finca Malaveïna, a Bordeaux-style blend, aged for 22 months and packed with dark fruit. perelada.com; tel +34 972 538 001; Paratge la Granja s/n, Peralada; tours by appointment 💲✗

05 MARTÍN FAIXÓ

The next day, head towards beautiful Cadaqués, which was adored by such artists as Dalí, Picasso, Duchamp and Miró. On a hilltop overlooking the Costa Brava is the farmhouse of Martín Faixó. Restored since 2004 by the family, the slate building itself dates from the 14th century and offers a clue to the local soil. Everything they do is designed to reduce impacts on the environment: no tractors are used, sheep graze the vines, grapes are harvested by hand, and waste is almost zero. As a coastal winery, the white Picapoll grape is a regional speciality and ideal with fish. Try the

Can Roca, this is their attempt at a down-to-earth bistro, serving Catalan dishes and local wines. With such starpower behind it, standards are high. *restaurantnormal.com; tel +34 972 436 383; Plaça de l'Oli 1, Girona*

CAN CANALLA
Enjoy a pre-dinner drink at this old-town wine bar. *Tel +34 972 604 213; Plaça Bell-lloch, 4 Baixos, Girona*

CELEBRATIONS
CASTELL DE PERALADA INTERNATIONAL MUSIC FESTIVAL
Staged annually over July and August, this is one of the world's eminent cultural festivals, showcasing opera and dance in the grounds of Peralada Castle. The festival was founded by the Suqué Mateu family, who own the castle and its associated winery. Future plans include spreading festival events throughout the year so check the website for details of performances. *festivalperalada.com*

WHERE TO STAY
With its appealing old town, set around the Onyar river, and good road and rail transport links, Girona makes for a great base for exploring the region. There's a wide range of accommodation but if you're staying in the city centre (recommended for ease of walking to restaurants), you will need a hotel with its own parking as on-street parking is very limited. However, many of the wineries featured in this trail also offer rooms for overnight stays, for various budgets, so visitors can stay en-route.

HOTEL CIUTAT DE GIRONA
This is a clean, stylish four-star hotel on the west bank of the Onyar, near the old town. Stroll across the bridges for an evening out. Secure underground parking. *hotelciutatdegirona. com; tel +34 972 483 038; Carrer Nord 2, Girona*

WHERE TO EAT
LA SIMFONIA
Choose between the sleek interior or a table outside in a quiet old-town square at this excellent little restaurant. It serves creative dishes at reasonable prices and has a wine list packed with local talent. *lasimfonia.com; tel +34 972 411 253; Plaça de l'Oli 6, Girona*

NORMAL
Devised by the brains behind El Celler de

BALEARIC
SEA

SÓLLER

Serra de Tramuntana

BADIA
D'ALCÚDIA

INCA

01

02   BINISSALEM

04

ARTÀ

MALLORCA

PALMA DE
MALLORCA

03

05

MANACOR

BAY OF
PALMA

LLUCMAJOR

FELANITX

MEDITERRANEAN
SEA

[Spain]

MALLORCA

Sun, sea, sand and surprisingly good vino: head inland and discover this holiday isle's wines, made in the shadow of the Serra de Tramuntana and on the central plains.

Mallorca, the largest of Spain's Balearic Islands, has been a wildly popular holiday destination for millions of northern Europeans for a hundred-odd years – but it has survived this invasion and prospered. A group of earlier invaders – the Romans – were evicted in 425 CE, leaving behind two things: vines and olive trees. A fair price, perhaps.

Since wine has been part of the landscape of this enchanting island for more than 2500 years, you can expect some old vines; grapes are routinely harvested from 60-year-old plants in Mallorca's two Denominació d'Origen (DO) zones, Binissalem and Pla i Llevant (the central plain). Most Mallorcan bodegas (anything from a warehouse to a stone cellar) concentrate on the island's traditional grape varieties: Callet, Mantonegro and Prensal Blanc. These are typically pepped up with dashes of Cabernet, Merlot or Shiraz. Malvasia, an ancient grape, is making a comeback on the terraced vineyards in the

slopes of the Serra de Tramuntana range, which runs along the west edge of the island and is the first land to meet incoming weather fronts.

Wine touring on Mallorca has two great joys: firstly, most of the bodegas are within a short drive of one another, and you're never more than a half an hour from a good restaurant, a beach or a sensational view. And, secondly, the vast majority of the island's bodegas are family-run businesses, often located in old sandstone buildings in the centre of towns. If you meet the families who make the wine, you'll catch some of their passion for this place and its food, wine, traditions and landscapes. The island has long produced rough-and-ready wines – dark and unfiltered from sun-baked vineyards – but with the combination of decades of tradition and the ambition of younger generations, Mallorcan wine is becoming more sophisticated. Only minuscule quantities are exported, which is all the more reason to investigate them in person.

GET THERE
The island capital, Palma, receives flights from all over Europe. There's also a slow ferry from mainland Spain.

01 Terraced vines on the west coast

02 Modern production, Bodegas Miquel Oliver

03 Tasting at Bodegas Miquel Oliver

04 Bodegas Ribas

① BODEGAS MACIÀ BATLE

'People thought we were crazy investing in wine rather than a golf course or hotel,' says Ramón Servalls i Batle, director of Macià Batle. 'But they're realising that there's so much more to Mallorca than sun and sand.' As one of the largest and most diversified wineries on the island – its shop stocks olive oils, chocolates and appetisers – Macià Batle stands at the opposite end of the winemaking spectrum to Miquel Oliver (see opposite). Here wines are blended in a high-tech laboratory (you can watch from behind a glass partition) and bottled by a €500,000 machine.

But for all the trappings of big business, Macià Batle remains a family-owned winery with a friendly welcome for all and a firm attachment to tradition. All Ramón's wines are based on indigenous grape varieties, such as Callet and Mantonegro, hand-picked from vines that can be more than 40 years old – in fact, some vines are so ancient that they produce just one bunch of grapes. The bodega has been on this site, in the foothills of the Serra de Tramuntana, just south of the wine-producing hub of Binissalem, since 1856 and the vines are managed with local know-how. 'Days are so warm that the grapes need a cooling breeze, so we take away leaves, letting the wind get to the grapes,' says Ramón. After pressing, some of the juice is matured in the crimson-painted cellars under the courtyard, where there's space for 850 barrels. A wide range of wines emerge, including a raspberry-scented Rosado, a Blanc de Blancs and several intense Mantonegro blends. *maciabatle.com; tel +34 971 140 014; Camí de Coanegra, Santa Maria del Camí; Mon-Sat by appointment* ⑤

② BODEGA RIBAS

Head north towards the foothills of the Tramuntana range to explore the oldest winery on the island: Bodega Ribas. Construction began on the winery at this grand country mansion in 1711. 'Wine was part of everyday life then

and the consumption was much higher than nowadays,' explains Araceli Server Ribas. 'Many families had a plot for their own consumption and it was part of the Mediterranean diet; even kids had it regularly mixed with water.' Today, Ribas' wines are powerful and best paired with the robust Mallorcan cuisine. The rare Ribas de Cabrera and the Ribas range blend Mantonegro grapes with Cabernet Sauvignon and Shiraz. 'The Mantonegro lends a fresh nose that complements the warmer mouth,' says Araceli. Unusually, a sweet wine, Sioneta, using Muscat grapes that have dried on the vine, is also made here. Tours are offered with tapas, food or musical accompaniment.

bodegaribas.com; tel +34 971 622 673; Carrer de Muntanya 2, Consell; Mon-Sat by appointment 💲 ✖

⑬ FINCA BINIAGUAL

If you want to get fit, work in a winery. From May to September workers patrol Bodega Biniagual's 148,000 vines three times a week, walking 10km (6 miles) each time. Everything is done with extra care here because the winery has been given a second lease of life. The family-run finca (estate), set around a handsome courtyard deep in the DO Binissalem, was a farming homestead in the days of Arab rule. Located at the crossroads of the island, its golden age was in the 17th century when new houses

were built and vines planted. But come the 20th century, phylloxera destroyed the vines and the community. Biniagual's resurrection began in 1999 when vines were planted once again.

Over the last two decades Mallorcan winemakers have learned how to make indigenous grape varieties the stars of authentic Mallorcan wines. 'You'll only find Mantonegro on the island, especially around Binissalem,' says winemaker José Luis Seguí. 'It requires a lot of work but gives the wines their personality and unique aroma.' In 2019 a cellar door, hosted by sommelier José García, was opened in which to try Biniagual's wines (especially the Finca Biniagual Mantonegro) with plates of Mallorcan tapas.

finca-biniagual.com; tel +34 971 870 111; Camí de Muro 11, Binissalem; daily, tastings by appointment 💲 ✖

⑭ BODEGAS MIQUEL OLIVER

This is a hard-working bodega led by the serious but enthusiastic winemakers Pilar Oliver and Jaume Olivella. You've now crossed over into the second of Mallorca's two Protected Designations of Origin (PDO): Vins des Pla i Llevant. This designation covers the terracotta plains of central Mallorca, where Miquel Oliver grows its Callet, Mantonegro and Prensal Blanc vines, divided by drystone walls from fields of almond trees (the trees blossom in February, making the

month a spectacular time to visit inland Mallorca). Pilar and Jaume opened a winery building and cellar door next to their vineyards in 2015, to mark the winery's 2012 centenary. The original winery in the centre of Petra has been restored and now offers an insight into the island's wine traditions – tours (some include tapas plates or Mallorcan meals) take in both venues before Pilar and Jaume show off their most successful creations: Ses Ferritges, a Callet, Shiraz, Merlot and Cabernet blend; and Aia, an award-winning Merlot.

Petra's claim to fame is that it is the birthplace of Father Junípero Serra, the priest who not only founded the Mexican and Californian missions that became San Diego,

Santa Barbara and San Francisco but also introduced vines to California. It is strange to think that Napa Valley's origins lie in a sleepy Mallorcan town that has changed little since Serra started his walkabout in 1749. Before leaving, catch the views from the padre's hilltop hermitage, just 4km (2.5 miles) out of town. *miqueloliver.com; tel +34 971 561 117; Carretera Petra-Santa Margalida km1.8, Petra; Mon-Sat by appointment* 🟢 ✕

05 VINS MIQUEL GELABERT

End the trail with some of the most garlanded Mallorcan wines, made on the east side of the island in a rustic estate just outside the workaday town of Manacor. From around 30 varieties of grape, some from old

vines of 40 to 65 years of age, wine magician Miquel Gelabert conjures fascinating wines that are aged in a cellar dating from 1909. Notably, he produces stellar white wines, slightly unusually on Mallorca, including the excellent Sa Vall Selecció Privada, blended from Giró Blanc, Viognier and Pinot Noir.

You're only a short hop from the quiet beaches of Mallorca's east coast, so end the trip with a chilled bottle, a bite to eat and the waves breaking on the sand. *vinsmiquelgelabert.com; tel +34 971 821 444; Carrer d'en Salas 50, Manacor; by appointment* 🟢 ✕

05 Bodegas Miquel
Oliver wines

06 Hiking in the
Tramuntana

WHERE TO STAY
LA RESERVA ROTANA
This luxurious finca sits in splendid isolation in 202 hectares (500 acres) of beautifully tended grounds just to the north of Manacor, with a private golf course, tennis court, pool, gym, sauna, own vineyard and fabulous restaurant. Rooms in the 17th-century manor house are grand, with countrified decor and the odd antique. *reservarotana.com; tel +34 971 845 685; Camí de Bendris km3, Manacor*

SA TORRE
Sa Torre is a very comfortable, midrange rural hotel with two swimming pools, bicycle storage and its own winery. Lying in the heart of Mallorca's wine country, just south of Binissalem, it has a highly regarded restaurant with a great collection of local wines. *sa-torre.com; tel +34 971 144 011; Carretera Santa Maria-Sencelles km7, Santa Eugènia*

WHERE TO EAT
RESTAURANT MARC FOSH
One of Mallorca's most renowned chefs, Marc Fosh has won a Michelin star for his restaurant in Palma's Hotel Convent de la Missió. Kitchen vegetables here are supplied by Fosh's own Mallorcan farm. *marcfosh.com; tel +34 971 720 114; Carrer de la Missió 7A, Palma*

ES VERGER
Grab a pew in this rustic restaurant, situated halfway up Àlaro mountain. The delicious shoulder of local lamb – perfect with one of the island's earthy reds – is one of Mallorca's essential dining experiences.

facebook.com/ EsVergeralaro; tel +34 971 182 126; Camí des Castell, Alaró; Tue-Sun

WHAT TO DO
WALK THE TRAMUNTANA
Walk off some of the food and wine along the Ruta de Pedra Sec (Dry Stone Route), a 170km (106-mile) path along the Tramuntana mountain range, skirting around sandy coves and trekking through aromatic patches of wild herbs and pine forest. The walk can be broken into eight stages and there are several refuges for overnight stays. The Consell de Mallorca hand out maps and can make refuge reservations for you. *conselldemallorca.net*

CYCLE THE ISLAND
Rent (or bring) a bicycle and explore the famously cycle-friendly island on two wheels. It's easy to follow signposted routes in the flatlands of Es Pla or into the mountains. You could even do this whole wine trail by bicycle, if desired.

CELEBRATIONS
BINISSALEM WINE FESTIVAL
Just after the annual harvest in September, Binissalem's wine festival concludes with the epic Battle of the Grapes: not a wine tasting but a full-on food fight – leave your best clothes at home. *seemallorca.com/ binissalem*

POLLENÇA WINE FAIR
In spring (often May), the Associació Vi Primitiu de Pollença hosts a weekend of wine tasting in the convent of Santo Domino in central Pollença. It's a good opportunity to taste wines from places that aren't usually open to the public. *seemallorca.com/ pollenca*

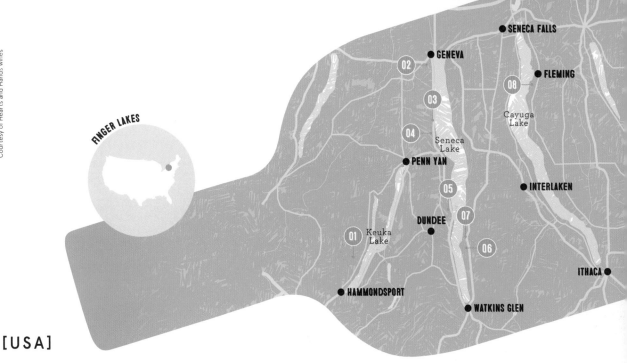

Courtesy of Hearts and Hands wines

Map labels: SENECA FALLS, GENEVA, FLEMING, 02, 03, 08, Cayuga Lake, 04, Seneca Lake, 05, PENN YAN, INTERLAKEN, 07, DUNDEE, 01, Keuka Lake, 06, ITHACA, HAMMONDSPORT, WATKINS GLEN, FINGER LAKES

[USA]

FINGER LAKES

An infectious sense of freedom – and gorgeous lakeside views – await you here, where European vines grow at the northern limit of the New World.

The Finger Lakes of New York represent one of the furthest limits of winemaking in North America. The winters can be very harsh; for most of its history only native American and hybrid grapes were planted here, with the belief that the higher-quality European *vinifera* vines wouldn't survive. While wine has been made here since the mid-1800s, with a boom in sparkling and sweet wine in the last half of that century, only in the 1960s, after the twin plagues of phylloxera and Prohibition, did *vinifera* grapes begin to be taken seriously. Their ability to thrive in the Finger Lakes is no longer in doubt. Today's pressing question is: which *vinifera* grapes, and where? How will the Finger Lakes identify itself?

The shores of four of the area's eleven lakes (Seneca, Cayuga, Keuka and Skaneateles) are home to the great majority of its wines, and these, in turn, are defined by a wide variety of soil types and exposures. In

dealing with that variety, every Finger Lakes winery has had to decide what to champion: a grape, its site, or the region at large. A number of winemakers believe that Riesling and Pinot Noir are the finest vehicles to discover and convey the Finger Lakes' terroirs. Others embrace a host of grapes, and consider questions of method most important: native or laboratory yeast, machine or hand-harvesting, oak or steel. There are a host of opinions in between. It's an exciting time to taste and explore the reality on the ground.

The beautiful, glacier-carved lakes are incredibly deep; their moderating influence is the chief factor that allows winemaking to happen here. They are also very long, as much as 64km (40 miles) north to south; plan your time carefully as you travel up and down them. The most convenient bases are the region's two city hubs, Watkins Glen or Ithaca, at the respective southern tips of lakes Seneca and Cayuga.

GET THERE
JFK or Toronto are the nearest major airports. Flights go from JFK to Ithaca, 85km (53 miles) from Hammondsport. Car hire is available.

① DR KONSTANTIN FRANK

Founded in 1962 by Ukrainian immigrant Dr Konstantin Frank, this pioneering estate is home to some of the first *vinifera* plantings in the region. Having transitioned into a fourth generation of family ownership, Dr Frank is now home to three tiers of wine: value-oriented Salmon Run; the old-vine, estate-driven Dr Konstantin Frank; and several single-vineyard wines, each named after a female member of the Frank family.

The wines to watch for here are Rkatsiteli, Grüner Veltliner, Riesling Semi-Dry and the aged sparkling wines – all best enjoyed on an expansive deck that offers panoramic views of Keuka Lake. *drfrankwines.com; tel +1 800-320-0735; 9749 Middle Rd, Hammondsport; 10am-5pm daily* $

② RAVINES WINE CELLARS

Ravines Cellars' Morten Hallgren grew up in Provence, France, and learned winemaking at his family estate, Domaine de Castel Roubine. After further training in Bordeaux and various locations in America (including six years at Dr Konstantin Frank), Morten and his wife Lisa secured a set of vineyards between two large ravines on the eastern shores of Keuka Lake in 2000.

Since then, they've gone from strength to strength and today, with wide distribution and the popular Ravinous wine club, are one of the most representative Finger Lakes wineries nationwide. Ravines' wines have an uncomplicated appeal, and while proud of his Riesling and Pinot Noir, Morten also bottles other grapes such as Cabernet Franc and Gewürztraminer, staking the

Finger Lakes' fame on quality. The Dry Riesling and Pinot Noir from the Argetsinger vineyard are two of their finest bottlings to date.

The tasting-room experience here, in a converted old barn, is especially warm. The building itself oozes memories of generations past and the kind, knowledgeable staff are eager to please; small plates are available, too. After your visit, take a short drive to the nearby city of Geneva. Some of the Finger Lakes' most significant history happened here, and it's easy to soak up via a stroll through the tree-lined streets. *ravineswine.com; tel +1 315-781-7007; 400 Barracks Rd, Geneva; by reservation 10am-5pm daily* $ ✕

③ FOX RUN VINEYARDS

Fox Run is situated in a converted century-old dairy barn overlooking

Seneca Lake. It includes a market and a cafe where artisanal Finger Lakes cheeses are paired with Fox Run wines. You can taste one of the widest stylistic arrays from a single estate in the Finger Lakes, from red and white to sparkling, from rosé to port styles. Winemaker Peter Bell has seen a transformation in Finger Lakes as a wine destination: 'Good food and lodging were pretty scarce 10 years ago. Now it's easy to find both,' he says. As well as newcomers like a white Pinot Noir, Fox Run's highlights include single-vineyard Riesling, Lemberger and Chardonnay bottlings. Kick back with a glass or two and enjoy the views of Seneca Lake on the back patio. *foxrunvineyards.com; tel +1 315-536-4616; 670 Rte 14, Penn Yan; 10am-6pm Mon-Sat, 11am-6pm Sun* Ⓢ✕

⓸ ANTHONY ROAD WINE COMPANY

Anthony Road's story is something of a mirror to that of the Finger Lakes as a whole. Ann and John Martini planted their first vines – all hybrids – in 1973, and have since replanted nearly all the vines to *vinifera* varieties such as Chardonnay, Riesling, Pinot Gris, Cabernet Franc and Merlot. Today, the great majority of their delicious bottlings are strictly *vinifera*, but they also offer a semi-sweet hybrid wine (of Vignoles), giving a window to the recent past.

Anthony Road is a super visit to make for wine education (especially if combined with Hermann J Wiemer), and much more. Very close to Seneca Lake, the bring-your-own-picnic-friendly open-lawn patio (local cheese also available) offers spectacular views. Inside, a gallery features frequently changing works by local artists. And don't miss the Art Series Riesling and winemaker Peter Becraft's experimental Grey Series wines. *anthonyroadwine.com; tel +1 315-536-2182; 1020 Anthony Rd, Penn Yan; tastings by reservation 10am-4pm daily, till 6pm summer* Ⓢ

⓹ HERMANN J WIEMER

In 1979 German-born Hermann Wiemer, one of the first to push for *vinifera* varieties in the region, founded his eponymous estate. Since then, his winery has earned a reputation among the best in the United States. Hermann retired in 2007 and his former assistant, Fred Merwarth, has taken over the winemaking, focusing on terroir, matching variety and style to the estate's varying vineyard sites. Oskar Bynke is Fred's partner in this project and often serves as the public face for the estate – his wine presentations are keenly insightful. All the wines here are made with an eye for detail, but don't miss the Magdalena Vineyard Riesling, the Magdalena Vineyard Cabernet Franc and the sparkling wines. Bynke is also keenly aware that this fast-rising region benefits his and other wineries in many ways. 'With quite a few options including

outdoor and water activities, museums, and authentic farm-to-table dining experiences that don't feel contrived, there is something for everyone,' he says. 'It just takes a drive around the lakes to see the abundant resources available.' *wiemer.com; tel +1 607-243-7971; 3962 Rte 14, Dundee; 10am-4pm Mon-Sat, 11am-4pm Sun* Ⓢ

⓺ BLOOMER CREEK

The Bloomer Creek tasting room is a short walk from the Stonecat Cafe in Hector, and if you visit on a weekend afternoon, you're likely to be served by a tall, affable gentleman named Kim Engle. Along with his wife, artist Debra Bermingham, Kim started Bloomer Creek some 30 years ago, and continues to make the wine with the help of only one employee. In a region where many growers focus on Riesling, and most harvest by machine, these wines stand out: here, the red wines of Loire, France, are the model; and natural methods, including hand-harvest and native yeast ferments, are the goal.

Kim makes terrific wines from Gewürztraminer, Pinot Noir, Riesling and other grapes, but it is his Cabernet Francs that most clearly give an original profile of Finger Lakes terroir. Be on the lookout for the lip-smacking Bloomer Creek rosé and the elegant, ageworthy White Horse Meritage Red. *bloomercreek.com; tel +1 607-546-5027; 5301 Rte 414, Hector; by reservation Sat & Sun* Ⓢ

07 FORGE CELLARS

Like a handful of others in the region, Forge Cellars work strictly with Pinot Noir and Riesling, believing that these are the best grapes for Finger Lakes' terroir. This focus allows the winery a meticulous approach to quality.

Forge Cellars is an exciting joint venture between two friends: New York-based Rick Rainey and Louis Barruol, born into a winemaking family from Gigondas in the Rhône. Working with a number of top growers and terroirs across the Finger Lakes, Forge ensures the grapes are hand-picked and makes its wine with minimal manipulation. The results are gorgeous, and speak for a great ageing potential.

The tasting room hosts seated tastings from Wednesday to Saturday (reservations required), while the Salon offers small plates and wine by the glass. Make reservations online and use map or sat nav to get there as there isn't a sign on the road (or on the building, for that matter).
forgecellars.com; tel 607-622-8020; 3775 Mathews Rd, Burdett; tastings by reservation Wed-Sat 💲✕

08 HEART & HANDS WINERY

If you're heading to or from Skaneateles from Ithaca, treat yourself to a lovely drive along the east side of Cayuga Lake on Rte 90 to visit this small winery that started the Riesling-and-Pinot revolution. A winding road takes you along the lake, past a wildlife refuge, beside open fields and through cute historical towns, until you reach the Union Springs and the winery of Tom and Susan Higgins, Heart & Hands. Consummate hosts, the Higgins' are passionate about three things: limestone soil, Pinot Noir and Riesling. Established in 2007, the winery is quietly making a convincing case for vineyard-specific Pinot and Riesling as the Finger Lakes' signature varieties; they also craft an extraordinary vintage sparkling Brut.
heartandhandswine.com; tel +1 315-889-8500; 4162 Rte 90, Union Springs; by reservation noon-5pm Thu-Sun 💲

ESSENTIAL INFORMATION

WHERE TO STAY
FROG'S WAY B&B
Get the full green Ithaca experience at this house in EcoVillage, a planned community just west of town that features conscientious design choices such as locally sourced materials and solar panels. Two rooms share a bathroom; breakfast is organic and local. *frogsway-bnb.com; tel +1 607-592-8402; 211 Rachel Carson Way, Ithaca*

INN ON COLUMBIA
This inn is spread across several homes clustered in a quiet residential area a short walk from downtown. The slick interior design is refreshingly contemporary. *columbiabb.com; tel +1 607-272-0204; 228 Columbia St, Ithaca*

WHERE TO EAT
DANO'S HEURIGER ON SENECA
Make sure you arrive here early in the evening; this traditional Austrian *heuriger* (wine tavern)

offers stunning views of the sun setting over Seneca Lake. The food is deliciously classic – schnitzel, currywurst, spätzle and Sacher Torte are among the staples –and the exciting wine list offers a selection of Austrian and German wines alongside a wide range of the best from the Finger Lakes. *danosonseneca.com; tel +1 607-582-7555 9564 Rte 414, Lodi; Thu-Sun*

STONECAT CAFÉ
All the locals swing through the Stonecat at some point; it's like a Cheers bar for wine lovers and winemakers. The atmosphere is relaxed and casual – it's easy to hang out here all day, thanks in part to the excellent selection of Finger Lakes wines and beers. The open-air back dining room gives onto a sloping garden where most of the food on the menu is sourced – it doesn't get more 'farm-to-table' than that! A perfect spot to recharge at the end of a long tasting day.

stonecatcafe.com; tel +1 607-546-5000; 5315 Rte 414, Hector; Wed-Sun

WHAT TO DO
Enjoy a morning hike through otherworldly cliffs of Watkins Glen State Park, where 19 waterfalls crash along a 3km (2-mile) course, and learn about the Finger Lakes' unique geology. (Don't forget to take a quiet moment to admire the Central Cavern Cascade.) *parks.ny.gov/parks/watkinsglen*

CELEBRATIONS
In the middle of July, Watkins Glen hosts the terrific Finger Lakes Wine Festival, where more than 80 wineries pour their new releases in a cheerful Woodstock-like scene of campers, wine lovers and live music. Over every weekend in December, Skaneateles is transformed into a Dickensian Christmas celebration, with costumed characters roaming the streets. *flwinefest.com; skaneateles.com*

Courtesy of Stonecat Café

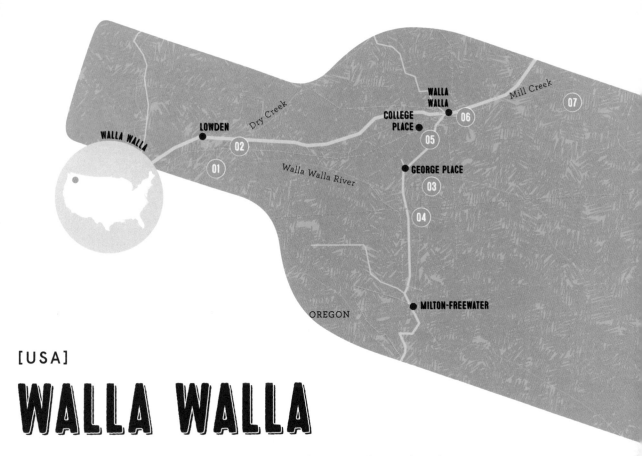

[USA]

WALLA WALLA

*A breadth of world-class wines, first-rate dining and spectacular scenery –
this is Washington at its best. As one winemaker says: 'We sold everything we
had in New York and moved to Walla Walla.'*

Beneath the Blue Mountains on the eastern side of Washington, the Walla Walla Valley has become a remarkable story of rural transformation. The area has always been known for its agriculture, but three decades ago the valley and the town were struggling. Then the grape vines arrived. Today, Walla Walla is one of Washington's most celebrated wine regions. It is also the state's best equipped for wine-country travel, with an enticing mix of tasting rooms, charming local eateries, comfortable B&Bs and luxury hotels.

Washington's desert country is quite a landscape, too: sweeping, arid, with wide-open sunny skies. The road from Seattle takes you over the Cascade Range, which in winter has some of the best downhill skiing in the Pacific Northwest (if driving at that time of year, check that roads are open and that you have snow tyres).

In the town of Walla Walla itself, tasting rooms can be found throughout the downtown area as well as at some wineries on the outskirts. Almost half of the Walla Walla AVA sits below the Oregon border just a few minutes south of town, but most of the wineries are located in the Washington half. If you're in the market for world-class Syrah, the Rocks District of Milton-Freewater AVA has become one of the new hot spots of the region. While tasting through the region, be sure to allow some time to enjoy a walk around the town of Walla Walla itself, which has developed a justified reputation for good wine and food – some of the best chefs in the state have relocated to open restaurants here.

GET THERE
Fly directly into Walla Walla regional airport, or drive 4hr east over the Cascade Mountains from Seattle.

01 WOODWARD CANYON

Founded by Rick and Darcey Fugman-Small in 1981, Woodward Canyon was only the second winery in Walla Walla, and today their children Jordan and Sager work in the vineyards and winery alongside Rick. The vineyards on the family farm are located in the Woodward Canyon for which the winery is named. The Fugman-Smalls have kept their focus on small-production, artisanal wine meant to celebrate the distinctive character of Washington. The tasting room stands in the family's restored 1870s farmhouse, and inside you'll find charming and well-informed staff. Keep an eye out for their Cabernet and Merlot, but you can also expect a few unusual varieties such as Dolcetto made in small lots. *woodwardcanyon.com; tel +1 509-525-4129; 11920 US-12, Lowden; 10am-5pm daily* ⑤

02 L'ECOLE NO 41

West of Walla Walla, the small community of Frenchtown was founded in the 19th century by French Canadians. Today the village is called Lowden and the original L'Ecole No 41, which became the Lowden Schoolhouse, serves as the tasting room for this third-generation family-owned winery. The Clubb family established L'Ecole No 41 in the early 1980s and led the charge for sustainable farming. When it comes to winemaking, L'Ecole believes 'in well-balanced wines, good acidity and firm but not overpowering tannins'. You'll find that class in their Ferguson Estate red, a blend of Bordeaux varieties grown in the region's highest vineyard. It's one of Washington's most distinctive wines and ages well. *lecole.com; tel +1 509-525-0940; 41 Lowden School Rd, Lowden; 10am-5pm daily* ⑤

03 AMAVI CELLARS

The name Amavi is a combination of 'amor' and 'vita'. And no one has done more than the winery's founder, Norm McKibben, to support the life of Walla Walla wine. He got started in grapes by getting started with apples. 'All I meant to do was help out a couple of friends who had [an apple] packing house and were struggling,' he says. Norm then got talked into planting wine grapes. Now, Amavi concentrates on wines made entirely from the Amavi Vineyards in Walla Walla, all certified sustainable. One of the state's most celebrated winemakers, Jean-François Pellet, maintains the soils; in the cellar the goal is transparency. A visit

From left: courtesy of Woodward Canyon; L'ecole no 41 / Sander Olson (2)

to the tasting room also offers beautiful vistas of that Walla Walla sky. Pop in for a flight of wines, or call ahead for a tour of the winery and vineyards followed by a private tasting in the barrel room. *amavicellars.com; tel +1 509-525-3541; 3796 Peppers Bridge Rd, Walla Walla; tastings daily by reservation* $

04 PEPPERBRIDGE

Pepperbridge is a collaboration between three families: the McKibbens, Murphys and Pellets. 'Terroir is a vague word but it means a lot to me,' says winemaker Jean-François Pellet. 'We all want that sense of place.' The wine programme is dedicated to Bordeaux varieties. The flagship wine, Trine, is a blend of the five Bordeaux varieties – Cabernet Sauvignon, Merlot, Cabernet Franc, Malbec and Petit Verdot – with the proportions changing by vintage. Pepperbridge also bottles varietally oriented wines, particularly Cabernet Sauvignon and Merlot. The latter has become one of the signature varieties of Walla Walla, with bursting fruits and savoury herbs followed by that crystalline acidity. Stop into the Pepperbridge tasting room for a flight of wines and views of the Blue Mountains. *pepperbridge.com; tel +1 509-525-6502; 1704 JB George Rd, Walla Walla; 10am-4pm daily; larger parties book ahead* $

05 GRAMERCY CELLARS

Master sommelier Greg Harrington spent his restaurant career overseeing some of the country's finest wine lists. 'Visiting Walla Walla, we realised that one could make earthy, balanced wines,' he says. 'We sold everything we owned in NYC and moved to Washington.' Harrington's Gramercy Cellars has become one of the most celebrated wineries in the state for making exactly those earthy, balanced wines from Rhone varieties such as Syrah, Grenache and Cabernet Sauvignon. Reserve in advance for a visit to the tasting room to enjoy its minimalist lounge feel and a flight of five to six Grammercy wines (mostly reds).

gramercycellars.com; tel
+1 509-876-2427; 625 N 13th
Ave, Walla Walla; Tue-Say
by reservation ⑤

06 SEVEN HILLS WINERY

Do you want to taste different single-vineyard expressions of Cabernet and Merlot from different Washington AVAs side by side? Then this elegant tasting room is for you. Established in the late 1980s by the McClellan family, Seven Hills works with some of the oldest Cabernet Sauvignon and Merlot vineyards in the Walla Walla Valley and beyond. Book ahead to taste through a flight across the portfolio, or schedule a more educational tasting accompanied by fabulous food from Kinglet, which is right next door in the former Whitehouse Crawford building. Seven Hills' tasting room is set a converted warehouse, with high ceilings, natural wood floors and tons of light flooding in. sevenhillswinery.com; tel +1 509-529-7198; 212 N 3rd, Walla Walla; by reservation 10am-5pm daily ⑤✕

07 ÀMAURICE CELLARS

Three generations of the Schafer family work the slopes of the Blue Mountains while also sourcing fruit from some of the finest vineyards in the state. Then daughter Anna Schafer gets to work in the cellar to create àMaurice's award-winning wines with a mix of white and red Bordeaux varieties as well as Malbec and Syrah. Wines are bottled with changing art-focused labels; the Artist Series wines, Cabernet Sauvignon-based Bordeaux blends, feature a different painting as the image for each vintage.

The tasting room is relaxed and welcoming, with an eclectic feel inside the converted workspace (keep an eye on the schedule for some interesting happenings). There is also outside seating, weather permitting. amaurice.com; tel +1 509-522-5444; 178 Vineyard Ln, Walla Walla; 10.30am-4.30pm Fri & Sat & by appointment ⑤

Courtesy of L'Ecole No 41 / Colby D Kuschatka; Leon Werdinger / Alamy Stock Photo

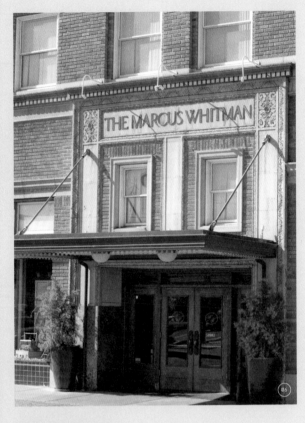

WHERE TO STAY
**MARCUS
WHITMAN HOTEL**
A landmark in the
middle of town, bringing
together classic styling
with contemporary
upgrades and modern
country-comfort in
a historic building.
Downstairs the hotel
includes the Marc
Restaurant, one of the
region's showpiece
culinary experiences,
as well as the Vineyard
Lounge for drinks.
*marcuswhitmanhotel.
com; tel +1 866-826-
9422; 6 W Rose St,
Walla Walla*

THE GG
Walla Walla has come to
be known for its B&Bs.
Recently refurbished,
the luxe GG stands in
one of the area's original
homesteads, with crisply
reworked rooms and
suites. Chill after dark
by the fire pit or enjoy a
the three-cource locally
sourced dinners cooked
up each Friday night.
*theggwallawalla.com;
tel +1 509-579 9739; 922
Bonsella St, Walla Walla*

WHERE TO EAT
KINGLET
The renowned
Whitehouse Crawford
restaurant helped usher
in high-end dining to
the Walla Walla area
when it opened in
2000, but closed as
the pandemic loomed
in 2020. A year later, a
new incarnation with
chef Maximilien Petty
at the helm revitalised
this historic former mill,
serving sublime seasonal
cuisine (including a five-
course tasting option),
all accompanied by an
expertly curated list of
local and global wines.
*kingletww.com; tel +1
509-676-4550; 55 W
Cherry St, Walla Walla;
Thu-Mon*

PASSATEMPO TAVERNA
Passatempo is a firm
Walla Walla favourite.
The seasonal menu
is inspired by the
dishes of Italy, using
local ingredients.
That 'locavore'
commitment carries
into the cocktails,
which are made fresh
with seasonal garden
ingredients.
*passatempowallawalla.
com; tel +1 509-876-
8822; 215 W Main St,
Walla Walla; Thu-Mon*

AK'S MERCADO
For a taste of
Washington-Mexican
cuisine, seek out the
new venture by chef
Andrae Bopp. Kick
back in the cosy lounge
or patio area to enjoy
huevos rancheros for
brunch or fresh-made
tacos alongside cocktails
and house brewed beer
later on.
*andraeskitchen.com;
tel +1 509-572-0728; 21
E Main St, Walla Walla;
daily*

WHAT TO DO
Burbank's McNary
National Wildlife Refuge
was formed to offset the
impact of the McNary
Dam. As well as serving
as home to a wealth
of indigenous wildlife
including a wide range
of birds, otters, beavers,
mule deer and migrating
animals, there are
multiple walking trails:
lace up your boots and
grab your binoculars
fws.gov/refuge/McNary

[USA]
WILLAMETTE VALLEY

Burgundian expats and Portland hipsters have helped turn this pocket of the USA's northwest into a food and wine powerhouse in just a few decades.

The achievements of Oregon's wine producers over the last 50 years are really quite remarkable. Before then, there was hardly a vineyard to be found in this densely forested state, but today its foremost wine region, the Willamette Valley, is renowned as one of the best places in the world to grow Pinot Noir. Anyone doubting this claim should talk to one of the numerous Burgundian expatriates who have enthusiastically established wineries here to produce delicate, elegant reds that bear more than a passing resemblance to the wines of their homeland. And white-wine lovers need not worry, as Pinot Noir is not the only game in town: Pinot Gris and Chardonnay also perform well here, while aromatic whites from Riesling and Gewürztraminer are getting better with every vintage.

The 11,008 hectares (27,202 acres) of vineyards in the Willamette Valley (the vast majority of which

GET THERE
Seattle-Tacoma is the nearest major airport, 300km (186 miles) from Forest Grove. Car hire is available.

are Pinot Noir) stretch out to the south and southwest of the state's largest city, Portland, which serves as an ideal staging post for visits to the region. Portland has a reputation for eccentricity (you may well see signs and graffiti imploring residents to 'Keep Portland Weird') and is rumoured to be the birthplace of the hipster, but it is also a vibrant city that offers visitors a dazzling array of great restaurants and places to drink. An abundance of organic produce, artisanal coffee, craft beer and street food are evidence of a foodie culture in which wine plays a leading role, and over 930 wineries are just a short drive away, making a trip to Oregon the ideal combination between a city break and rural wine-tasting experience.

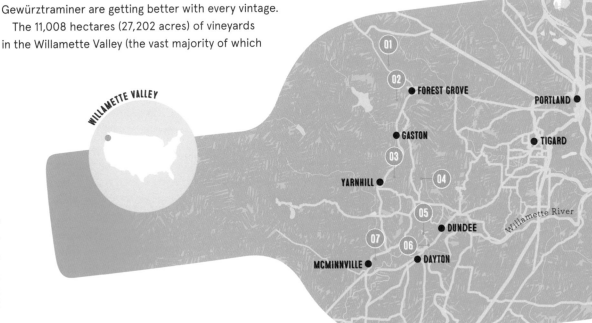

WILLAMETTE VALLEY

FOREST GROVE
PORTLAND
GASTON
TIGARD
01
02
03
04
YARNHILL
05
DUNDEE
Willamette River
07
06
MCMINNVILLE
DAYTON

David H. Collier @ Getty Images

01 DAVID HILL

This beautiful estate has more history than most in the Willamette Valley – wine was being made here way back in the late 1800s, long before it was considered a sensible pursuit for an Oregonian. But in 1919 Prohibition put paid to all that, and it wasn't until the mid-1960s that people started planting vineyards again. When that happened, the place originally known as 'Wine Hill' (the name was later changed to honour the local David family) was one of the first to see grapevines – and it continues to thrive to this day, with many of the original vineyards still intact.

Pinot Noir wines form the bulk of the line-up here, but David Hill also produce wines from a range of other varieties and even has some fortified port-style wines.

Visiting the winery is a relaxed affair, worthwhile as much for the stunning views as for the wines. A tasting gets you a choice of seven pours from their range; you can also book wine and cheese pairings, or add on cheese and charcuterie platters to tastings.
davidhillwinery.com;
tel +1 503-992-8545; 46350
Northwest David Hill Rd, Forest
Grove; by reservation 11am-5pm
daily 💲 🍴

02 MONTINORE

Established in 1982, Montinore is a great place to get to grips with what makes Willamette so special. Pinot Noir is the most important variety here, as it is throughout the valley, but owner Rudy Marchesi is also very fond of aromatic white wines – his Riesling, Gewürztraminer and Pinot Gris are some of the region's best. Willamette Valley has a remarkably high number of biodynamic practitioners; the Montinore estate is Demeter-certified, so anyone interested in seeing the realities of biodynamic agriculture can learn more about this fascinating method.

The tasting room overlooks the estate's 81 hectares (200 acres) of vines and offers a flight of five wines. If the weather is good, Montinore is also the perfect place to bring a picnic and take a wander through the vineyards.
montinore.com; tel +1 503-359-5012; 3663 Southwest Dilley Rd, Forest Grove; by reservation 11am-5pm daily (S)

03 WILLAKENZIE ESTATE

WillaKenzie is a splicing-together of the names of the Willamette and McKenzie rivers, which between them are responsible for the distinctive soil type found in this part of the region. The Lacroute family that founded the estate back in 1991 have French roots (Burgundy, naturally) and their belief in the Willamette Valley's terroir (highlighted by estate's 'place matters' tagline) prompted them to adopt the practice of making single-vineyard wines from their most interesting parcels of vines. WillaKenzie is considered to be one of the foremost players in the drive for quality in the Willamette Valley, but it's also one of the best set up to receive visitors.

The 'Perspective of Place' flight offers a block-by-block tasting of WillaKenzie's Pinot Noirs, accompanied by cheese and charcuterie and a screening of drone-filmed views of the estate. You can also try your hand on the pétanque courts.
willakenzie.com; tel +1 503-662-3280; 19143 NE Loughlin Rd, Yamhill; by reservation 11.30am & 2.30pm Fri-Sun (S)

04 BERGSTRÖM WINES

When many Burgundians were coming over to Oregon to establish wineries, Josh Bergström (son of the founders of Bergström Wines) was heading in the opposite direction. After learning to make wine in Pinot Noir's spiritual home (and meeting his wife Caroline in the process), Josh returned to the Willamette Valley and has since established a reputation as one of the very best winemakers in the state. He will tell you that the secret is conscientious farming: no pesticides and chemicals are used on the 70 hectares (173 acres) of vineyards, and Josh also farms biodynamically to ensure the fruit is perfect.

If you want to get to grips with how good Oregon Pinot Noir can be, this is the place to do it, as everything from their Cumberland Reserve up to the Bergström Vineyard is superb. Josh is a dab hand with Chardonnay too, so be sure to taste the whites while you are there. Reserve ahead to pop into the charming winery and Ekollon tasting room for a flight of these benchmark wines ($80).
bergstromwines.com; tel +1 503-554-0468; 8115 NE Worden Hill Rd, Dundee; by reservation Thu-Tue (S)

05 DOMAINE DROUHIN

One of the region's true destination wineries, Domaine Drouhin stands at the top of the Dundee Hills with exceptional views of the entire valley. On a clear day, Mt Hood, Mt Jefferson and the Three Sisters are all visible from the deck.

Domaine Drouhin is the Oregon outpost for Burgundy's famed Joseph Drouhin winery, and it is here that Véronique Boss-Drouhin brings the finesse of French winemaking to the fruit of Oregon. The high-ceilinged tasting room is one of the Willamette Valley's more palatial experiences – soak it up by pre-booking the seated Drouhin Oregon Experience, tasting four wines from the Dundee and Eola-Amity Hills sub-appellations

including the estate's flagship Cuvée Laurène; in good weather permitting, they also offer tastings on a deck beside the vineyard. *domainedrouhin.com; tel +1 503-864-2700; 6750 NE Breyman Orchards Rd, Dayton; by reservation 11am-3pm daily* 🅢

06 SOKOL BLOSSER

This family-run winery was established in 1971 by Bill Blosser and Susan Sokol Blosser, and has long played a pioneering role in the Willamette Valley's wine scene. Sure, they were one of the first wineries in the region, but they were also the first to open a tasting room to welcome visitors (back in 1978), and their innovative range of wines has always kept them at the forefront of the region's wine scene. The customary Pinot Noir forms the core of the Sokol Blosser range, now overseen by second-generation winemakers Alex and Alison Sokol Blosser, but there are other varieties

available and their Evolution red and white blends are some of the best-value wines in Oregon.

Guests are not just in for a sensory treat with the wines – the visitor centre itself is an architectural gem. Beautifully designed, with incredible views of their vineyards and the Cascade Mountains, it offers tastings of four flights of Sokol Blosser wines. In the summer, you can also hike through the vineyard to learn about winemaking here, finishing with snacks and a glass of wine. There's also a restaurant, Farm & Forage, with six-course tasting menus and paired wines. If there's one winery that you must visit during your trip to Oregon, this is it. *sokolblosser.com; tel +1 503-864-2282; 5000 NE Sokol Blosser Lane, Dayton; tastings by reservation 10am-4pm Wed-Mon* 🅢✕

07 EYRIE VINEYARDS

A tour of the Willamette Valley is not complete without visiting Eyrie,

the first vineyard to plant vines here in the 1960s. Founder David Lett recognised the potential of the region's cool climate for making Pinot Noir and its sibling varieties Chardonnay and Pinot Gris – which are what Eyrie is renowned for to this day.

Today, son Jason Lett leads Eyrie, making wine in the historic winery space established by his father. The tasting room maintains its historic feel, but with its location in the heart of McMinnville it's also an easy walk to local food favourites, coffee shops and other tasting rooms. Best of all, a stop into the tasting room includes not only four or seven wine flights from across the Eyrie portfolio, but also the option to add from a revolving collection of older vintages. With a library of wines from over 50 vintages, there is no better place to taste wines built to age. *eyrievineyards.com; tel +1 503-472-6315; 935 NE 10th Ave, McMinnville; by reservation noon-5pm daily* 🅢

WHERE TO STAY

KENNEDY SCHOOL

One of the McMenamins group of hotels, Kennedy School is a converted schoolhouse classed as an historic landmark. Nowadays this quirky venue is home to a brewery, numerous bars, a gym that doubles as a live-music venue and 57 well-appointed guest rooms. *mcmenamins.com; tel +1 503-249-3983; 5736 NE 33rd Ave, Portland*

JUPITER HOTEL

Those looking for a cool, comfortable crash pad in central Portland should consider the Jupiter Hotel. It has the feel of a deluxe motel, with spacious rooms and a lively bar – the Doug Fir Lounge – that is an attraction in itself. *jupiterhotel.com; tel +1 503-230-9200; 800 East Burnside St, Portland*

WHERE TO EAT

LE PIGEON

Although small in size, Le Pigeon is big in influence – Portland's food lovers will tell you that it was one of the restaurants that kick-started the city's contemporary dining scene, offering a five-course seasonal tasting menu. *www.lepigeon.com; tel +1 503-546-8796; 738 East Burnside St, Portland; by reservation only Tue-Sat*

STAMMTISCH

Dig into serious German food – with a beer list to match – at this dark and cosy neighborhood pub. Don't miss the Maultaschen (a gorgeous pasta pocket filled with leek fondue in a bright, lemony wine sauce), the clams with knackwurst sausage and white beans in a white wine sauce, or the paprika-spiced roast chicken. *stammtischpdx.com; tel +1 503-206-7983; 401 NE 28th Ave, Portland; daily*

WHAT TO DO

With more breweries than any other city on Earth, Portland is a craft-beer lover's dream. Plan a DIY itinerary at www.portlandbeer.org, or take an organised

tour with Brewvana. The city's street food scene is taken just as seriously, so check out Food Carts Portland for up-to-date information about what's cooking. *experiencebrewvana. com; foodcartsportland. com*

CELEBRATIONS

A packed calendar of events includes the Portland Rose Festival (May/June), World Naked Bike Ride (June) and the Adult Soapbox Derby (August). Weekly markets are also important to Portlanders and the best are Portland Saturday Market and the Portland Farmers Market; the latter has a weekly programme of live music and cooking demonstrations by top chefs. *rosefestival.org; pdxwnbr. org; soapboxracer.com; portlandsaturday market.com; portlandfarmersmarket.org*

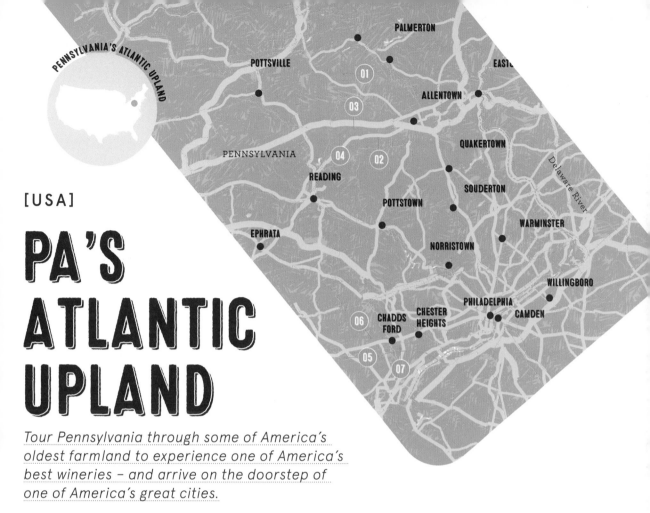

PENNSYLVANIA'S ATLANTIC UPLAND

PALMERTON

POTTSVILLE

01

EAST...

ALLENTOWN

03

QUAKERTOWN

PENNSYLVANIA

04

02

SOUDERTON

READING

POTTSTOWN

Delaware River

WARMINSTER

EPHRATA

NORRISTOWN

WILLINGBORO

PHILADELPHIA

CHADDS FORD

CHESTER HEIGHTS

CAMDEN

06

05

07

[USA]

PA'S ATLANTIC UPLAND

Tour Pennsylvania through some of America's oldest farmland to experience one of America's best wineries – and arrive on the doorstep of one of America's great cities.

One of the 13 original US colonies, Pennsylvania is a state where you're enveloped in the past, from the Liberty Bell and Independence Hall in Philadelphia to the weathered log cabins at Valley Forge to the silence of the open fields at Gettysburg.

Amid the refurbished buildings and historic markers that reflect the deep ties to America's history are a group of pioneers with comparatively shallow roots. While grape growing and winemaking date back to the 1600s, the Limited Winery Act was passed as recently as 1968. Today, around 300 wineries operate statewide.

Many benefit from the rolling terrain spilling off the Allegheny and Pocono Mountains that provides elevation and a drying breeze. Pennsylvania's diverse topography also produces a variety of climates, but don't worry – though cold winters and humid summers are typical, extremes in those seasons rarely endure.

Most of the state's wineries are clustered across the eastern and south-central sections and along Lake Erie, in the northwest corner. The vast majority of operations are family-owned, many with vineyards. While you'll find *vinifera* such as Chardonnay, Cabernet Sauvignon and Cabernet Franc, you'll also come across samples of hybrids such as Chambourcin and Traminette, both made in a variety of styles and improving in quality by the year. Native American grapes such as Niagara and Concord satisfy a local sweet tooth. That said, the greatest gains are being made in the production of premium dry wines, from red and white blends to experimentation with newcomers such as Grüner Veltliner, Albariño, Zweigelt and Blaufränkisch.

Weekends from March through October offer a variety of events, from summer concerts to harvest festivals.

GET THERE
Allentown has an airport or use Philadelphia. Or try Jim Thorpe as an historic option or West Chester in the reverse direction.

01 GALEN GLEN

It may be one of the state's most rural wineries, but it sports an international reputation for its Riesling and Grüner Veltliner. Tucked into a valley between the Blue and Mahoning mountains, Galen Glen offers an airy tasting room and a 32km (20-mile) view from the back patio.

Galen Troxall and his wife Sarah still work on the farm that has been in Galen's family for decades, but have handed over much of the winemaking and viticultural responsibilities to their daughter, Erin. Both come from scientific backgrounds. 'We farm wine. Period. Not grapes. Responsibly and sustainably,' says Sarah. 'We are obsessed with aromatic white wine: Riesling, Grüner Veltliner and Gewürztraminer.' Try Galen Glen's reds, too, such as Zweigelt and Chambourcin.
galenglen.com; tel 570-386-3682; 255 Winter Mountain Dr, Andreas; noon-6pm Fri & Sat, Sun noon-5pm Ⓢ

02 CLOVER HILL

It was several years after the passage of the Limited Winery Act that Pat, a teacher, and John Skrip, a civil engineer, decided to plant grapes as a hobby at their home outside Allentown. Today, Clover Hill (with son John Jr as winemaker) is among the state's biggest producers, operating out of a spacious, modern tasting room that looks out over the hilly terrain of eastern Pennsylvania. Visitors will find a diverse list of products, with several styles of Chambourcin, a low-tannin red hybrid that grows plentifully throughout the region, and offerings such as frizzante, dessert wine and port. Meats and cheeses are available for purchase.

> ## 'We farm wine. Period. Not grapes. Responsibly and sustainably. We are obsessed with aromatic white wine'
> *– Sarah Troxell, Galen Glen*

01 Historic Jim Thorpe
town in Pennsylvania

02 The tasting room at
Galer Estate

03 Winemaker Sarah
Troxell at Galen Glen

04 Antipasti platters at
Folino Estate

cloverhillwinery.com; tel +1 610-395-2468; 9850 Newtown Rd, Breinigsville; 10am-5.30pm Mon-Sat, noon-5pm Sun 💲

03 FOLINO ESTATE

A head-turner. There's no other way to describe the Tuscan-style villa that comprises Folino Estate's winery, tasting room, market, restaurant and events hall, built on a 22-hectare (54-acre) property, some 5.6 hectares (14 acres) of which are dedicated to vines. Around the winery are a sprawling patio and bocce court. 'Seeing our dream come to life has been an experience like no other,' says Andrea Folino.

You could probably count the number of regional wineries that have full-service restaurants on one hand, but Folino Estate focuses on Old World-style wines to pair with the pizzas and pastas produced on site. Wines range from Pinot Grigio and Moscato to Pinot Noir and a Bordeaux blended red called Lorenzo Forte. *folinoestate.com; tel +1 484-452-3633; 340 Old Route 22, Kutztown; 11am-8pm Wed-Sun* 💲 🍴

04 SETTER RIDGE

Many regional wineries shy away from Pinot Noir; Setter Ridge, operated by the Blair family, embraces this finnicky grape, not only growing it on parts of 12-hectare (30-acre) vineyard but using it in several wines, including a varietal.

'We're blessed with a climate that allows us cooler days, with less humidity than surrounding areas,' says Rich Blair, who opened the winery in 2010. At the end of a twisting driveway, past the vines, is an A-frame with a covered porch. Pick your spot to sample a list of quality dry wines (the winery name – and the canine portraits on their bottles – are a nod to the family's fondness for English setters). *setterridgevineyards.com; tel +1 610-683-8463; 99 Dietrich Valley Rd, Kutztown; 11am-5pm Thu-Tue* 💲

05 VA LA

Va La is not merely recommended, it is unmissable. The winery is unparalleled in its consistency for excellence – indeed, a national

blends accounting for the more
than 150 awards garnered since the
winery opened in 2011.
*galerestate.com; tel +1 484-899-
8013; 700 Folly Hill Rd, Kennett
Square; noon-8pm Fri-Sat, noon-
7pm Sun* $

07 PENNS WOODS

A former wine importer, Gino
Razzi earned 95 points from *Wine
Spectator* magazine for his first
commercially produced wine. Still,
he says that there were plenty
of self-doubts when he created
Penns Woods in 2001.

Razzi's winery, which now
involves daughter Carley in many
aspects of the operation, first
and foremost sells the consistent
quality of its full line of wines,
mostly *vinifera* and primarily
estate-grown. 'I think for my father
the most satisfying part of opening
his winery was allowing his hobby
and dream to become a true
reality,' Carley says.

The tasting room and wine shop
overlook rolling vineyards. While
some are drawn by a busy events
schedule that includes music and
yoga in the vineyard, many just
spread a blanket or settle in at one
of the picnic tables on the lawn.
*pennswoodswinery.com; tel +1
610-459-0808; 124 Beaver Valley
Rd, Chaddsford; 12-6pm Mon-Thu,
11am-7pm Fri & Sat, 11am-6pm Sun*
$ ✕

website annually lists it among
America's top wineries.

Owner Anthony Vietri is the fifth-
generation of his family to farm the
2.8 hectares (7 acres) of northern
Italian and French varieties of
grapes on a farm that dates back
to the original 405 hectares (1000
acres) of the John Miller estate,
deeded to Miller by William Penn,
founder of Pennsylvania, in 1713.

Also the winemaker, Anthony
makes just six or seven field-blend
wines a year. 'We strive to offer dry
table wines that are unique to this
site and specifically designed to
shine with food,' he says.

Wines are offered by the glass
or bottle in the two-level tasting
room inside the century-old barn.
A $20 flight features four wines
accompanied by bites of local
specialities and seasonal tidbits
from the farm. Out the back,
a porch and lawn place visitors
alongside the vines.

*valavineyards.com; tel +1 610-268-
2702; 8822 Gap Newport Pike (Rt
41), Avondale; 12-6pm Fri-Sun* $ ✕

06 GALER ESTATE

The tagline for this suburban
Philly winery is 'blending nature,
science and art' – appropriate
for a producer that neighbours
the nationally known Longwood
Gardens in Chester County.

Wine-tech connoisseurs will
appreciate the gravity-flow winery,
with a specialised fermentation
room that feeds into a
subterranean barrel room. Lele and
Brad Galer run the place, which
brings us to the art: artist Lele
shows her own work and that of
regional artists and craftsmen in a
rustic tasting room. (Accompanying
charcuterie and local cheeses
available.) Dry, premium *vinifera*
make up the wine list, with
Chardonnays from several vineyards
and rosé along with Bordeaux

WHERE TO STAY

THE DOLON HOUSE

A must-stay B&B in the must-see Victorian town of Jim Thorpe. The structure was built in 1844, but owners Michael and Jeffri have turned it into their own trip through time with pieces collected over their 40 years of travels, and serve up fabulous breakfasts. *dolonhouse.com; tel +1 570-325-4462; 5 W Broadway, Jim Thorpe*

WHERE TO EAT

BOLETE

Bolete is the marriage of a couple's love for food: says Lee, the chef, of the farm-to-table venue he runs with partner Erin: 'We do not rush what we do and we don't want you to rush through your dining experience with us.' The result has drawn

praise both regionally and nationally. *boleterestaurant.com; tel +1 610-868 6505; 1740 Seidersville Rd, Bethlehem; Thu-Sat*

SAVONA BISTRO

Seasonally sourced produce cooked up in fine style (from wood-fired pizza to gourmet sandwiches) in this highly regarded locals' favourite in Kennett Square. *savonabistro.com; tel +1 610-444-5600; 696 Unionville Rd, Willowdale; Tue-Sat*

MARION HOSE BAR

Beer and bar food with atmosphere at a renovated vintage firehouse in Jim Thorpe. *marionhosebar.com; tel +1 570-732-1968 16 W Broadway, Jim Thorpe; Thu-Mon*

WHAT TO DO

NORTHERN PA

The Valley Preferred Cycling Center is a world-class biking facility in Trexlertown which also offers track racing to amateurs; in Kempton, Hawk Mountain Sanctuary is a nonprofit wild bird sanctuary, operating since 1934 and with a visitor centre, trails and overlooks. *thevelodrome.com; hawkmountain.org*

SOUTHERN PA

Seek out Kennett Square and the world-famous mushroom country that surrounds it, as well as gorgeous Longwood Gardens and the Brandywine River Museum of Art, which specialises in Wyeth family artworks and the art of Chester County.

historickennett square.com; longwoodgardens.org; brandywine.org/museum

PHILADELPHIA

Stop at the National Constitution Center and Reading Terminal Market. To the west is Amish Country and the splendour of Hershey and its huge theme park. *constitutioncenter.org; readingterminalmarket. org; discoverlancaster. com; hersheypa.com*

CELEBRATIONS

The Lehigh Valley Wine Trail is one of the region's most active, with special events throughout the year featuring tastings, vineyard and winery tours, food and wine pairings and live entertainment. Other wine-related festivals can be found on the state's wine association website. Among the metro events worth checking out are Philly Wine Week, held each March. *lehighvalleywinetrail. com; pennsylvaniawine. com; phillywineweek.org*

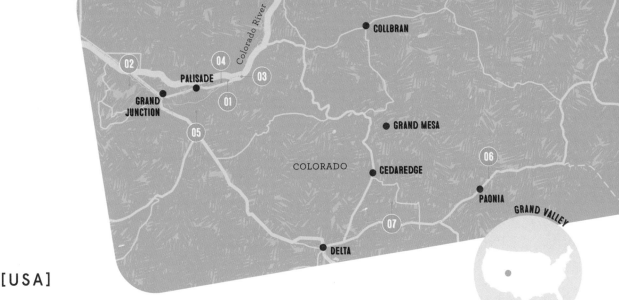

COLLBRAN

Colorado River

02 · 04 · 03
PALISADE · 01
GRAND JUNCTION · 05

GRAND MESA

COLORADO · CEDAREDGE

06

PAONIA

07 · GRAND VALLEY

DELTA

[USA]

GRAND VALLEY

With some of the highest-elevation vineyards in the world, Colorado wineries offer soul-stirring vistas of mountains and the Colorado River, plus a refreshing twist on traditional wine styles.

Colorado has long been known for its fantastic skiing, alpine hiking and a flourishing craft-brew culture. But the Centennial State is also home to an eclectic community of grape-growers and winemakers – a passionate, curious bunch who produce iconoclastic wine styles brimming with personality that comes from alkaline soils and thin mountain air. This unique terroir rewards patience and perseverance, and Colorado's winemakers have both in spades. On a visit, you'll be greeted with generous hospitality and an infectious enthusiasm for what's possible in a place that remains a well-kept secret in the wine world.

Colorado winemaking is still a new frontier. While it has roots in the 1800s, only five wineries were in operation as late as 1990. Now, around 150 wineries lie scattered across the state – from the front range (Boulder/Denver) to the four-corner town of Cortez near the grand Mesa Verde. However, the largest concentration of vineyards can be found hugging the Rocky Mountains' western slopes around

Grand Junction, where the low humidity and intense sunshine of the high desert make it possible to grow a wide range of grapes despite a shortened season.

The Grand Valley AVA is home to the highest concentration of vineyards in Colorado. Many of them sit at around 1372m (4500ft), soaking up the sunshine that radiates off the valley's chalky Book Cliffs. It's unlikely you'd find these exact growing conditions anywhere else in the world and, perhaps surprisingly, Bordeaux, Rhône and Italian varieties all thrive here, despite a short, challenging season in comparison to other regions that champion these classic longer-growing varieties.

About an hour's drive (120km/75 miles) southeast, the Delta region in the West Elks AVA offers an extremely different microclimate, home to Pinot Noir, Riesling, Pinot Grigio and Pinot Meunier that manage to grow at 2134m (7000ft). Dovetailing these two areas makes an ideal weekend getaway, offering a broad perspective on what is going on in Colorado's wine scene.

GET THERE
A 370km (230-mile) drive west from Denver to the Grand Valley passes the Continental Divide. Or, fly into Grand Junction's airport (GJT).

01 TWO RIVERS WINERY

In 1999, Bob and Billie Witham opened Colorado's 44th winery, with a vision of making high-quality wine in their home state. The couple still live amid their vines, off the beaten path in the Redlands area at the mouth of the Colorado National Monument, attracting visitors from all corners of the world. French wines inspire them, as is made clear in their variety of choice (Cabernet Sauvignon, Merlot, Riesling, Chardonnay, Syrah) – and also by the property's countryside château-styled buildings. Stay the night at the winery's Two Rivers' Wine Country Inn.

tworiverswinery.com; tel +1 970-255-1471; 2087 Broadway, Grand Junction; 10am-5pm Mon-Sat, 12pm-5pm Sun $

02 RED FOX CELLARS

'Respectful but unbound by tradition' is the proud motto Red Fox uses to blaze trails in Colorado's wine industry. Not only does this winery play with Italian varieties like Nebbiolo, Dolcetto and Teroldego, it also experiments with ageing traditional grapes in spirit-seasoned barrels from local distilleries. A smooth, long-lasting Bourbon-barrel-aged Merlot is Red Fox's bestseller; in 2017, the winery took home a silver medal at the Governor's Cup for its tequila-barrel-aged Chardonnay (with surprisingly chipper lime-like notes and bright acidity). Founders Sherry and Scott Hamilton are inspired by Colorado's craft-beer movement and don't see why the wine industry can't have a little more fun, too.

Their 'urban barn' in the heart of Palisade is a relaxed, social space with a rustic feel. In addition to signature wines, it offers food, house-made cider on tap and creative wine cocktails.

facebook.com/Red.Fox.Cellars; tel +1 970-464-1099; 695 36 Rd C, Palisade, CO 81526; 11am-5pm daily, till 7pm Fri & Sat $ ✗

03 PLUM CREEK

It began in 1976 with a few friends – Doug and Sue Phillips, and Erik Bruner – playing with Colorado grapes. By 1984, Plum Creek had become the 10th bonded winery in Colorado; it's still the state's oldest continually active winery, focusing on high-quality winemaking using only Colorado fruit. Thick wooden beams set the tone for Plum

Stone Cottage Cellars prides itself on having the highest Merlot vineyard in the world, at 1980m (6200ft)

Creek's warm, welcoming winery, while local art and sculpture bring depth to its landscape. Each vintage dictates the team's focus in the cellar, but the Old World guides stylistic choices, with Cabernet, Merlot and Chardonnay leading Plum Creek's award-winning wines. Corey Norsworthy heads up the winemaking team alongside Joe Flynn, with endless ideas for how to keep Plum Creek at the forefront of Colorado's wine tradition. Drop in for tastings or book tours ahead. *plumcreekwinery.com; tel +1 970-464-7586; 3708 G Rd, Palisade; 10am–5pm daily* 💲

04 COLTERRIS

Set among vineyards, orchards and lavender and rose gardens, Colterris has created quite the stir in recent years. Scott and Theresa High's winery – the 'Col-Terris' name is a spin on their 'from the Colorado land' tagline – is built on high aspirations, with a talented team of experienced vineyard-focused winemakers and 100% estate-grown fruit. The couple have lived in Tuscany, Umbria and Bordeaux and investigated land in Mendoza, eastern Washington and Sonoma. But, in the end, the challenging singular climate and geography of Colorado presented unbeatable appeal. Scott explains how, with Colterris sitting at over 1432m (4700ft), 'the intense sunlight gives unique character to these wines; thick skins give way to distinctive flavour and incredibly deep colour.'

The Highs have two talented winemakers in charge, Bo Felton and Justin Jannusch, under whose watch Colterris prides itself on being a Bordeaux-style winery. In summer and on winter weekends, visit the separate Colterris at the Overlook tasting room for panoramic views of the Colorado River, Grand Valley and majestic Book Cliffs. At both sites, private tours can be booked ahead, or just drop by for tastings. *colterris.com; tel +1 970-464-1150; Colterris Winery: 3907 North River Rd, Palisade; 10am–5pm daily;*

Colterris at the Overlook: 3548 E 1/2 Rd, Palisade; 10am-5pm; daily Jun-Oct, Nov-May Fri-Sun Ⓢ

05 WHITEWATER HILL

Whitewater Hill was established in 2004 by John Behrs and Nancy Janes, who were drawn to Colorado's dramatic day-to-night temperature changes, which swing from highs of 30°C/86°F down to lows of 12°C/54°F in the fruit-maturation months of August and September. Growing in ancient marine limestone within a high-desert terrior, Whitewater Hill's grapes develop thick skins to defend against this extreme climate; this gives them a character unlike any other, with the red wines taking on hints of cloves and nutmeg, and the whites haunting spice notes. Melanie and Jeff Wick took over as owners in 2022, with Chloe Nicoson staying on as winemaker and the Wicks' developing the food options, starting by opening up a food truck selling charcuterie and panini.

Whitewater Hill is one of the few Colorado wineries to make ice wine: their delectable Zero Below late-harvest Chardonnay is only picked frozen so isn't always available. *whitewaterhill.com; tel +1 970-434-6868; 220 32 Rd, Grand Junction; 10am-5.45pm daily Ⓢ✕*

[Delta/Paonia]

06 STONE COTTAGE CELLARS

Around 113km (70 miles) southeast of Grand Junction, the northern Fork/Delta/Paonia wine country is higher than the Grand Valley AVA – averaging 1980m to 2133 (6500ft to 7000ft). Stone Cottage's owner Brent Hellickson explains that 'growing grapes at this elevation is hard and different to anywhere else; wineries here are more intimately attached to the mountains.'

His vineyards sit upon a south-sloping mesa – good for aspect and draining off cool weather. The family farm rests on clay-based rocky soils with a sublayer of calcium marl, basalt boulders and volcanic material, allowing vineyard roots to draw mineral character into the wines; this Old World expression makes Chardonnay a favourite. Wine acidity here is higher than elsewhere in the state, producing other subtle, light styles: Alsatian varieties like Gewürztraminer and Pinot Gris.

The winery radiates an old-Colorado Western charm (enjoy this with a stay at the Stone Cottage), and prides itself on having the highest Merlot vineyard in the world (1890m/6200ft), framed by the distant West Elk Mountains. Tours are available by appointment. *stonecottagecellars.com; tel +1 970-527-3444; 41716 Reds Rd, Paonia; tasting room 11am-6pm daily May-Nov Ⓢ✕*

07 JACK RABBIT HILL

It isn't every day someone moves from California to Colorado to make wine, but that's what Lance Hanson did in 2001. He had no script when founding Jack Rabbit Hill – just a desire to understand this marginal, high, dry climate and its unusual challenges, and grow grapes in the most sustainable, ecologically thoughtful way possible. He converted to biodynamic farming in 2006 – Jack Rabbit Hill is Colorado's only Demeter-certified winery.

These wines are some of Colorado's most Old-World-style drops. Hanson's love for Loire, Burgundy and Beaujolais wines speaks to his surprisingly elegant, soft-spoken expressions born of Pinot Noir and even Pinot Meunier, a red grape often seen in Champagne that imbues deep colour and a morello-cherry-like flavour to a blend. Organic ciders, estate-distilled gin, vodka and brandy are also on offer. Only 18 of 72 acres are under vine here; the rest is livestock pasture, ponds and a medicinal garden. And this high-in-the-sky winery gives views of the grand mesa to the west and of the Black Canyon of the Gunnison National Park. *jackrabbithill.com; tel +1 970-234-9463; 26567 North Rd, Hotchkiss; by appointment Ⓢ*

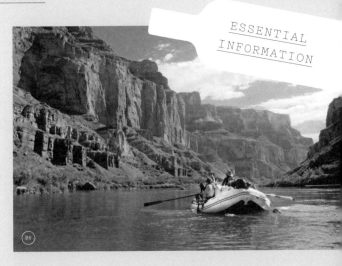

ESSENTIAL INFORMATION

WHERE TO STAY

WINE COUNTRY INN
Sleep among vines at this château-like pick at Two Rivers Winery, where rooms are plush yet charming, and the Champagne Suite comes with a four-poster bed. *tworiverswinery.com; tel +1 970-255-1471; 2087 Broadway, Grand Junction 81507*

HIGH LONESOME RANCH
A remote, five-star experience in homestead cabins or even safari tents, with excellent cuisine to boot. *thehighlonesomeranch. com; tel +1 970-283-9420; 275 County Rd 222, DeBeque*

BROSS HOTEL
Retreat to a slower pace in Paonia, where this snug B&B is known for its hospitality, charming frontier ambience and fruit-named rooms. *paonia-inn.com; tel +1 970-527-6776; 312 Onarga Ave, Paonia*

WHERE TO EAT

TACOPARTY
A fun, casual scene, where fresh local ingredients fuel the Mexican menu and there's deliciously creative gelato – a must during sweetcorn season. *tacopartygj.com; tel +1 970-314-9736; 126 S 5th St, Grand Junction; Tue-Sat*

BIN 707
A formal local favourite for Colorado-sourced farm-to-table fare. No reservations – it's just first come, first served. *bin707.com; tel +1 970-243-4543; 225 N 5th St, Grand Junction; Tue-Sat*

IL BISTRO ITALIANO
Italian-born Brunella brings her north-Italian tradition to Grand Junction with authentically delicious bites like prosciutto platters and butternut-squash ravioli. *ilbistroitaliano.com; tel +1 970-243-8622; 400 Main St, Grand Junction; Tue-Sat*

626 ON ROOD
Elegant and inventive, this is contemporary American at its best. Artful mains change seasonally and are paired with an excellent wine list. Servers know their stuff and can highlight regional wines, many of which are sustainable and biodynamic. *626onrood.com; tel +1 970-257-7663; 626 Rood Ave, Grand Junction; Tue-Sat*

KANNAH CREEK BREWING COMPANY
Craving a pint and a pizza after a long day of tasting wines? Kannah's Broken Oar is probably the best IPA on the Western Slope, and the Black's Bridge Stout – an Irish-style dry stout with lots of depth – isn't fooling around either. *kannahcreekbrewingco. com tel +1 970-263-0111; 1960 N 12th St, Grand Junction; daily*

WHAT TO DO
This region is a delight for outdoors enthusiasts. There are endless biking and horse-riding trails, hikes within Colorado National Monument, and great tubing down the Colorado River to Fruita. Go rock climbing and kayaking or hike the inner canyon of Black Canyon of the Gunnison National Park. Or take a break from wineries and visit peach orchards and lavender farms for an inside look at Colorado's other agricultural industries. *colorado.com*

CELEBRATIONS
Regional festivals range from the Lavender Festival in July to the Colorado Mountain Wine Festival during September harvest. Or kick off the summer with the Palisade Bluegrass and Roots Music Festival in June. *coloradolavender.org; coloradowinefest.com; palisademusic.com*

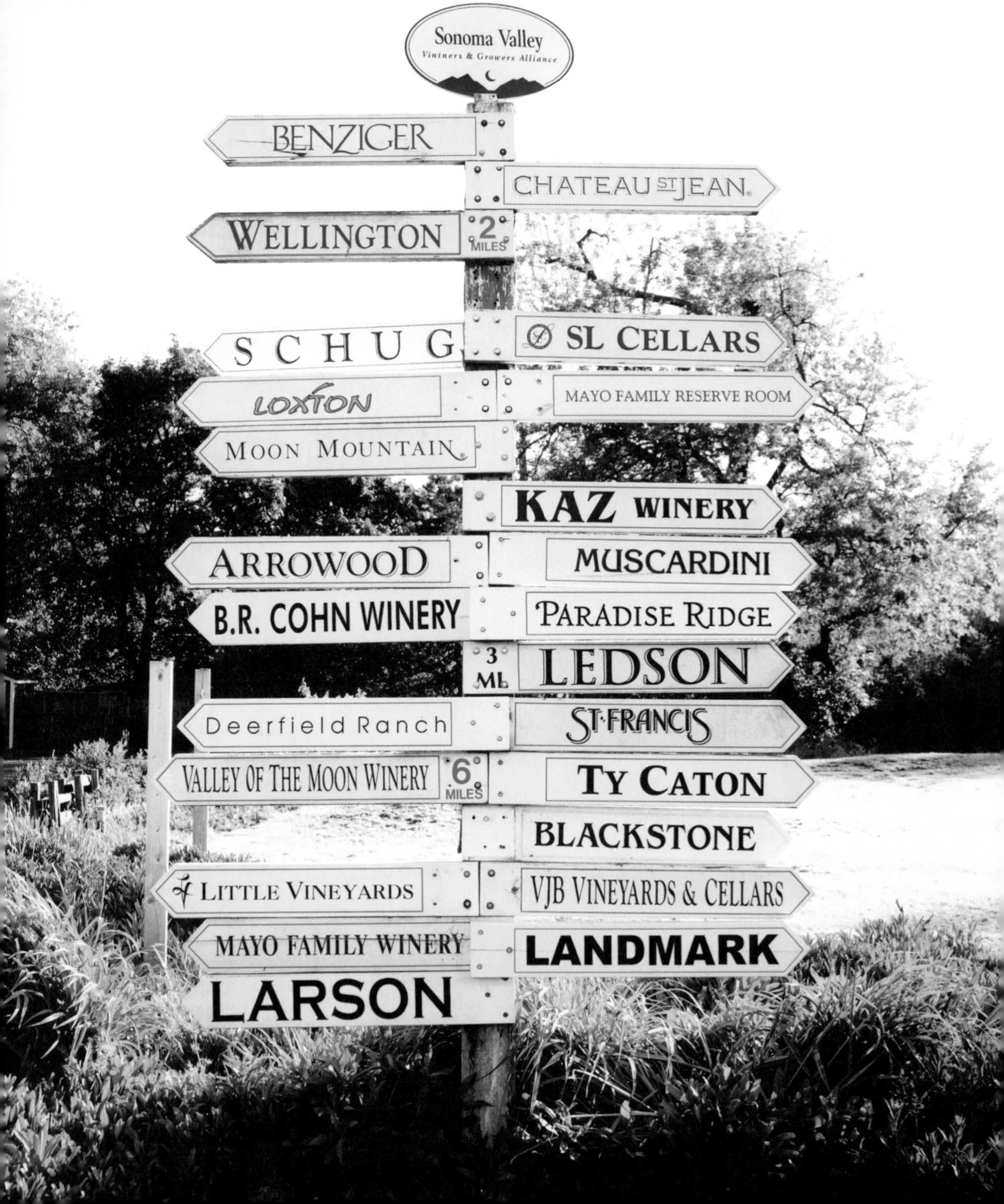

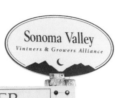

Sonoma Valley
Vintners & Growers Alliance
BENZIGER
CHATEAU ST JEAN
WELLINGTON
2 MILES
SCHUG
SL CELLARS
LOXTON
MAYO FAMILY RESERVE ROOM
MOON MOUNTAIN
KAZ WINERY
ARROWOOD
MUSCARDINI
B.R. COHN WINERY
PARADISE RIDGE
3 MI
LEDSON
Deerfield Ranch
ST FRANCIS
VALLEY OF THE MOON WINERY
6 MILES
TY CATON
BLACKSTONE
LITTLE VINEYARDS
VJB VINEYARDS & CELLARS
MAYO FAMILY WINERY
LANDMARK
LARSON

SONOMA

[USA]

SONOMA

Sonoma Valley's astonishingly varied geography and climate, plus its bold and exciting winemakers, make for some of California's best wines.

Stunning Sonoma is a diverse patchwork of microclimates and terroirs, where many of the best estates treat their land with a reverence usually reserved for Old World vineyards. It is also home to many of California's most skilled and forward-thinking winemakers. Pinot Noir and Chardonnay are the star grape varieties (though Zinfandel and Syrah are also very successful), and the region's best wines are becoming increasingly collectable. You could say that if the Napa Valley is California's answer to Bordeaux, then Sonoma shares many similarities with Burgundy (although the locals are fiercely proud of the many things that make their region unique).

While today's Sonoma is certainly at the cutting edge of the state's wine scene – thankfully, its wineries largely escaped

the ravages of the 2020 Glass Fire – it's also where California's first commercial winery was established back in the 1850s. This long history is evidenced in many gnarled old vineyards, some of which are over 100 years old. It is a land of huge diversity – baking hot inland, but downright cold out on the wet and windy 'Extreme' Sonoma Coast (where some of the state's most awe-inspiring vistas are to be found). In between, there is a variety of geographies and microclimates suited to a range of different grape varieties, and this results in a wide variety of wine styles.

Wine and food are embedded in the culture of this part of Northern California, something that's evident in the first-rate tasting rooms and restaurants in Healdsburg town, the ideal place to base yourself here.

GET THERE
San Francisco is the nearest major airport, 92km (57 miles) from Sonoma. Car hire is available.

01 CLINE CELLARS

Fred Cline grew up surrounded by a wealthy family. His grandfather – a certain Mr Jacuzzi – spent time on the family farm in Oakley, instilling a love of the land into his grandson. These old vineyards, planted with Zinfandel, Mourvèdre and countless other red and white grapes, inspired Fred to learn winemaking and set up Cline Cellars. It moved from its original home to an incredible 140-hectare (350-acre) property in Carneros in 1993. Since then, Cline has focused on gutsy, full-bodied wines that fly the flag for some of the lesser-known Californian varieties, and therefore represent some of the best value in the state.

There are a range of tasting flights of vintage and exclusive wines, conducted by spring-fed ponds or in the tasting room; cheese and charcuterie boards are available.

clinecellars.com; tel +1 800-546-2070; 24737 Arnold Drive, Hwy 121, Sonoma; tastings by reservation daily (S)

02 HANZELL

California's oldest continuously-producing Pinot Noir and Chardonnay vines can be found at Hanzell, which makes its wines using the world's first stainless steel temperature-controlled tanks; considering that this technology now serves as the backbone of winemaking worldwide, that's no small feat. Tastings at outdoor platforms at the Ambassador's 1953 vineyard block take in three current-release wines, and give background on Hanzell's integrated farming and winemaking philosophies.

Founded in the 1950s, Hanzell has held on to its historical feel by conserving its original winery and older vine plantings, though outdoor art and sculptures from natural materials also lie dotted around the property. Surrounded by forests, with panoramas of San Francisco Bay, this is one of the prettiest spots in Sonoma County to taste wine. *hanzell.com; tel +1 707-996-3860; 18569 Lomita Ave, Sonoma; by reservation 10am–3pm daily* (S)

03 LITTORAI

One of the Sonoma wine trade's deepest thinkers, not to mention most talented winemakers, Ted Lemon of Littorai is a man who takes farming very seriously. The fruit that he harvests from his biodynamic vineyards and the resulting Chardonnay and Pinot Noir wines are among the region's best, and a visit here is a must for anyone interested in what makes Sonoma so special. Having inspired a new

01 Showing the way in
Sonoma

02 Paradise Ridge
champions the arts

03 Barrel ageing
at Emeritus

04 Emeritus Vineyards

generation of young winemakers with his dedication to crafting artisanal wines, Ted hasn't forgotten about inspiring the public. In the tasting room, two options are available to visitors. The Single Vineyard Tasting is a 45-minute exploration of Littorai's vineyard-designated releases ($65), while the longer Gold Ridge Estate Tour & Tasting will also lead you through the vineyards and explain Littorai's farming methods ($85). *littorai.com; tel +1 707-823-9586; 788 Gold Ridge Rd, Sebastopol; by reservation Mon-Sat* $

04 EMERITUS VINEYARDS

Emeritus creator Brice Jones has founded some of Sonoma County's most influential wineries, and headed up the petition that made one of its biggest AVAs, the Sonoma Coast, officially recognised. In 1999, he turned his focus to Emeritus

Vineyards, to deliver handcrafted Pinot Noir from exceptional Sonoma growing regions. Revolving around vineyards close to the coast, Emeritus offers distinctive single-vineyard Pinot Noir with backbone.

Though all Emeritus vineyards sit on the far western side of Sonoma County, each has its own elevation, soil and growing conditions – and the particular characters of these sites show in the glass. But though the wines come from multiple locales along Sonoma's Coast, the tasting room is a true reflection of the Russian River Valley. You can also book a Hallberg Ranch vineyard tour that concludes with a tasting of single-vintage Pinot Noirs. *emeritusvineyards.com; tel +1 707-823-9463; 2500 Gravenstein Hwy N, Sebastopol; by reservation: tastings 10am-3pm daily, tours 10am-noon Thu-Sun* $

05 PARADISE RIDGE

The Russian River Valley is one of Sonoma's most famous American Viticultural Areas (AVAs) and is full of excellent wineries worth visiting. What sets Paradise Ridge apart, in addition to its well-made Pinot Noir, Chardonnay and Sauvignon Blanc wines, is their love of the arts. An open-air sculpture gallery set in the meadows and woodlands of the winery's grounds, Marijke's Grove features a biannually changing selection of works centred on various themes.

The 'Estate' tasting offers flights of two white or light-red Russian River Pinot Noirs; the 'Explorer' four Bordeaux-style reds from Sonoma County's renowned Rockpile AVA. *prwinery.com; tel +1 707-528-9463; 4545 Thomas Lake Harris Dr, Santa Rosa; tastings by reservation 11am, 1pm & 3pm daily* $

Ø5

Ø5 Dine at Rustic, the restaurant at Francis Ford Coppola Winery

Ø6 The spa retreat at Fairmont Sonoma Mission Inn

06 COPAIN

The beautiful surroundings at Copain are enough to make you want to pack it all in and move to California to make wine. Of course, the reality is a bit more complicated than that, and Wells Guthrie spent many a year apprenticing with some of France and California's most respected winemakers before setting up on his own in 1999. His wines became progressively more silky and elegant in style, cementing Copain's reputation for quality, and though Guthrie sold up and moved on in 2016, current winemaker Ryan Zepaltas has maintained the same high standards.

The tasting rooms offer impressive views and a variety of top-notch tasting experiences ($65-$95) that offer a great introduction to the wines of Copain, and also tell the story of the surrounding region. All are small-group experiences guided by a dedicated host; you can also book a 'Classic Food & Wine Experience'

to taste Copain's signature wines paired with locally sourced bites. *copainwines.com; tel +1 707-836-8822; 7800 Eastside Rd, Healdsburg; by reservation 10am-4pm daily* 💲

07 BANSHEE

The town of Healdsburg is a great place to base yourself for a wine-tasting trip, as not only do you have the region's vineyards and wineries on your doorstep, but also the town's numerous tasting rooms. Banshee, just a stone's throw from the main plaza, is the best of the bunch: great wines, friendly, knowledgeable staff and a lively but relaxed atmosphere. Having honed her skills at wineries in Australia, Italy, Argentina and South Africa, the California-born winemaker Alicia Sylvester has a stellar pedigree – you can be sure that whatever you choose to taste, it will be delicious.

With a comprehensive list of wine flights starting at $40 (charcuterie boards are available to add on), Banshee is a great place to come

and learn more about Sonoma wine. *bansheewines.com; tel +1 707-395-0915; 325 Center St, Healdsburg; 11am–7pm Thu–Sun* 💲

08 FRANCIS FORD COPPOLA

Not content with being one of the most influential people in Hollywood, Francis Ford Coppola has also played a leading role in the modern Californian wine industry. In 1975 he purchased one of the most historic estates in the Napa Valley (Inglenook – though it wasn't until 2011 that he was able to reunite the property with its brand name, which was sold separately), and since then every new hit movie has seen his wine operations expanded.

The Sonoma winery produces a wide range of wines and has set the standard for wine tourism – visitors can expect everything from the usual tasting flights ($25 to $40, depending on what you taste) to a variety of wine experiences that include a private wine tasting combined with a spot of bocce ball ($50). There is also a restaurant, café and deli as well as the Zoetrope cinema, a gallery of movie memorabilia, two popular swimming pools and a calendar of events for the whole family. *francisfordcoppolawinery.com; tel +1 707-857-1471; 300 Via Archimedes, Geyserville; 11am–5pm Thu–Mon* 💲🍴

WHERE TO STAY

H2

This swanky boutique hotel delivers beautifully attired rooms, a pool and a perfect location just off the main plaza. It also has a great bar and restaurant (Spoon Bar), worth visiting even if you're not staying here. *h2hotel.com; tel +1 707-431-2202; 219 Healdsburg Ave, Healdsburg*

VINTNERS INN

Surrounded by beautiful vines and gardens, Vinters Inn blends business-class amenities with vineyard chic; there's an award-winning restaurant (John Ash & Co), too. *vintnersresort.com; tel +1 800-421-2584; 4350 Barnes Rd, Santa Rosa*

WHERE TO EAT

CAMPO FINA

In an 1884 storefront, Campo Fina maintains Healdsburg's Spaghetti Western traditions with pasta and wood-fired pizza – go classic buffalo mozzarella and basil, or gourmet *cardoncello* mushrooms and sausage. Family recipes inspire tomato-braised chicken with polenta and 'old school in a skillet' meatballs with housebaked ciabatta. *campofina.com; tel +1 707-395-4640; 330 Healdsburg Ave, Healdsburg; Tue-Sun*

EL MOLINO CENTRAL

Rustling up home-cooked Mexican classics with seasonal flare, this locals' favourite is a homey, comfortable spot designed for nice weather. For picnics, grab a takeaway plate or a bag of the delicious tamales. *elmolinocentral.com; tel +1 707-939-1010; 11 Central Ave, Sonoma; daily*

WHAT TO DO

There's plenty of history in Sonoma, and much of it can be found in Sonoma State Historic Park, with its collection of historic attractions relating to the founding of the state of California. Hikers (and drinkers) will love the 5km (3 mile) countryside trek that begins at Bartholomew Park Winery; the thermal hot springs at Fairmont Sonoma Mission Inn and Spa are the perfect place to relax afterwards. *parks.ca.gov; bartholomewestate.com; fairmont.com*

CELEBRATIONS

October's Sonoma County Harvest Fair promises wine, beer and cider tastings, seminars and cookery demos. Sebastopol's famous Gravenstein apples are honoured every August, while the LGBTQ+ community come out in force for the Pride Parade and the Gay Wine Weekend in June. *harvestfair.org; gravensteinapplefair.com; outinthevineyard.com*

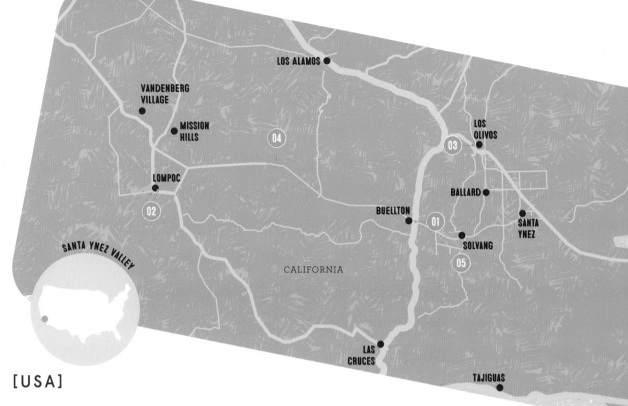

Santa Ynez Valley

CALIFORNIA

[USA]

SANTA YNEZ VALLEY

*This California trail, from Lompoc to Buellton, begins in a buzzing converted industrial
quarter of tasting rooms and concludes at one of the region's signature estates.*

To the wider world, Santa Barbara is possibly best known as a playground for the well-heeled of Los Angeles, 161km (100 miles) to the southeast. Its wine country was also the setting for the misadventures of Miles and Jack in the 2004 film Sideways, as they sip their way through their midlife crises. For oenophiles, though, this beautiful stretch of coastline jutting into the Pacific north of Los Angeles – the so-called American Riviera – is notable for other reasons. Along the west coast of the US, Santa Barbara county is the only well-established winegrowing region fully exposed to the fogs and cool weather of the Pacific. Consequently, it has the longest growing season in California, with sunny days but cool temperatures. The results include some of the best Pinot Noir in the state, but there are wines across all varieties with lots of flavour concentration and fresh acidity. Vineyards planted closest to the ocean tend to offer lighter-bodied wines, while the warmer temperatures found inland create bolder, more full-bodied reds and whites.

Hwy 101 crosses the full length of the county, north to south, so it's easy to pay a visit to the region. The beach-loving community of Santa Barbara itself faces south, so you can expect warmer temperatures here than in the town of Lompoc in the more exposed north. East of Lompoc, temperatures rise as you progress away from the coast and into the desert hills – locals like to say temperatures go up one degree per mile. So, while travelling Santa Barbara wine country, pack with layers. You'll want a mix of clothes for warm weather as well as for chilly moments.

GET THERE
Fly into Santa Barbara airport, then drive 30min; or if you start in LA, drive along the coast 3hr to begin the tour in Lompoc.

❶ PALMINA NOT UPDATED; MERGING WITH VEGA WINES, HAVE EMAILED

For over 20 years Palmina has focused on crafting food-friendly wines from Italian varieties grown in Santa Barbara county. 'The intention with Palmina is to share the perspective of Italian culture through the wines,' says owner Steve Clifton, 'with a little California lifestyle and personality thrown in.' New releases are offered alongside a recipe developed in the Palmina kitchen (pair grilled pork chops with fennel and radicchio with Palmina Nebbiolo Rocca, for instance; wine club events include Clifton's cooking as well). Tasting room options include aromatic and refreshing Malvasia, charming and delicious

Dolcetto, or serious and beautiful Nebbiolo, as well as a range of other distinctly Italian varieties, and single-vineyard options from throughout the region. The tasting room sits alongside the winery, which has been fitted into a converted warehouse space for a friendly, urban feel. Walk-ins are welcome but call ahead for larger groups. *palminawines.com; tel +1 805-735-2030; 1520 E Chestnut Court, Lompoc; 11am-5pm Thu-Sun & by appointment 52*

❷ LONGORIA

It's hard to find a winemaker that has had more influence on the development of the Santa Barbara County wine region than Rick Longoria. Arriving in the region's

01 Vines at Brewer-
Clifton

02 Autumn at Melville
vineyard

03, 04 & 05 Harvest
time at Melville

06 Pea Soup
Andersen's Inn at
Buellton

early days in the 1970s, Longoria helped found some of the area's most important wineries, while also advising on vineyards throughout the region. At the forefront of Longoria's own winemaking is his Fe Ciega Pinot Noir, the wine he makes from his own vineyard. In all Longoria's wines, the goal is to create a wine that delivers in its youth but is built to age. 'In the beginning the wine has youthful tenacity but as they mature, they become more complex and bigger than their skeleton.'

Expect an array of other single-vineyard Pinots and Chardonnays from the famed Sta Rita Hills. Longoria has a love for the wines of Spain as well, so he's included a few Spanish varieties such as Albariño and especially Tempranillo. Next to the winery is the tasting room, in a historic former clubhouse building for business leaders of the last century (charcuterie and nibbles are available).
longoriawine.com; tel +1 866-RLWines; 415 E Chestnut Ave, Lompoc; 11am-4.30pm Sat-Wed $

03 BREWER-CLIFTON

Winemaker Greg Brewer has spent his winemaking career in the world-famous Sta Rita Hills and helped create the official AVA, and in 2020 Wine Enthusiast named him their Winemaker of the Year. His single-vineyard Pinot Noir and Chardonnay showcase the sun-ripened flavours of California sun, with the savoury accents and mouthwatering acidity redolent of farming along the coast. The winery is built into a converted warehouse space in the centre of Lompoc; the tasting room is to the east, in the town of Los Olivos, with knowledgeable staff guiding you through tasting flights of Brewer's vineyard-designated wines. If you enjoy Chardonnay, be sure to ask if any of wines from his small production Diatom label are also available. Schedule tasting room visits in advance; private tastings at the Lompoc winery are sometimes available too, strictly by appointment only.

brewerclifton.com; tel +1 805-866-6080; tasting room 2367 Alamo Pintado Ave, Los Olivos; 10am-4pm Thu-Mon by appointment $

04 MELVILLE

The Melville family was among the first to develop vineyards and full-estate winemaking in their corner of the Sta Rita Hills, and along with other founding winemakers they helped define the conditions of this famed region. The winery sits along Hwy 246 between Buellton and Lompoc, in the heart of the Sta Rita Hills AVA and surrounded by some of the Melville vineyards and the region's rolling desert hills. In the accompanying tasting

room – a relaxed adobe-style affair – explore their Chardonnay, Pinot Noir and Syrah. Enjoy a flight of wines at the bar or, weather permitting, a bottle on the outdoor patio. Book ahead for a longer 90-minute vineyard tours along with your tasting.

melvillewinery.com; tel +1 805-735-7030; 5185 E Hwy 246, Lompoc; 11am-4pm daily, till 5pm Fri & Sat $

05 ALMA ROSA

Founder Richard Sanford planted the Alma Rosa vineyards deep in the Sta Rita Hills at the start of the 1970s. In doing so, he established the very first vineyard

there, effectively launching what is today recognised as one of California's pre-eminent Pinot Noir regions. At the tasting room in downtown Solvang, try a flight of five wines from across the Alma Rosa portfolio of Pinot Noirs, Chardonnays, Rhone varietals and sparkling wines in a handsome, spacious indoor-outdoor setting; cheese plates are on offer, too. Private tours and seated tastings at the Alma Rosa Ranch House, and hikes around the estate, are also available by prior appointment.

almarosawinery.com; tel +1 805-691-9395; 1623 Mission Dr, Solvang; tasting room 11am-7.30pm Thu-Sat, 11am-6pm Sun-Wed $

WHERE TO STAY

PEA SOUP ANDERSEN'S INN

A relaxed roadway style inn, Pea Soup Andersen's is a regional classic. If you've ever done a road trip across California, you've probably seen the billboards advertising its adjoining restaurant – it does offer more than split-pea soup. The hotel is simple, comfortable and central. From here it's easy to get anywhere in the county. *peasoupandersens.com; tel +1 800-732-7687; 51 East Hwy 246, Buellton*

SANTA YNEZ VALLEY MARRIOTT

Buellton's Marriott is urban in design, and offers access to the wineries and surrounding landscape in Santa Ynez Valley (the building has also been certified sustainable). Rooms are spacious and comfortable. You'll also find a fitness centre and pool onsite, and the hotel is pet friendly. *marriott.com; tel +1 805-688-1000; 555 McMurray Rd, Buellton*

WHERE TO EAT

INDUSTRIAL EATS

The Industrial Eats Restaurant & Butcher Shop offers a menu of wood-fire pizzas, seasonal salads and a selection of daily specials. Beer and local wines are served on tap. Food is available via walk-up counter service to eat on site, or take away deli-style. *industrialeats.com; tel +1 805-688-8807; 181 Industrial Way, Buellton; daily*

THE HITCHING POST II

Made famous by the movie *Sideways*, the Hitching Post is a long-established restaurant serving up steakhouse-style cuisine, local wines and classic cocktails. Expect Western-style decor with mood lighting and friendly service. *hitchingpost2.com; tel +1 805-688-0676; 406 E Hwy 246, Buellton; Wed-Sun*

FIRESTONE WALKER BREWING COMPANY

Need some time away from the vine? At the Firestone Walker Brewing Company in Buellton you can do a barrel tasting and take self-guided brewery tours, but most come here to enjoy craft ales brewed using locally foraged ingredients. *firestonebeer.com; tel +1 805-697-4777; 620 McMurray Rd, Buellton; Wed-Mon*

WHAT TO DO

OSTRICHLAND

Those curious about giant flightless birds can feed them at Solvang's Ostrichland or take a self-guided tour to learn more about these striking animals. There is an educational gift shop offering insights about both ostriches and emus. *ostrichlandusa.com*

LA PURISIMA GOLF COURSE

If you want to fit in a round during your visit to wine country, the La Purisima Golf Course hosts 18 holes and sits on the eastern side of Lompoc. It's a public green so available for out-of-town guests looking for some tee time. *lapurisimagolf.com*

INDEX

Second Edition
Published in February 2023 by Lonely Planet Global Limited
CRN 554153
www.lonelyplanet.com
ISBN 978 1838 69601 6
© Lonely Planet 2022
Printed in China
10 9 8 7 6 5 4 3 2 1

VP Print, Publisher Piers Pickard
Associate Publisher Robin Barton
Editor and indexer Polly Thomas
Art Direction Daniel Di Paolo
Layout design Jo Dovey
Cartographer Rachel Imeson
Print Production Nigel Longuet

Cover images: Matt Munro, Justin Foulkes, Mark Read, Andrew Montgomery © Lonely Planet

Authors: Ashley Hausman, Christina Rasmussen, Elaine Chukan Brown, Paul Vigna, Bob Campbell, Huon Hooke, Robin Barton, Michael Ellis, Anne Krebiehl, Benjamin Kemper, Caroline Gilby, John Brunton, Regis St Louis, Sarah Ahmed, Tara Q Thomas

Lonely Planet Global Limited

Digital Depot, Roe Lane (off Thomas St), Digital Hub, Dublin 8, D08 TCV4 IRELAND

STAY IN TOUCH lonelyplanet.com/contact

Paper in this book is certified against the Forest Stewardship Council™ standards. FSC™ promotes environmentally responsible, socially beneficial and economically viable management of the world's forests.